D0205925

PUBLIC SCHOOL REFORM
IN PUERTO RICO

PUBLIC SCHOOL REFORM IN PUERTO RICO

Sustaining Colonial Models of Development

JOSÉ SOLÍS

Contributions to the Study of Education, Number 60

Greenwood Press
Westport, Connecticut • London

Library of Congress Cataloging-in-Publication Data

Solís, José.
      Public school reform in Puerto Rico : sustaining colonial models
of development / José Solís.
         p. cm.—(Contributions to the study of education, ISSN 0196–707X ;
no. 60)
      Includes bibliographical references and index.
      ISBN 0–313–28978–6 (alk. paper)
      1. Educational change—Puerto Rico.   2. Education—Social aspects—
Puerto Rico.   3. Education—Political aspects—Puerto Rico.
4. Education—Puerto Rico—American influences. I. Title.
II. Series.
LA501.S58   1994
371'.01'097295—dc20   93–15841

British Library Cataloguing in Publication Data is available.

Library of Congress Catalog Card Number: 93–15841
ISBN: 0–313–28978–6
ISSN: 0196–707X

First published in 1994

Greenwood Press, 88 Post Road West, Westport, CT 06881
An imprint of Greenwood Publishing Group, Inc.

Printed in the United States of America

The paper used in this book complies with the
Permanent Paper Standard issued by the National
Information Standards Organization (Z39.48–1984).

10 9 8 7 6 5 4 3 2 1

DEDICATION

Para mi compañera, Tita, mi familia, y todos aquellos Puertorriqueños, los
anónimos que luchan y los Presos Políticos y Prisioneros de Guerra quienes,
a través de las rejas de las prisiones Estadounidenses, forjan un Puerto Rico
libre del colonialismo.

Little girl, daughter of a farm laborer, near Caguas (1941). From *Puerto Rico Mio*, photography by Jack Delano, published by the Smithsonian Institute. Washington, D.C., 1990.

CONTENTS

ACKNOWLEDGMENTS

This book is but a moment in the rich history of literature on colonialism in Puerto Rico. The contents grow out of a drive to attempt to understand not why Puerto Rico remains a colony under the veil of insidious U.S. domination, rather what requirements must we as a people fulfill in the process of liberating ourselves from such an existence. The developments in this book have been inspired by the voices of many compañeras(os), friends, and skeptics, all worthy of my sincerest gratitude. To Walter Feinberg and Ralph Page I extend my appreciation for their constant critique and enthusiasm. Thanks to José López, a leader and friend whose commitment to Puerto Rico's struggle educated me profoundly. The Juan Antonio Corretjer Puerto Rican Cultural Center in Chicago, of which José López is director, provided resources unavailable in any library or other setting. Rafael Marrero was responsible for putting much of this book in its form. His interest in computer technology was of fundamental significance in the book's presentation. I must include others whose kind assistance made finalizing this work possible. I am especially grateful to Jack Delano for the use of his photography which has and continues to convey some special messages for all who experience his art. Thanks to Lisa Klermund for being there when finalizing the work became critical, to Joe Baker and Tom Roser at the LA&S Computer Skills Center at DePaul University, to the staff at the Puerto Rico Collection Department of the José M. Lázaro Library at the University of Puerto Rico, and to Jesús Delgado and the staff of the Puerto Rico Teachers Federation. Special gratitude is extended to Sally Scott for her suggestions and persistence in reviewing the layout of the text. What makes music of lyrics is like that which makes worlds of words, my deepest felt gratitude to Luis Alfredo "Firo" Colón Osorio and Linda Backiel. Finally, none of this would have been possible without the enormous display of patience by my children, Willie, Michelle, Kris, Nicol, and Aurora; may they choose to do their part for the improvement of their people and as such the world.

Sunrise in the Cayey valley (1982). From *Puerto Rico Mio*, photography by Jack Delano, published by the Smithsonian Institute. Washington, D.C., 1990.

INTRODUCTION

*P*uerto Rico's status as a colony has been recognized by virtually every international organization while it is generally evaded by the United States. The most fundamental meaning of colonialism states that it is "the establishment and maintenance, for an extended period of time, of rule over an alien people that is separate from and subordinate to the ruling power."[1] Any examination of the development of any part of or of an entire nation under colonialism has to be understood within the context of the colonial reality characterizing it. Once we acknowledge the colonial reality of any people, our points of reference are more lucidly capable of explaining the dynamics of colonialism in the twentieth century. In the case of Puerto Rico, we need to make the case that it is a colony.

Rather than entering into an extensive historical argument establishing the evidence of Puerto Rico's colonial reality, I will rely upon the principles of international law and the legal foundations explaining Puerto Rico's situation.

SELF-DETERMINATION AND PUERTO RICO

The principle of free determination of all peoples has been consecrated in the U.N. Charter (Art. 1.2); concretized in General Assembly resolutions 1514 (XV) and 2675 (XXV); and recognized as a fundamental right in Article 1 of the Civil, Political, Economic, Social, and Cultural International Compacts: "All peoples on Earth have the right to freely determine, without external interference, their political condition and to continue their economic, social and cultural development." As an explanation of the colonial identity of a people, the law through Resolution 1514 (XV) states that colonies are

territories which are geographically separated from the country which controls them and . . . different from that country in their ethnic or cultural aspects . . . that there be administrative, political, juridical, economic or historical factors that exert influence over the relationships between the metropolitan State and the territory, in such manner as to arbitrarily render such territory to a subordinate state or condition.[2]

With the above internationally agreed-upon characterization and principles explaining a colonial people, the development of any or all institutions in Puerto Rico must be examined within the context of the colonial reality inasmuch as the following conditions obtain:

• Puerto Rico is separated geographically from the United States and its population is ethnically and culturally different from that of the United States.
• The administrative, political, and juridical organization of Puerto Rico places the island in a subordinate position in regard to the United States. This is especially evident in the organization of its juridical powers, which allows for the applicability of the federal grand jury on legal matters concerning Puerto Rico, as well as the limitations imposed by the United States on the Puerto Rican Senate and House of Representatives in the adoption of resolutions concerning the people of Puerto Rico.
• The militarization of the population and the territory of Puerto Rico exceeds the limits required by its civil defense and national security, thus serving the geostrategic interests of the United States (as expressly and publicly acknowledged by the U.S. representative before the U.N. Committee of the 24— the committee whose focus is to examine the decolonization process throughout the world).
• The model of economic development, based on payments to external factors (the exportation of capital to the United States) and on net unilateral transfers from the United States to Puerto Rico, creates arbitrary factors of subordination and dependency on the United States.
• Finally, from a historical point of view, Puerto Rico was a Spanish colony ceded to the United States by virtue of the Treaty of Paris of 1898; this cession places the people of Puerto Rico in a condition of complete dependency on the United States, because it is clearly stated in Article IX of the treaty: The civil rights and the political condition of the inhabitants of the territories henceforth ceded to the United States, will be determined by the United States Congress.[3]

The legal rights acquired by the United States through the Treaty of Paris reflected the validity, under international law, of the treatment of colonial possessions at the time. However, they sparked serious debate in Puerto Rico and in the United States, both for and against imperial expansion through colonialism. Spain had signed the Autonomy Charter of 1897 with Puerto Rico, granting the island unprecedented autonomy in political and economic matters, thereby complicating the legitimacy of the Treaty of Paris between the United States and Spain in regard to dominion over Puerto Rico. The strongest opposition in the United States organized the American Anti-imperialist League. The league was "composed of diverse strands of opinion, including those who feared an influx into the continental United States of uncivilized colored people, with economic and political threats to white dominance."[4]

Today, much of the language regarding Puerto Rico's status reiterates similar colonial posturing. In a 1991 column, Senator Paul Simon (D-Ill.) asserts that "commonwealth status for Puerto Rico is pre-packaged colonialism."[5] He goes on to say that

No matter how you cut it, the present commonwealth status is simply old-fashioned colonialism, attractively packaged. . . . Commonwealth status is fine for some major American corporations avoiding income taxes, but that is a high price to pay for second-class citizenship for Puerto Rican citizens. Eventually, commonwealth status will go, just as other forms of colonialism around the world have gone. Puerto Rico will either become a state or become independent.[6]

For Senator Simon, as for many other Democrats, the preference seems to be statehood, primarily because statehood would probably expand the strength of the Democratic party, which Puerto Ricans have historically favored. Here we have an anti-colonial position that can be explained by the political advantage gained through a decolonization effort favoring statehood. The intention here is to demonstrate how an anti-colonial resolution can be defended from the colonizer's position in such a way that resolving the status issue provides a beneficial situation for the colonizer. This however does not explain how a Republican would defend statehood. Suffice it to say that military and industrial interests transcend strict political party affiliations when it comes to developing strategies for sustaining lucrative profits from a colony.

Another example can be drawn from the more conservative elements in the United States. Patrick J. Buchanan's 1991 article "Don't Make Puerto Rico 51st State"[7] is an apparent call for a continued Puerto Rican colony. While recognizing the volatile situation in Puerto Rico, Buchanan nevertheless, stresses the need to avoid any discussion or action for the resolution of the status issue. His article refers to Law Num. 4 of April 5, 1991 by which then Governor Rafael Hernández Colón wrote into law Spanish as the official language of Puerto Rico, overturning the Official Languages Act of 1902, which essentially asserted that English would enjoy considerable power in the governance of the country. Notwithstanding, Buchanan noted that the new legislation was equivalent to a declaration of independence and that Puerto Rico's resident commissioner, the island's nonvoting delegate to Congress, asserted that "Puerto Rico is a Spanish speaking country . . . if this happens to give some people more concern, so be it." The following exerpt from the Buchanan article serves the purpose of supporting the argument that the appearance of an anti-colonial, even a pro-independence position can be appealed to with self-interested colonial motives.

That vote [referring to the language legislation] may have saved the island, and the mainland from a bad marriage and a bloody divorce. President George Bush, chief sponsor of statehood, may yet be spared a tragic error that could put us on the road to a constitutional crisis of the sort now faced by Prime Minister Brian Mulroney in Quebec. . . . If Puerto Ricans voted 55–45 for statehood, we could well have created a Northern Ireland in the Caribbean and scheduled our own *intifada* for the new century. . . . Americans ought to empathize with the desire of Puerto Rican patriots to maintain a separate identity, as well as the right to one day declare independence. . . . The move to have the island vote on statehood, commonwealth status or independence has been put on the back burner in the Senate committee. Leave it there, and turn the burner off.[8]

In this case we have a position that condemns the propensity for a decision because such is, for the most part, tantamount to waking up a sleeping dog. Yet, resistance to colonialism is not new nor has it been asleep. Buchanan's point is that to bring the issue to the fore is to invite almost certain disaster. However, while appearing to rely upon the principle of self-determination, Buchanan is actually urging that the whole process be discontinued. He senses that a crisis is coming, yet he feels that fuel should not be added to the fire. In any case, the right to self-determination is not at the heart of his argument. His primary concern involves the political and security threat that forcing a culturally different people into statehood poses for the United States. For Simon and Buchanan the underlying motive is self-interest. This is an unmistakable trait of the colonizer. Even in the process of attempting to carry out decolonization, the colonizer seeks first to measure the benefit derived from decolonization. Most recently, local newspapers in Puerto Rico have run various articles citing Senator Daniel Patrick Moynihan's (D-NY) comments regarding the results of the planned plebiscite on Puerto Rican status, scheduled to take place in November of 1993. The comments by the senator from New York assert that the U.S. administration's acceptance of a softer 936 plan (936 corporations are those U.S. multinational interests who enjoy a "tax holiday" in Puerto Rico under the Internal Revenue Service's Code item 936) means, "there will not be a shock in Puerto Rico."[9] In the same article Moynihan was further reported as stating that the U.S. Senate would not approve statehood for Puerto Rico, even if the island residents chose it. Soon after the publication of the senator's comments, proponents of statehood for Puerto Rico rushed to ascertain that such comments were not direct quotes. Obviously, the point was to undermine the accuracy or redirect the meaning of the comments. Through these articles these men provide evidence that the anti-imperial position of today is much as it was at the turn of the century— a combination of concern for the benefits derived from an anti-colonial position and the threat that peoples of colonies, people of color, might present for the security of U.S. domination. Yet Puerto Rico has a constitution and is what is commonly referred to as a free associated state or commonwealth.

The establishment of the free associated state or commonwealth was actually a well calculated evasion of the colonial status that defines Puerto Rico's reality. Public Law 600 defined the new political alignment and replaced earlier arrangements.

The people of Puerto Rico were given only the option of adopting a domestic consultation within the Estado Libre Asociado (ELA or free associated state) framework, and even here the character of this Puerto Rican consultation was subjugated to wide preemptory powers exclusively retained by the U.S. Government, including complete control over foreign policy and national defense. When drafters sought to include welfare provisions relating to guarantees of basic human needs such as . . . health, housing, education, and work, they were stricken from the document as "socialistic," and incompatible with the dominant legal instrument— namely, the U.S. Constitution.[10]

The design and implementation of the ELA has served only to disguise the colonial reality of Puerto Rico, and has been a charade before the international community, leading many to believe that the United States has no colonial possessions— such a fact would have fundamental significance in describing and challenging the character of U.S. democracy. Despite the fundamental problems with the legitimacy of the ELA status, a plebiscite to decide Puerto Rico's political state was held in 1967.

The plebiscite, conducted under the auspices of the colonial administration, resulted in a victory for the pro-commonwealth factions.

Pro-independence forces were widely suppressed and harassed, no transfer of power preceded the plebiscite, the U.S. Congress never indicated a willingness to accept a pro-independence or even a pro-statehood outcome, and there was no opportunity to vote against the plebiscite.[11]

Any plebiscite concerning Puerto Rico will have to comply with international law that outlines such an exercise. First, The United States would have to recognize the sovereignty of Puerto Rico. Second, U.S. troops must vacate the island. Third, all U.S. intelligence agencies and judiciary control must be removed. Fourth, all political prisoners and prisoners of war must be freed and allowed to participate in the process. The likelihood of this happening is left for the reader to decide. Nevertheless, according to international law, these constitute the minimal requirements for the exercise of a plebiscite.

That Puerto Rico remains a colony is a generally accepted verity. Why this reality has been avoided since 1898 by many who today call it a colony will not be examined here. Suffice it to say that time is an important factor in motivating action; and when the objective reality and the subjective combine, the possibilities for deriving benefit from an action are best secured.

The importance of Puerto Rico's public school system in sustaining the colonial relationship has often been explained in the context of cultural invasion or through an examination of such colonial practices as language imposition. This volume, however, will outline how a particular conception of development, embedded and advanced in the colonial relationship, has been reproduced in the schools, particularly in the reform initiatives and reform language throughout Puerto Rico's colonial history under the United States. A significant outcome of the development project has been the evolution of a rationality that mediates the tension between the colonized and their potential to make critical assessments of different situations and the relationship of the colonized with the colonizer.

The struggle waged between conceptions of development based on growth and those based on political-economic explanations continues in Puerto Rico. In the process, the public school system has suffered the consequences of colonialism and the contradictions that characterize exploitation. Nevertheless, the objective conditions have become such that the subjects involved may, by exercising their vision of education and development, challenge the present reality and wage their own battle, on their own terms, between competing models of development. This could, for the first time in the history of Puerto Rico's public schools, constitute a development project, an act of self-determination.

Self-Determination: the right by virtue of which all peoples are entitled freely to determine their political status and to pursue their economic, social and cultural development. All peoples may, for their own ends, freely dispose of their natural wealth and resources without prejudice to any obligations arising out of international economic cooperation, based upon the principle of mutual benefit and international law. In no case may a people be deprived of its own means of subsistence.[12]

Throughout this volume, I will examine the impact that a particular conception of development under U.S. control has had on Puerto Rico's public school system. This will be accomplished by articulating certain aspects of Puerto Rico's economic history and the concurrent reform initiatives arising from the school system in response to the economic situation. The emphasis upon the school system's reactions to U.S. development projects will raise the issue of rationality. That is, as the language of schooling confined itself to the language of growth-as-development, the possibilities for expanding any conception of development and forging a critical awareness of being became progressively constrained by a rationality consistent with the model of development.

Chapter 2 will outline two models of development. One of these, it will be argued, characterizes Puerto Rican development under the United States. Chapters 3 and 5 will present general outlines of Puerto Rico's economic history during U.S. colonialism. This history is divided into the period of monocultural production, roughly between 1898 and 1940, and the period covering the 1940s through the 1980s, during which industrialization recast the character of the Puerto Rican economy. Chapters 4, 6, and 7 will examine some of the most significant educational reform initiatives and policies that arose during those historical periods, as these initiatives and policies responded to U.S. development projects for Puerto Rico. Within the volume different sections will be dedicated to the concept of rationality and its dynamics in the context of a changing economic and social environment in the colony. It is hoped that this volume will provide a critical awareness of Puerto Rico's colonial situation generally, as well as some insight into the complexity and necessity of overcoming such a situation in its most overt form and in more subtle and insidious forms that continue to hinder human potential, regardless of place.

NOTES

1. Rupert Emerson and D.K. Fieldhouse, "Colonialism," *International Encyclopedia of the Social Sciences* (New York: Macmillan, 1968), vol. C, 1-3.

2. Permanent Peoples' Tribunal, *Tribunal Proceedings and Findings* (Barcelona: January 27–29, 1989), 16–17. The document was prepared by an international tribunal whose intent it was to continue to internationalize the issue of Puerto Rican colonialism. Such tribunals have jurisdiction under accepted principles of international law in accordance with the precedents of the Nuremburg and Tokyo tribunals, following procedures approved by the Economic and Social Council of the United Nations (Resolution 1503 [XLVIII]).

3. Ibid., 20.

4. Ibid.

5. Paul Simon, " Commonwealth status for Puerto Rico is pre-packaged colonialism," *Extra*, March 13, 1991, 8. *Extra* is a bilingual community newspaper serving the Latina(o) communities of Chicago.

6. Ibid.

7. Patrick J. Buchanan, "Don't make Puerto Rico 51st State," *Chicago Sun–Times*, March 16, 1991,17.

8. Ibid.

9. Daniel Patrick Moynihan in "U.S. may not afford statehood for P.R." Robert Friedman, *San Juan Star*, July, 25, 1993, 2.

10. Permanent Peoples' Tribunal, 22.

11. Ibid.

12. International Human Rights Covenants (1966), Common Article 1 (1).

Mathematics class at an elementary school in Caguas (1946). From *Puerto Rico Mio*, photography by Jack Delano, published by the Smithsonian Institute. Washington, D.C., 1990.

2

DEVELOPMENT: TWO MODELS

At stake, therefore, is something more than a war of words; the battle lines are drawn between two conflicting interpretations of historical reality, two competing principles of social organization.[1]

S ince 1898 the labor of defining and realizing development in Puerto Rico has been promulgated within the context of a political-economic relationship with the United States sustained under colonialism. This context, in some important ways, accounts for the developments experienced in the public education system of Puerto Rico. Furthermore, the possibilities for expanding the dialogue and efforts to reform Puerto Rico's educational system are influenced by a particular conception of development grounded in the colonial relationship. Since this volume focuses on an assessment of the relationship between the history of educational reform policies in Puerto Rico and the issue of development, the meaning and context of development need to be articulated. The first task, then, is to present the concept of development, and to elaborate upon some of its socioeconomic implications, and how these implications contribute to a particular vision and implementation of policies consistent with that concept.

The two models of development examined here are taken from the work of Charles Wilber and Kenneth Jameson. The first section, on the orthodox model, will outline the general characteristics of the model and responses to some of its problems. The second section on the political economy model, contains two general positions: Marxist theory and dependency theory. The examination of development through these paradigms allows the diversity of development theory to be contained within a framework narrow enough for an elaboration of some economic and educational developments in Puerto Rico.

My intention is not to imply that somehow decolonization automatically brings with it an expanded conception of development, though some explanations of decolonization do allude to this concern: "Decolonization is quite simply the replacing of one 'species' of men by another 'species' of men."[2] Nor is the presentation regarding the orthodox and political economy models an exhaustive one. Rather, it is intended to introduce one aspect (the political economic) of the interconnectedness between economic conceptions of development and the implementation of educational policy and reform initiatives— which, in the case of Puerto Rico, are intimately linked to its relationship with the United States.

Webster's Ninth New Collegiate Dictionary defines development as "the act, process, or result of developing: the state of being developed." Implied is a gradual unfolding by which something is developed— a gradual advance or growth through progressive changes. The gradual unfolding implies that inherent in development there is a progressive process of becoming; a gradual unfolding or a passing through stages, each of which prepares for the next.[3] Charles Wilber notes that from the definition, there is another sense in which history remains important. Suggested in the language of "unfolding" is an implicit correspondence to the idea that an essential or true nature of an entity, for whatever reason lacking, remains to be revealed through the passage of time. There appears, then, a teleology of sorts characterizing the propensity of an end toward which history tends or should tend. Development thus is more than change; it is change in a particular direction.[4]

THE ORTHODOX MODEL

In the United States, development arguments have been predominantly grounded in an orthodox model.[5] Generally speaking, Walter Rostow's "high mass consumption" stands as the paradigm's primary objective. In the case of Puerto Rico, the country's position as the seventh largest customer in the world for U.S. goods in 1978,[6] should indicate the degree to which development has unfolded and the stage in which the country finds itself. Yet the relationship with the United States reveals that in a very important sense "high mass consumption" may not be a sufficient indicator of development. Coupled with this, the high dropout rate and the rise of illiteracy confront us with some important contradictions regarding development measurement from the perspective of "high mass consumption."

The orthodox model takes per capita income as the prime indicator of economic development.[7] Yet in Puerto Rico per capita income has proven problematic as a prime indicator of development. For instance, during the 1930s per capita income fell so that by 1933 it was 30 percent below what it had been in 1930.[8] The presence of many more Puerto Ricans in school during the period had minimal bearing on the course of development. The role of the school was to prepare workers to respond to the demands of the economy— in this case, an economy whose principal focus was to enrich the capital owned and controlled by the colonial power. The problem of explaining development from the perspective of per capita income growth and its correlation to schooling long characterized one aspect of Puerto Rico's reality. This is not to say, however, that policy makers did not continue to appeal to schooling as the "great equalizer."

More recent evidence helps to support the argument that the problem remains intact. During the 1980s, 70 to 80 percent of the population was eligible to receive food stamps by virtue of their low incomes.[9] In Puerto Rico, then, the growth of per capita income was directly related to particular welfare policies (food stamps) that increased spending power while obscuring Puerto Rico's underdevelopment and actual state of poverty. Regardless of the high rate of school enrollment and attendance, the potential for development, through the contributions made to the local economy by the educated, was tempered by the lack of a locally owned and controlled industry. What little the Puerto Rican economy could offer to these educated sectors of the society could not compare with the possibilities of personal and professional growth available outside Puerto Rico.

Development and progress are often presented as constituents of some kind of natural law from which history gathers its momentum and gives meaning and legitimacy to the process and progress of development.[10] The ideas of the naturalness of development and progress, and of the continuum of history, pose important implications for schooling and its policies. If history and progress are natural and lawlike, then what could possibly explain Puerto Rico's failure to overcome its underdevelopment or misdevelopment? Some of the more popular arguments charge that the schools are not educating the students for the competitive world of tomorrow. Others argue that the government needs to allocate more money to do the job. Still others assert that the problem resides in the very nature of the relationship with the United States: that as long as Puerto Rico's development is overwhelmingly defined by another nation, the other nation will seek what benefits its well-being and not necessarily that of the colony. If history and progress are lawlike, then those most advanced are so because of their affinity with nature and progress; and, conversely, those not as far along need only to continue to drudge away in the wake of the more advanced. Two of the arguments mentioned may be closely related to this lawlike configuration. The third could also find its roots in the same explanation. However, there is also the possibility that the third argument views the advanced not as explainable according to some natural law or Hegelian explanation of historical progress but, rather, according to man-made policies and exploitation. The notion of the relationship of development to history is present in different theories of the orthodox paradigm.

The most widely read analysis of the historical development view was articulated by Walter Rostow's stages-of-growth model. On Rostow's account, today's underdeveloped countries remain characterized by "traditional" ways and economies whose progress at best represents the basic preconditions for the kind of development experienced by Western developed nations.[11] The most productive and democratic road to development is viewed as the one that is least restrictive to the lawlike nature of development left to the "free" and creative spirits of clever entrepreneurs.

Since an uncoerced person can be depended upon to act rationally to maximize her/his individual self-interest, it is thought that an automatic, self-regulated mechanism . . . emerges in the course of history. These free choices are expected to overcome scarcity and result in progress through the automatic adjustments of free exchange in markets.[12]

Any deficit in development is seen as a problem born out of the constraints perpetrated by a people: their lack of achievement, the preservation of traditional cultural forms in the economy and values generally, and their "nonrational" behavior, among other sociocultural factors that hinder the process and progress of development.[13] Interestingly, in the case of Puerto Rico, the country inherited by the United States in 1898 had already experienced profound internal transformations in its production and class relations.[14] Indigenous capital had developed in agriculture, among other areas of the country's economy. When the United States invaded Puerto Rico, the country was experiencing a growth in the working class and wage labor. One wonders whether capitalist development would have prevailed. Nevertheless, one thing is certain: Puerto Rico's development changed, and the direction was both controlled by and aimed at the enrichment of U.S. interests.[15]

From the beginning of the U.S. presence in Puerto Rico, the U.S. military government found it difficult to purge the country of its "nonrational behavior." In his 1899 *Report on Civil Affairs*, Governor George W. Davis, concerned about the U.S. development plans for Puerto Rico, asked:

How could we expect to accomplish the successful implementation of the new dispositions, the Puerto Ricans tenaciously cling to local customs and laws with which they are familiar. The accomplishment of a reform or the instituting of innovations will present many difficulties, not precisely because the public is tied to antiquated customs, rather because many of them cannot understand the measures being proposed as substitutions for these customs. They prefer to maintain the old institutions and laws, though these may be defective, in the eyes of a new administration, with its unfamiliar procedures and codes.[16]

Education played a pivotal role in the endeavors to avoid some of these obstacles facing development, as viewed by the new government. For example, in an attempt to ensure the success of the new administration, in most elementary schools, girls spent more than half their time learning needlework skills.[17] From the U.S. point of view, important reasons for expanding education in Puerto Rico were to teach and to inculcate "American values."

A second obstacle to growth, according to Rostow's model, is the creation of government regulation and participation in the economy.[18] The rise of industrialization in Puerto Rico during the early 1940s marked the initiation of such a project through state capitalism, exemplified under Operation Bootstrap. The timing of the founding of the Government Development Bank and the Government Development Company, the offspring of Operation Bootstrap, was, to some, a particularly strategic necessity and possibility given the higher insular revenues brought about as a result of World War II. Economic progress in Puerto Rico was swift in coming, in part because of the colonial government, which remained loyal to U.S. interests after World War II, and in part because the economic crisis that fell upon the people cried out for urgent and immediate remediation, with little attention given to Puerto Rico's long-term development requirements.[19] The thrust of the government's involvement in the country's development came with the institution of the Government Development Bank and the Compañía de Fomento (the Government Development Company). Both were instrumental in undertaking the effort to "convince the citizens of the need for modernization and to develop a coherent view of the economy; and by forcing this on the actors of the economy through the various means at its disposal."[20]

Having progressed in the number of school facilities, expansion of teacher certification, increased expenditures for educational development, and, to some degree, literacy, education in Puerto Rico by 1948, half a century after U.S. occupation, nevertheless remained painfully inadequate. Juan José Osuna asserted that the educational situation in Puerto Rico for 1940 in terms of literacy, achievement, and enrollment was worse than that in Hawaii, Louisiana, or Alaska.[21] Thus, the meaning and relationship of education to Puerto Rican development remained questionable. Faced with the continued debate over the language of instruction or the value given to the English language over Spanish, and with the problem of teacher resistance to educational policies originating outside of Puerto Rico, among others, the above statistics can only account for the empirical evidence of what could be considered a more profound dilemma— one grounded in a conception of development unable to articulate persuasively how and why growth could take place while development, and one of its most important aspects, education, remained inadequate. Government involvement in the economy, in this context, while confronting what Rexford Tugwell perceived of as the exploitative side of laissez-faire, contributed to the preservation of an orthodox conception of development through the implementation of U.S.-sponsored economic policies that addressed the "colonial crisis" while maintaining the colonial relationship.

Both the regulation of the economy by the government and the laissez-faire position respond to the obstacles mentioned above from within the context of the orthodox paradigm. In responding to these obstacles, the laissez-faire position defends itself primarily in two ways.[22] If problems such as market failures and monopoly power can be dismissed as nonexistent or causing minimal economic loss, then the policy of laissez-faire continues to be viable and indeed desirable, from a developmental standpoint.[23] That is, if we can attribute the problems in development to irrational behavior, what Wilber and Jameson call a "protean" nature or even a moment in the natural development scheme, then market failures are not failures as such but are explained through appeals to the behavior patterns demonstrated by individuals or groups. In this case, an argument for the continuation of laissez-faire policies remains viable and maybe even encouragable. Again, time (i.e., history) will provide the fundamental vehicle through which the stages of development will be experienced in the underdeveloped countries.

The second response from the laissez-faire position admits to certain deviations from laissez-faire.[24] As was remarked above regarding the institution of the Government Development Bank in Puerto Rico, the degree of government penetration in many Third World economies is great. Governmental institutions in these countries often regulate prices by nonmarket considerations, distorting the operation of labor markets through minimum wage legislation and through provisions for employment in the government sector.[25] Commenting on this aspect of the laissez-faire strategy as characterized through the structural adjustment projects of the World Bank, the International Monetary Fund, and the Agency for International Development, Kathy McAfee remarks that

"Structural adjustment," the catch-phrase for the latest version of the market-driven private-sector-led development model, is in essence a "recolonization" of the Caribbean by foreign capital. Structural adjustment is based on two notions: that poor nations can work their way out of debt by providing even more cheap labor and raw materials to the industrialized nations; and that the private sector should determine how a society's resources are used. The first is an old story, dusted off and modernized to justify the continued removal of the region's resources. It has the added effect of placing Caribbean nations in competition to undersell each other's exports, thus derailing efforts at regional integration. The second is equally convenient for justifying foreign control, since the "private sector" really amounts to foreign investors.[26]

Structural adjustment lending is aimed at providing loans to client countries whose efforts at development focus on less government involvement in the economy through a withdrawal of guarantees of a minimum wage, freezing wage increases, constricting credit extensions, and other government spending cuts.

Aside from the laissez-faire response to the obstacles facing development, there is the position advanced by the advocates of a planned economy. Proponents of this position advocate the necessity of governmental involvement in the economy in order to offset any restraints arising in the development program, that is, nonrational behavior and government regulation and participation.[27] The government, for example, might embark upon a campaign to convince its citizens of the need for and desirability of modernizing the society while contributing its own resources to that process.[28] Again, this was evidenced by the establishment of the Government Development Company and Government Bank.

One could well argue that with the invasion by the United States and the subsequent occupation, Puerto Rico's development, or modernization, would remain contingent upon the economic, military and social advantages derived from the U.S. presence, which the United States intimated was advantageous to Puerto Rican development needs. The rapid shift in Puerto Rico from a predominantly agricultural society to an industrial one proved both beneficial and tangibly disadvantageous. While Puerto Rico experienced higher levels of production and per capita income, and expanded education and housing, the price tag for these improvements included greater underemployment and unemployment, greater trade dependence, more migrants to the United States, and a progressively higher private and public debt.[29]

Despite the differences between the laissez-faire and planning positions, both focus on the growth of GNP in the "developing" countries. Yet the orthodox strategy failed in some crucial areas, according to the advocates of growth-with-equity. There are continued high rates of unemployment, increased income inequality within and among nations, and the stagnation of real income levels among the poorest.[30] According to many economists and sociologists, Puerto Rico has been plagued by unemployment since the beginning of U.S. colonization. In part this can be explained by the characteristics of industries like sugar, which employs relatively few people permanently; most of its workers are seasonal and usually spend the remainder of the year unemployed. In addition to unemployment, the second change that is apparent in the data regarding the failure of the orthodox strategy is an increase in the inequality of income distribution in underdeveloped countries.[31] In 1946–47, the poorest 80 percent of families in Puerto Rico received only 44 percent of total income. In 1955 the poorest 80 percent received 48 percent of total income.[32]

Yet another problem is that of absolute poverty and a people's inability to provide basic necessities. The impact of food stamps upon the modification of poverty in Puerto Rico was mentioned earlier in this chapter. According to the doctoral dissertation of Edwin Irrizary Mora, coordinator of the Economic Research Program at the University of Puerto Rico at Mayagüez, the rise in Puerto Rico's poverty is, in an important way, due to the increase in payments generated toward capital and away from workers in the form of wages. In 1987 only 27 percent of payments generated went to workers, while 73 percent went to capital.[33] If per capita income contributes to an understanding of the level of poverty in a country, and in the case of Puerto Rico is restricted to consuming predominantly U.S. goods, then it is worth noting that Puerto Rico has a per capita income between 50 and 70 percent less than that of the poorest state in the United States, Mississippi.[34] On the other hand compared with many other countries of the Caribbean, Puerto Rico appears rich.

As a result of the persistent failures in the orthodox strategy, an attempt to curtail the continuation of such shortcomings is presented in the growth-with-equity theory. Orthodox economic theorists were faced with the test of striking an equilibrium between growth and equity. The view that development equals growth in per capita GNP now had to be met with an equal vision of benefits to the poorest derived from GNP growth; thus there emerged a third major response within the orthodox paradigm, one that has been termed "growth-with-equity."[35] There was, to be sure, a correspondence between the liberal and conservative arguments for this development option. Growth-oriented theory could be accommodated as a conservative posture on the basis of its emphasis upon the arguments that income inequality provided the necessary space for individuals to invest and take risks which would maximize total income and provide what is commonly referred to as the "trickle down" effect. The liberal posture proposes that state redistribution of benefits would regulate incentives, thus securing the space needed to provide for growth.[36] The defendants of growth-with-equity argue that there are three primary reasons for both the problems of execution and, more important, the problems of strategy, in the "grow now, trickle later" approach. A country cannot grow now and redistribute later because of the structures that develop with unequal growth. The case of Puerto Rico is of particular importance in that the economic and political restraints placed upon the country by its relationship with the United States determine, to a great degree, the scope and sequence of any attempts at redistribution.

Citing a second problem with the growth strategy, growth-with-equity advocates argue that strict orthodox strategies underestimate the great numbers of people who move to urban regions and the complexity of the effects that urban life has on economic and social mobility in any country.[37] The urbanization of Puerto Rico during and following the period of industrialization, accompanied by the rising rate of unemployment in the growing urban centers and the problems of redistribution, reflect but one of the difficulties confronting the possibilities for successful implementation and development of an orthodox economic theory (orthodox theory suggests that there is a correlation between the growth of a country in terms of the distribution of capital and growth, and the mobilization to urban centers). While researching labor migration, the Center for Puerto Rican Studies (CENEP) discovered that between 1940 and 1950 the rural population grew 1.0 percent while the urban population grew 58.0 percent.[38] In Puerto Rico the movements from rural to urban settings took a unique form. Migration from the island to the United States was most pronounced, and levels of unemployment rose significantly during the period when Puerto Rico was experiencing its most rapid GNP growth.[39] Migration to the United States acted as a safety valve for an economy whose growth would have appeared less appealing if the migrants had remained in Puerto Rico and been factored into the growing ranks of the unemployed.

The last argument by adherents of the growth-with-equity theory asserts that other significant areas of development have been ignored. One of these key areas is agriculture.[40] In many cases agriculture has been important, inasmuch as it has provided the necessary fuel for the introduction of industrialization. But, as Charles Wilber and Kenneth Jameson contend, "It turns out that this was at the expense of the vitality of the sector." In Puerto Rico, ignoring agriculture gravely hurt the economy. This, however, does not mean that industrialization per se is the culprit. More important has been the structure and direction that capitalism has taken in Puerto Rico. "Operation Bootstrap, the penetration of U.S. advertising, and the demonstration effect of well-stocked supermarkets have exacerbated the problem."[41]

Citing development in some Asian countries, most growth-with-equity advocates believe that the poor can improve their lives without recourse to political and social revolution. Nevertheless, one needs to consider different variables present in some of the Asian countries. While many growth-with-equity economists cite the success of industrial growth in Taiwan and South Korea, this success can be partially explained by different factors. After the Korean War, for example, South Korea continued to develop agriculture for local consumption, land distribution remained broadly geared toward some degree of equitable holdings, farming and manufacturing were closely tied and shared in developing advances of mutual benefit, and imports were subject to restrictions in order to protect local manufacturing— a far cry from attempting to explain Puerto Rico simply by appealing to the cases mentioned with no reference to mediating conditions.[42]

Two other points that unite the growth-with-equity critique are worth mentioning. First, the proponents of this view regard people in the poor countries as responsive to economic opportunities. Poor countries like Puerto Rico are the result of the failures of the wealthy (or in this case the colonizer) to provide creative opportunities for the colonized to engage productively in the economy. Development has been structured by a hierarchy that is "out of touch with the common folk" and whose interests remain misguided and tied to a select few at the expense of the many. This seems obvious enough. Yet resolution is certainly not explained simply on the basis of misguidance.[43]

Last, while focusing narrowly on economic factors such as land, labor, and capital, the growth-with-equity proponents preclude the importance of culture, social, and political factors in terms of the contributions they make to development or underdevelopment.[44] Nevertheless, the government intervention characterizing the planned approach of the equity-with-growth response challenges the faith in the automatic workings of the market, especially in an era of international oligopolies with extensive market power and price-fixing arrangements, and it assigns an important role to government actions.[45] In the case of Puerto Rico it seems that such attempts merely bring out many of the contradictions in a colonial relationship that tries to achieve social justice through the enrichment of cultural, social, and political factors and economic growth. Referring to the Puerto Rican goverment's industrial development plans, Agustín Cueva notes that "Operation Bootstrap signaled the end of the growth-with-equity model and a springboard for newly organizing growth first initiatives."[46] This vision of development as growth, as we will see throughout this volume, constitutes part of a common thread running through the history of Puerto Rico's educational development, contributing to a particular conception of development in the language of educational reform policy.

POLITICAL ECONOMY MODEL

Competing with the orthodox paradigm of development is the political economy approach. While the laissez-faire and planning economists of the orthodox school focus on the role that economic growth plays in determining development and the growth-with-equity theorists concentrate on the distribution of benefits to the poor, the political economists are more concerned with the nature of the process by which economic growth is achieved. Central to the growth economists is the articulation of people as means. Thus a prerequisite to growth may include a society's commitment to change some of its values for the sake of effecting growth. But for political economists, one goal is to enhance what people value. Development or growth is embraced only if it enhances a people's deepest values.[47] In one sense, then, development, in the political economy paradigm, is consistent with "history equals progress," since development is a means toward the enhancement of a people's values; and these values, according to this argument, representing their deepest interests, will historically evolve to the benefit of their development. "Development is thus seen as the unfolding, in human history, of the progressive emancipation of peoples and nations from the control of nature and from the control of other peoples and nations."[48]

Within the political economy paradigm we find primarily two schools of thought. One, the Marxist, focuses on the centrality of class structure in determining the control of the economy; and the other is the dependency theory approach, which emphasizes the relationships between nations. Both schools concern themselves with aspects of each other's approach, yet understanding the differences is important for a clear view of the political economy paradigm. Remarking on the general field of inquiry characterizing this paradigm, Wilber and Jameson note:

The economic or social surplus is viewed as a residual factor— that which remains after necessary consumption has been extracted from total output. Political economists argue that control of this economic surplus determines the nature of the development process. . . . The degree of foreign control of the surplus also will shape the strategy of development. The economic surplus concept is used by both Marxists and dependency theorists to analyze historical development and explain the existence of underdevelopment.[49]

Invariably, the form that development or underdevelopment takes will fundamentally contribute to the advancement of particular conceptions of education and the language surrounding educational reform. Thus, from a political economy perspective, in the case of Puerto Rico, the language of development, and more specifically the language advancing the reform of educational policies, is predominantly motivated by the exigencies of foreign control. Such exigencies often impede education's contribution to the country's development and instead have as their primary concern the preservation of control. For example, Puerto Ricans historically have been told that Puerto Rico is too small and overpopulated for self-government, that its high population density explains the low levels of employment and low living standards. Though New York City, populated by great numbers of Puerto Ricans, is more densely populated than Puerto Rico, no one asserts New York's population density accounts for the low standards of living and high unemployment among Puerto Ricans there. Furthermore, if we remove the population density numbers from San Juan in an analysis of Puerto Rican population, we will discover that the density issue is lessened considerably.[50] Foreign control, both economically and, subsequently, in education, has more to gain, in terms of its preservation, by advancing the population density and resource argument as a natural outcome of history rather than attempting to look carefully and critically at how foreign control of surplus contributes to a general state of underdevelopment, and how the language of educational reform is limited by including only those conceptions of development that act as appendages to that control.

The political economy paradigm focuses on the theory of underdevelopment, asserting that only by understanding the forces of underdevelopment can the contradictions be located and the struggle launched to resolve them.[51] The most likely place to begin would be with a general treatment of the development of capitalism, since the latter acts as a springboard for both the Marxist and the dependency theorists. While Wilber and Jameson do treat the relationship between those in control and those in subordinate roles in the above statement on underdevelopment, they have not explained how capitalism failed to experience the same results in the areas that fall under the category of "underdeveloped." Their theory rests on a diffusionist foundation on which beliefs about the rise of European "modernization" are based. In his work, "Colonialism and the Rise of Capitalism," James Blaut states:

It is still critically important to demonstrate that European social evolution has always been self-generated, owing nothing important to the non-European world, that Europe (or rather Western Europe, "the West") has always been, and remains today, ahead of the rest of the world in level and rate of development, that its economic system, capitalism, is the core of its uniquely progressive character, and that progress for the non-European world can only come via the diffusion of European-based multinational capitalism.[52]

Thus, even before we enter into a study of underdevelopment as stated by Wilber and Jameson, we need to understand how competing conceptions of capitalist development focus upon particular conceptions of development to resolve the problems facing underdevelopment. In Puerto Rico, the newly arrived business class was made up of those from the United States whose capital turned Puerto Rico into a "classical monocultural colony, directed by U.S. business interests and dominated by capitalist methods of production, with sugar becoming the leading export crop."[53] According to Wilber and Jameson's account, this may suffice to explain why underdevelopment may occur; yet Blaut insists that we further investigate the experience of the underdeveloped country and the relationship to the developed country. In Puerto Rico, for example, agriculture and other industries had begun to play an important role in the development of the country for over a third of a century before the U.S. invasion and occupation. "Technology improved as financing made its purchase easier, and production became more 'rationalized' accompanied by a growing working class."[54] Whether capitalism's development would have flourished without the U.S. invasion would be idle speculation at this point; what is certain is that a tendency in that direction was developing. Wilber and Jameson continue by affirming that a large share of the potential social surplus is used by the aristocratic landlords in excess consumption and the maintenance of unproductive laborers as a strategy for social and economic control. Change is thus opposed to the degree that it threatens the power held by the ruling classes and the governments legitimizing that power.

In his work on colonialism and the rise of capitalism, Blaut argues that the triumph of capitalism, occurring first in Europe, is not because of uniquely European facts but because of colonialism.[55] He argues that the rise of capitalism in Europe is more the result of sixteenth and seventeenth century colonialism.[56] Blaut goes on to demonstrate how the development patterns in Europe and outside were quite even throughout the Middle Ages and that after 1492, though the main characteristics of preindustrial capitalism were already in place in Europe as well as in other areas, this mode of production was dominant only in small sections of the European landscape and did not have the force of state power behind it.[57] This mode of production was unable to accumulate capital, increase production, or increase the wage work force quickly. "Colonialism removed the constraints," remarks Blaut. It provided capitalism in this region with the resources needed to increase its scale and its political power.[58]

Generally speaking, Wilber and Jameson's Marxist account of the development of capitalism as it relates to underdevelopment falls dangerously into the realm of diffusionism, which many theorists from the "underdeveloped" areas of the world strongly criticize for its approximation to imperialism. Furthermore, this account, though Marxist, disallows the legitimacy of different conceptions of development originating in the "underdeveloped" areas by stressing the centrality of Europe as the hub of all development, without a proper account of its relations to the rest of the world. Conceptually speaking, this kind of theoretical supremacy makes it difficult for the meaning of development to expand significantly.

The second theory within the political economy model is referred to as dependency theory. "The development of capitalism and the world market is seen as a twofold process": the underdevelopment of Africa, Asia, and Latin America is the consequence of the process of development of Europe and North America.[59] Dependency, in this account, signifies that many of the most important decisions about development strategies are those of entities external to the country.[60] As was stated earlier in this chapter, Puerto Rico's development since 1898 has been directed toward U.S. interests. The meaning and role of development have generally reflected the maintenance of dependency. The possibilities for expanding the meaning of development and enlarging a conception of education remain circumscribed by a language of educational reform that includes only conceptions of development that continue to encourage external control.

According to Gunder Frank, considered the father of dependency theory, a central thesis shared by both neoclassical and orthodox Marxist theories of development (and of which he was critical) was the necessary and normal stage of capitalism in the developmental hierarchy.[61] Both of these positions accepted what Frank refers to as a "dualistic view of the Third World." For the neoclassical, capitalism stood as the end of development; for the orthodox Marxist, capitalism remained a necessary stage in the transformation toward socialism.

In the neoclassical view, the degree to which a country is able to transform its traditional sector into a working part of the modern sector determines growth. Also, the neoclassical view understands development ultimately in terms of the market behaviors of individual actors.[62] Again, the notion of "proper" or "rational" behavior and conditions conducive to growth are appealed to by the neoclassical views. Frank rejects both the neoclassical and the orthodox Marxist theories. His confidence that future historical research will support this position, may have been enriched by the research of Blaut and a host of others whose work challenges basic elements of the above mentioned Marxist positions.

The second thesis of dualism that Frank rejects is that the present condition of the undeveloped countries is similar to some original, predevelopment stage of the presently developed countries.[63] This is what Blaut alludes to in his work on the relationship between colonialism and capitalism's development. That is, if at some point in history, "Europe had no advantage over Africa or Asia as to level and rate of development out of feudalism and toward capitalism," then the present condition of underdeveloped nations is not original, primal, or traditional; rather, this state is a product of the historical development of capitalism on a world scale.[64] This argument is important for at least two reasons. First, the arguments advanced by different conceptions and trajectories of development gain theoretical relevance and support as they challenge the neoclassical and orthodox Marxist positions. Second, since development is a product of historical sequence,

it is no longer correct to refer to the present conditions of the less-developed nations today as undeveloped— the now developed countries were never underdeveloped, though they may have been undeveloped— this accounts for the use of the term underdeveloped.[65]

An examination of colonialism and dependency in Puerto Rico might be more conducive to an accurate explanation of underdevelopment. "The experiment of development programs based upon capital-intensive, foreign owned, vertically integrated, and export oriented corporate expansion has been carried out more fully in Puerto Rico than in any other country in the world."[66] It is within this logic of orthodox economic planning in Puerto Rico that the strategies for developing educational reform policies develop.

For dependency to exist, then, there must be present two parts: the dominant and the dependent. The key to the relationship is control. Thus, though the metropolis may depend upon the satellite, to borrow Frank's terms, the overriding aspect favoring the metropolis is the control it exerts on economic and social determinations.

In conclusion, we are reminded that the determination of dependency, though seemingly simple to identify, requires a careful understanding of the economic and political forces both within and outside the dependent country that nourish the dependency relationship. For example, a society can undergo profound changes in its production system without the creation of fully autonomous decision-making centers; or a national society can achieve a certain autonomy of decision without thereby having a production system and an income distribution comparable with those in the central developed countries or even in some peripheral developing countries.[67] This account of dependency is not intended to imply that a country can "go at it alone" in today's world—if a country ever could. However, it does have the intent of presenting a second theory that accounts for underdevelopment in the world; a theory which raises questions regarding not only the possibilities of development but also the conceptual framework from which such possibilities will arise. Thus, if one position sees development in terms of maximizing rational behavior conducive to market expansion, the conceptions of development (including the role that social institutions like education play in advancing this rationality) will correspond to a particular language regarding development.

The attitudes related to the development plan are characterized by a particular technological rationality conducive to that conception of development, a rationality that becomes instrumental in the development of a country's educational programs.

"The instrumentalistic conception of technological rationality," remarks Herbert Marcuse, "is spreading over almost the whole realm of thought and gives the various intellectual activities a common denominator. They become a kind of technique, a matter of training rather than individuality, requiring the expert rather than the complete human personality."[68]

In this context, the language of educational development can appeal to one of at least three alternatives. First, education can be seen as divorced from the economic developments in the country, since education's role is not limited to the demands of preparing a work force. Second, education might attack the economic problems by focusing on the economic situation, in which case the role that politics plays in education, in terms of the dependency relationship, will have to deal with some rather profound contradictions. And last, education might try to strike a balance between the preparation for a vocation and a less circumscribed notion of development, as in appeals to truth, some forms of critical thinking, virtue, or the quest for knowledge. This is not to say that the three do not or cannot overlap. However, it is important to understand that from a position of power, the language of development regarding education may be different from that expressed from a position of vulnerability (or, in this case, dependency). Yet in a dependent relationship very often the language of educational reform echoes the language articulated by the metropolis. Thus the ideological relationship is preserved and the economic arrangement remains intact.

Again, dependency is not responsible for the perpetuation of an "instrumentalistic conception of technological rationality." Instrumentalism can exist in different settings laying claim to different ideological, political, and economic beliefs. Nevertheless, this instrumentalistic rationality for development does contribute to the perpetuation and standardization of the language of development. For Max Weber,

Rationalization is the key to all modernization and industrialization and represents the historical (originally under capitalism) penetration of all spheres of social life: the economy, culture (art, religion and science), technology, laws and politics, and everyday life by a single logic of *formal rationality*. This "logic" is defined by the principle of orientation of human action to abstract, quantifiable and calculable, and instrumentally utilizable formal rules and norms. The key to formal rationality is the phrase "without regard for persons."[69]

If Weber and Herbert Marcuse are correct, then the culture, the belief system, and maybe perhaps even the language and the physical geography of a country are subordinate to the prerequisites undergirding a rationalization for modernization— a technical rationality. Such a logic is consistent with the orthodox paradigm of economic development that we noted earlier, and its attempts to explain the absence or failure of development in terms of deficiencies (i.e., nonrational behavior, cultural dualism accounting for a lack of achievement, or other social, cultural, or psychological constraints).[70] The predominance of such a logic and rationality constrains the possibilities for expanding the language of development, and in turn education then suffers from underdevelopment in some important ways and becomes essentially a training ground for initiation into the "rational world of work."

The orthodox and political economy paradigms attempt to explain both the causal and the procedural aspects of development and underdevelopment. Both can be characterized by a type of teleology. The orthodox paradigm asserts that development is dependent upon the maximizing of rational behavior within a market-based economy, while the political economists insist that the nature of the economic process is central to determining the possibilities and limits underlying development and underdevelopment. Wilber and Jameson illustrate this teleology through the equation history equals progress. In general, for the orthodox economist, the removal of constraints upon the market, given the rational nature of self-interested individuals, will enhance development in a progressively unfolding manner. For the political economist, development is seen as the unfolding, in human history, of the progressive emancipation of peoples and nations from the control of nature and of other peoples and nations.[71]

The difficulty with both paradigms is that they attempt to explain very complex issues of political and economic change in oversimplified and predominantly Eurocentric terms. What remains of importance to this work however, is the relationship that the orthodox conception of development has to the language of educational development and reform. Both the orthodox and political-economic theories, given their adherence to specific economic agendas with related values, are directly and indirectly connected to different political agendas. Regarding this point, Daniel Ruccio and Lawrence Simon remark, "Radical theorists tend to be more upfront about their political interests. Orthodox theorists, concerned to claim the mantle of science, tend to shy away from stating explicitly the political dimensions and implications of their approach."[72]

If it is true that each of the paradigms is connected to a political agenda, then the conceptions of educational development would differ for each. The orthodox view of education will focus on the instrumentalistic features of an education that promotes and inculcates the maximization of rational behavior within a market-generated economy. The political economy view might then focus on the development of an educational program directed at overcoming control or dependence by concentrating on the local or national needs and aspirations as articulated by the culture. Yet if we agree that both paradigms oversimplify the issue of development by reducing their explanations to some ultimately determining factor, then are we not also compelled to examine more carefully and critically the relationship of development dynamics to educational reform?

The history of Puerto Rico's economic development and the role of schools are closely linked to the history of the country's political status. The power and popularity of the orthodox view persist. Education has played a major role in contributing to the preservation of the orthodox model of development. The attempts to reform education have historically failed to alleviate some of the country's greatest problems: unemployment, a growing rate of illiteracy, and high dropout rates. To assert that independence would reverse underdevelopment would be an oversimplification of the reality. However, in the present situation, the legitimacy of different conceptions of development, whether regarding the country at large or education in particular, is determined by the relationship Puerto Rico has with the United States. This circumscribes the possibilities for expanding the meaning of development. In other words, the very language of educational development is underdeveloped.

The first requirement, and quite possibly the most important, with respect to the expansion of a particular conception of development is agreement upon a language of development and its inculcation. In the case of Puerto Rico, this occurred in two general periods of the country's economic and social history. The first is here referred to as the "monocultural" period of development (see chapter 3); the second is referred to as the period of "growth" and "underdevelopment" (see chapter 5). Although the work will rely heavily on the economic analysis of James Dietz, that reliance is not meant to preclude the validity of other arguments. However, Dietz's analysis offers an element of consistency for the debates regarding development and school reform policy in Puerto Rico.

NOTES

1. Dennis Goulet, "Development . . . or Liberation," in *The Political Economy of Development and Underdevelopment*, ed. Charles Wilber (New York: Random House, Business Division, 1988), 484.

2. Frantz Fanon, *The Wretched of the Earth*, trans. Constance Farrington (New York: Grove Press, 1963), 35.

3. Charles Wilber and Kenneth P. Jameson, "Paradigms of Economic Development and Beyond," in *The Political Economy of Development and Underdevelopment*, ed. Charles Wilber, (New York: Random House, 1988), 5.

4. Ibid., 6.

5. Ibid., 7.

6. Frank Bonilla and Ricardo Campos, "A Wealth of Poor: Puerto Ricans in the International Order," *Daedalus* 110 (Spring 1981): 146.

7. Wilber and Jameson, "Paradigms of Economic Development," 7.

8. James Dietz, *Economic History of Puerto Rico : Institutional Change and Capitalist Development* (Princeton: Princeton University Press, 1986), 139.

9. Richard Weiskoff, *Factories and Food Stamps: The Puerto Rican Model of Development* (Baltimore: Johns Hopkins University Press, 1985) 136.

10. Wilber and Jameson, "Paradigms of Economic Development," 7.

11. Ibid., 8.

12. Ibid.

13. Ibid.

14. Dietz, *Economic History*, 98.

15. Ibid.

16. George W. Davis, *Report of the Military Governor of Porto Rico on Civil Affairs* (Washington, D.C.: U.S. Government Printing Office, 1900), 14.

17. Marcia Rivera Quintero, "Educational Policy and Female Labor, 1898–1930," in *Intellectual Roots of Independence: An Anthology of Puerto Rican Political Essays*, ed. Iris M. Závala and Rafael Rodríguez (New York: Monthly Review Press, 1980), 350–51.

18. Wilber and Jameson, "Paradigms of Economic Development," 8.

19. Dietz, *Economic History*, 185.

20. Wilber and Jameson, "Paradigms of Economic Development," 9.

21. Juan José Osuna, *A History of Education in Puerto Rico* (Río Piedras: University of Puerto Rico Press, 1975), 603–04.

22. Wilber and Jameson, "Paradigms of Economic Development," 9.

23. Ibid.

24. Ibid.

25. Ibid.

26. Kathy McAfee, "Hurricane: IMF, World Bank, U.S. AID in the Caribbean," in *NACLA Report*, vol. 23, No. 5, (February 1990): 13.

27. Wilber and Jameson, "Paradigms of Economic Development," 9.

28. Ibid.

29. Dietz, *Economic History*, 183.

30. Wilber and Jameson, "Paradigms of Economic Development, " 10.

31. Ibid., 11.

32. Agustín Cueva, *El desarrollo del capitalismo en América Latina* (Mexico City: Siglo XXI, 1977), 23–24.

33. Candida Cotto, "Aumenta la Pobreza en Puerto Rico," *Claridad*, vol. 1921, December 1–7, 1989, 4.

34. Weiskoff, *Factories and Food Stamps*, 2.

35. Wilber and Jameson, "Paradigms of Economic Development," 11.

36. Ibid.

37. Michael Todaro, "A Model of Labor Migration and Urban Underdevelopment in Less Developed Countries,"*American Economic Review* vol. 58 (Mar. 1969): 138–48.

38. Centro de Estudios Puertorriqueños (CENEP), Labor Migration and Capitalism: The Puerto Rican Experience (New York: Monthly Review Press, 1980), 180–81.

39. Dietz, *Economic History*, 227–28.

40. Wilber and Jameson, "Paradigms of Economic Development," 12.

41. Dietz, *Economic History*, 295.

42. McAfee, "Hurricane," 16–17.

43. Wilber and Jameson, "Paradigms of Economic Development," 12.

44. Ibid., p. 13.

45. Dietz, *Economic History*, 243.

46. Cueva, *Desarrollo del capitalismo,* 221.

47. Wilber and Jameson, "Paradigms of Economic Development," 15.

48. Ibid., p. 14.

49. Ibid., p. 15.

50. Dietz, *Economic History*, 287.

51. Wilber and Jameson, "Paradigms of Economic Development," 15.

52. James Blaut, "Colonialism and the Rise of Capitalism," *Science and Society* 53, no. 3 (Fall 1989): 261.

53. Dietz, *Economic History*, 99.

54. Ibid., p. 98.

55. Blaut, "Colonialism and the Rise of Capitalism," 263.

56. Ibid., p. 268.

57. Ibid., p. 290.

58. Ibid.

59. Wilber and Jameson, "Paradigms of Economic Development," 19.

60. Ibid.

61. David F. Ruccio and Lawrence H. Simon, "Radical Theories of Development: Frank, The Modes of Production School and Amin," in *The Political Economy of Development and Underdevelopment*, ed. Charles Wilber (New York: Random House, 1988), 124.

62. Ibid.

63. Ibid., p. 125.

64. Ibid., p. 126.

65. Ibid.

66. Dietz, *Economic History*, 309.

67. Fernando H. Cardoso and Enzo Faletto, *Dependency and Development in Latin America,* trans. Marjory Mattingly Urquidi (Berkeley: University of California Press, 1979), 18–19.

68. Herbert Marcuse, "Some Social Implications of Modern Technology," in *The Essential Frankfurt School Reader*, ed. Andrew Arato and Eike Gebhardt (New York: Continuum, 1982) 153.

69. Andrew Arato, "Esthetic Theory and Cultural Criticism," in *The Essential Frankfurt School Reader*, ed. Andrew Ararto and Eike Gebhardt (New York: Continuum, 1982), 191.

70. Wilber and Jameson, "Paradigms of Economic Development," 8.

71. Ibid., p. 14.

72. Rucio and Simon, "Radical Theories of Development," 166.

A sugarcane cutter in Guánica (1941). From *Puerto Rico Mio*, photography by Jack Delano, published by the Smithsonian Institute. Washington, D.C., 1990.

Reconstituting the Economy: Orthodox Development as a Form of Control

"We will not renounce our part in the mission of our race, trustees under God, of the civilization of the world," said Senator Albert Beveridge. "God has not been preparing the English speaking and Teutonic peoples for a thousand years for nothing but vain and . . . idle contemplation and self-admiration. No! He has made us the master organizers of the world to establish system where chaos reigns. He has made us adept in government that we may administer government among savages and senile people."[1]

*I*n Chapter 2 we examined two different paradigms of development. The orthodox paradigm centered on the growth of per capita income and high mass consumption, while the political economy paradigm focused on the nature of the process of economic growth. The former admits that a prerequisite for growth may include a society's commitment to change some of its values; the latter insists that one goal is the emancipation of peoples from control by other peoples and nations. In the orthodox paradigm, the primacy of growth and the prerequisite that people's values change according to what is referred to as the requirements for the maximization of rationalization (i.e. the articulation of a development model that adheres to a notion of rationalization consistent with a predominantly market-driven economy) place cultural values second to the efficiency and "matter-of-factness" that the growth-as-development paradigm advances. The second paradigm places more emphasis upon people's values and their culture in the development project. Development here is contingent upon more than the advancement of people and labor as instruments of expediency. The contingency of the meaningfulness of human agency in the evolution of such a development paradigm plays a more significant role.

A country's public school system will invariably contribute to the reproduction and reinforcement of that society's conception of development; different conceptions of development imply differences in the forms of education. Our vision of development and education will influence, and is influenced, by the language we employ in aspiring to such development; and our language is intimately linked to the values we hold in our culture as these are exercised in the production and reproduction of that which sustains our lives. Schools, then, become paramount institutions in preparing us to speak a particular language of development, one that finds its logic and meaning in the everyday life of people as they make choices and decisions about what is valuable.

This chapter will examine Puerto Rico's first experiences with the orthodox paradigm of development as it was articulated through the political economy into its public school system and culture generally under U.S. colonial control. In its initial phase, the orthodox model contributed to the development of a monocultural society whose predominant source of economic livelihood was the production of sugar. The character of such an economy had a profound impact upon the vision and disposition of educational policies implemented in Puerto Rico's growing public school system. The time frame covers the period from 1898 to roughly 1940.

In discussing the monocultural period, the chapter focuses on the evolution of an economically orthodox model of development as it became entrenched in Puerto Rico through its colonial relationship with the United States. This examination relies upon an understanding of the economic situation evolving during the period. The chapter argues that within the development project a system of values predicated upon the silencing of the culture, in the political-ideological sense, aimed at securing the well-being of a U.S.-directed orthodox economics in Puerto Rico. This chapter is divided into four sections. The first section presents an account of Puerto Rico's first experiences with U.S. economic development plans through the implementation of economic and political controls upon the island. The country's development was reinforced by policies aimed at rationalizing the role and leadership of the United States in Puerto Rico.

The second section examines the economic environment in the primary stages of U.S. colonialism as Puerto Rico's economy remained monocultural with the substitution of sugar for the once dominant coffee industry. This transition was important in that it allowed the United States to reconstruct the economy without disturbing the colonial single-crop emphasis. Such dynamics figured significantly in the development of policies and a rationale for public schooling.

The third section concerns the impact that the dominant sugar industry had on the lives of Puerto Ricans and the overall contribution that the sugar economy made to improvements and changes in Puerto Rican development. The final section of the chapter briefly analyzes some of the implications of the economic development plans in Puerto Rico for U.S.-Puerto Rican relations under colonialism— that is, how the development model could be understood as a form of control or domination through the incorporation and inculcation into the economy of production relations whose logic would reside in the rationalization of production under the aegis of the colonial power.

The issue here is not an argument attacking rationalization. It is an examination of how the process of rationalization in a colonial context transforms the identity of the colonized.

PREPARING THE LANDSCAPE

On July 28, 1898, three days after the invasion and U.S. occupation of Puerto Rico, evidence of the impending changes in the language and practice of development was first presented by General Nelson Miles in a declaration that reads in part:

The primary effect of this occupation will be the immediate transition from your former system of government, desiring that you accept with joy the system of government of the United States'. . . . we have come to bring protection, not only to you, but also to your property, promoting your prosperity and bestowing upon you the guarantees and the blessings of the liberal institutions of our government.[2]

Some months later, in 1899, Governor George W. Davis, in an attempt to draw support for the americanization of Puerto Rico, appealed to an implicit sense of progress that only the United States could afford Puerto Rico:

How could it be expected [changes in dispositions], the Puerto Ricans cling tenaciously to the uses, customs and local laws, with which they are familiar. The implementation of a reform or the instituting of an innovation will present many difficulties, not precisely because the public is linked to its former customs, rather because many of them cannot understand the measures proposed to substitute said customs. They prefer to maintain the former institutions and laws, though these may result defective. [3]

Both expressions are examples of the language that came to characterize, and influence the scope of legitimacy within which competing conceptions of development could be articulated. At the level of direct governance, the United States controlled political matters of the state. According to General Miles, this meant that a value system that protected the rights of private property and embraced a conception of liberalism brought to Puerto Rico, but neither created by nor an outcome of the participation of the Puerto Rican people, would be implemented. The transition of government from a Spanish colony to a U.S. colonial arrangement meant the restructuring of the economy and civil institutions, including the schools, so that these would reflect not only the understandings of what the different institutions meant according to the United States, but also the assurance that United States' interests in Puerto Rico would be secured through the transformation or silencing of the culture by, among other means, inculcating and eliciting agreement on a U.S.-controlled orthodox model of development through a newly institutionalized public school system. Furthermore, Davis's report implied the need to incorporate English into the Puerto Rican society, since the ability of Puerto Ricans to understand what the United States had in mind for their country's development was limited by their attachment to familiar customs and a language barrier that kept them tied to Spain and unable to understand the new administration and its function. The first organic laws governing Puerto Rico attested to the political and economic character being forged under the new colonial regime.

In 1900 Senator Joseph Foraker, from whom the Foraker Act received its name, affirmed that Puerto Ricans, "have not been prepared for any kind of experience for participation in government."[4] Yet Puerto Rico had gained an autonomy never since experienced under U.S. colonialism by the Autonomy Charter of 1897, signed by Spain and the result of much struggle and resistance to Spanish colonialism. Foraker's statement however becomes significant in the context of U.S. social and economic development plans for Puerto Rico and the need to implement a particular set of activities, including the establishment of a school system, that would create support among the people for U.S. tutelage. In addition, Foraker made it clear that the primary focus of the Puerto Rico-United States relationship was the expansion and security of U.S. interests:

We have reached the point in the development of our resources and the multiplication of our industries where we are not only supplying our home demands, but are producing a large surplus, constantly growing larger. Our greatest prospective and commercial need is for markets abroad. We cannot find them in the countries of Europe. Their demand upon us is limited. They strive to supply themselves and to compete with us in the markets of the world.[5]

Foraker was making a number of inferences. First, he suggests that in Puerto Rico the demand for U.S. goods and industries would be great. Second, that the Puerto Rican market would provide some of the U.S. commercial needs. And third, that commercial development in Puerto Rico would simply be a matter of expanding the range of the U.S. market. Furthermore, the statement is important when juxtaposed to U.S. policy in Puerto Rico at the time. Avoiding any delays, the following day the United States implemented the Foraker Law. Signed by President McKinley on April 12, some two weeks earlier, this first organic law established the legal framework for the organization of a colonial government in Puerto Rico. Again, the role that Puerto Rican participation would play in the creation of the infrastructure would be determined from abroad. Such an alienating prescription for development would prove detrimental to Puerto Rican development, while allowing some growth. The development of future markets abroad required the organization and implementation of practices that would maximize a conception of rational behavior consistent with the envisioned model of orthodox economic development in Puerto Rico.

This behavior may best be described as a logical response to the market. In other words, rational economic behavior refers to a particular disposition or behavior consistent with market demands. Logically, then, the lower the price the more a consumer is willing to buy; consumers seek to maximize the satisfactions they obtain from the use of their resources. They would not be "rational" if they did not.[6] Thus, maximizing rational behavior, dependent upon a host of factors, contributes to the predictability and security of rational behavior in regard to the market. Some of these factors include the role of advertising, the widening of choices, and the distribution of income; all of these support the process of maximizing rational behavior. The schools then become a central institution for the development of behavior patterns and cognitive responses compatible with the maximization of rational behavior.

The rapid economic developments that characterized the United States during the late nineteenth and early twentieth centuries, as Foraker so lucidly expressed, placed expansionist economic policies at the forefront of U.S. plans for political-economic supremacy. The expansion of public schooling, and in particular the role of English as the language of instruction and the highly centralized school administration, responded carefully to a set of requirements forged by the U.S. interests in creating a new and politically captive market within the context of a monocultural economy.

THE TRANSITION TO SUGAR

Before the U.S. invasion and occupation of Puerto Rico, the leading Puerto Rican cash crop was coffee. Two primary reasons accounted for the decline in coffee production and the change to sugar production as the leading crop. The first was natural: the destruction of Puerto Rico's coffee plantations by hurricane San Ciriaco on August 8, 1899, wiped out as much as 80 percent of the coffee crop.[7] However, human efforts contributed to a more permanent disposition that in the final analysis destroyed the coffee economy. During the last decade of the nineteenth century, Puerto Rico's coffee exports to the United States represented less than 1 percent of its worldwide market.[8] Once the U.S. acquired jurisdiction over Puerto Rico, Spain, considering Puerto Rico a foreign country, raised the import tax on its coffee. This left Puerto Rico with the United States, which had no tariffs on coffee imports because there was no domestic product to protect against foreign competition. Puerto Rico's coffee entered the United States on the same terms as any country's coffee, but it was more expensive than South American coffee.[9] Since Puerto Rico was not considered part of the United States, its coffee remained unprotected by special tariffs; but its unincorporated status did not prevent sugar from receiving special tariff protection.[10] So, in effect, Puerto Rico's livelihood had been dealt a strong blow as a result of factors related to the new colonial economy and changes in the international coffee industry.

The precipitous drop in the value of coffee production between 1899 and 1940 was exacerbated by two additional factors: the disruption of the European markets during World War I and hurricane San Felipe in 1928, which destroyed the great majority of the coffee crop and most of the plants.[11] This did not mean that production of coffee ended. At times the relative value of coffee exports decreased while the absolute value and quantity increased.[12] The loss of markets, higher tariffs, the hurricane, and the Great Depression were all factors in the devastation experienced by the coffee industry.

Historically, life and work in the coffee sector were characterized by high levels of poverty and long periods of unemployment. In 1917, the Bureau of Labor reported that there were 156,700 persons in the coffee industry, including workers and individual owners. Wages for workers in the coffee industry were considerably lower than for the other two major agricultural industries, sugar and tobacco. Coffee workers were paid between 15 and 60 cents per day, according to age and sex.[13] The wages were low and the employment seasonal, so the little earned by the coffee workers was unlikely to ease the pain of poverty during the long periods of no harvest. The first three decades under U.S. colonial rule saw Puerto Rico's coffee industry dwindle. In 1895 the volume of coffee exports was approximately 40 million pounds; it dropped to approximately 800,000 pounds by 1935.[14] The leading consequence of the decline of Puerto Rico's coffee industry throughout the first three decades was the growth of wage labor.[15] By 1930 sugar production had increased to more than ten times that of 1900. Investments in sugar became more efficient and reliable, with a considerably lessened risk of losses due to natural catastrophes like hurricanes or to competition from within and abroad. Thus, one single-crop economy was replaced by another form: sugar replaced coffee.

SUGAR AS KING

Increased investments in the industry and the improved methods of production soon gave sugar the dominant position over all other exports. Again, the reality of a single-crop economy was not changing under U.S. colonial rule. Sugar replaced coffee. Yet the educational demands in terms of development remained quite low. There was no need for a highly skilled and educated population in such an economic environment. Nevertheless, the need to inculcate and secure the internalization of the values and logic of orthodox economics remained important.

Resistance to U.S. sugar imports from Puerto Rico was strongly articulated. Chief among those resisting the free entry of Puerto Rican sugar into the U.S. were the beet sugar producers. The concern was that Puerto Rico's cane sugar, should it be allowed to enter unrestricted, might attract other U.S. sugar clients and set a free-trade precedent sending the wrong message to other territories under U.S. control.[16] This is not to say that all U.S. interests favored a tariff on Puerto Rico's sugar. Gordon Lewis reminds us:

The U.S. consul in San Juan spoke of the several thousand letters he had received from continental business men seeking information about investment opportunities, in part because they had heard of the island people that ". . . they are not a class of people acquainted with strikes."[17]

With this kind of perceived environment, U.S. investment found the temptation to open businesses in Puerto Rico both lucrative and politically secure. The free traders won, and Puerto Rico's sugar was shielded from the full force of foreign competition. Production in 1930 was more than ten times the level of 1900. Though the increase in production was interrupted by hurricane San Felipe in 1928, the annual production during the later 1920s was greater than during the last decade of Spanish rule.[18] The force that sugar gained as the leading export while restricted primarily to one market created a dangerous situation for the Puerto Rican economy and development. Most of the sugar produced was targeted for the United States, progressively committing the island to a monocultural export economy; further, factors like drops in prices, natural disasters, and economic recession in the United States would, should any one or a combination of these occur, prove devastating to Puerto Rico, reducing its ability to purchase necessary goods.[19]

Furthermore, the United States was importing raw sugar and the refining took place in the United States. Thus the value added in production was created within the U.S. economy and accrued to U.S. companies.[20] This provided evidence of the stagnation of technological development in Puerto Rico. Reserving the implementation of the more technologically sophisticated practices for the United States retarded technological research and development in Puerto Rico. Researching this concern, Daniel Headrick reminds us:

Technology, however, is not monuments but knowledge and activity. Its transfer, to be complete, involves the spread of activity and knowledge not only from one area to another, but also from one people to another. Hence our question becomes: How much, and for what reasons, did Asians, Africans, and Latin Americans learn about Western technology in the colonial period? And what was the role of schooling in that learning process?[21]

As the coffee industry declined, growers moved to the coastal areas where sugar plantations were being formed. This meant that population was concentrating in these areas. Landless laborers were increasingly moving to the sugar lands, as it became more difficult to survive on the coffee and tobacco plantations of the highlands. The population of Puerto Rico grew by more than 17 percent in the first decade of U.S. occupation, and changes in population for the sugar-growing municipalities averaged an increase of almost 46 percent (in Guánica, the largest sugar municipality, the population increase was an approximately 122 percent).[22] One might say that sugar cane production created a rural proletariat as a result of U.S. sugar investment that drew thousands of landless people from the mountains to the coastal sugar plantations.[23] The point is that the restructuring of the economy around sugar, including the effect of containing the population through a particular economic scheme, laid the infrastructural ground for one part of the total development picture. Given a particular objective reality, a sugar-based economy, the appeals regarding the development of other needs, such as education and its administration to the culture found some of their legitimacy in the established economic character of the country.

Finding it difficult to survive in the highlands, many of the coffee and tobacco growers migrated to the sugar lands in search of employment. What the Spanish had done to control labor and its activities under the *libreta* system, the United States was doing under a redesigned system of labor management— scientific management. Male migrants often exceeded female migrants by as much as 50 percent.[24] The United States in order to administer labor production needs, continued the *libreta* system by expanding sugar while reducing other sectors, concentrating land, and expanding the capitalization of the Puerto Rican culture.[25]

Advances in the technology and rationalization of sugar production resulted in the expansion of the industry. The coastal plains were dotted with huge sugar mills (*centrales*), whose modern technology processed the sugar harvested by cheap labor. The technology of irrigation brought formerly unusable and marginal land into use. Even land once used for domestic food production and pastures was engulfed by the growth of the sugar economy.[26] These advancements in technology (read "efficiency of production") reduced both the number of workers needed and the time that they would work (and hence earn wages). While this may seem a desirable development in the technological sense, such a shift left many former sugar workers unemployed. In 1917, for example, 40,000 sugar-cane workers in 32 municipalities went on strike for over five months. This was accompanied by strikes among workers on the docks and in the tobacco industry. In both cases, issues of employment, job security and development, in the midst of a changing economy, were the drving force. The changes in production however demonstrated the vulnerability of the Puerto Rican worker to the dictates of the economy and the model of development under the control of the United States. Thus, the colonial environment not only came under the tight control of the colonizer's economic plans but also given the need to alleviate the increasing economic strain, provided the colonizer with the space and legitimacy for disseminating and inculcating those values and means for alleviating the economic strain consistent with the economic plan.

With the growth of the sugar industry came the concentration of the island's population into the sugar-producing regions. At the same time the concentration of farmland came under U.S. control through legislation allegedly aimed at controlling the potential for monopolization of land ownership. In 1930 the number of farms with 500 or more acres was only 0.7 percent, yet these controlled 33.7 percent of all land. Though the Foraker and Jones acts forbade farms in excess of 500 acres, U.S. sugar interests were exempt from such regulation because they were often cooperative corporate ventures.[27]

Sugar-processing mills also came under U.S. control. Nearly 30 percent of the *centrales* in the decade of the thirties was owned by four U.S. firms.[28] These four companies accounted for more than 50 percent of Puerto Rico's total sugar output.[29] This is not to say that some Puerto Ricans did not have large landholdings. However, U.S. capitalist interests were the dominant economic force controlling Puerto Rico's production and wealth.[30]

The prosperity of the sugar industry was not reflected in the lives of the workers. While plantation workers in Hawaii and Cuba earned $.97 and $1.26 respectively, Puerto Ricans were being paid 63 cents per day. Averaging $3.34 per week in earnings on the plantations, Puerto Ricans spent over 94 percent of this on food, generally rice imported from the United States.[31]

Labor found it difficult to organize and challenge the persisting discrepancies between profits, prices, and wages because many were searching for jobs. Virtually every major product of the Puerto Rican export-oriented economy— coffee to some degree; sugar, tobacco, fruits, and other manufactured goods, to greater degrees went into the U.S. market. Profits were realized outside Puerto Rico, and wages, in the interest of production, had to be kept down. Wages were nothing more than a cost; they did not represent purchasing power for the commodities produced, since nearly all of the output was exported.[32] While sugar, it was argued, exceeded the value of other crops, as in the case of subsistence or locally marketed foods, gains did not accrue to the workers because profits contributed little to wages.

In addition to the sugar industry, exports of tobacco, mainly in the form of cigars, contributed to Puerto Rico's economy. Yet this should not be overestimated, since the land dedicated to tobacco was roughly one-sixth that of sugar. A large number of women found employment in the tobacco economy. During the period 1898–1940, the tobacco economy had more women employees than any other crop.[33] Like sugar, tobacco was controlled by the United States (80 to 85 percent). As in coffee, tobacco growers represented small landholders. By the 1930s, cigarmaking had become mechanized and cigar workers constituted a considerable part of the new urban proletariat.[34] Faring no better than sugar plantation workers, cigar workers earned $1.27 per week in 1933, while women in needlework factories earned $3.32 per week.[35] Whether for rural or urban work, women received less pay than men for the same job. More revealing is the fact that in tobacco 80 percent of the workers were women, while in the garment industry the representation was 85 percent.[36]

Survival for Puerto Ricans continued to be a serious burden. Consonant with the model of dependency engendered by the United States, the organic acts governing the island stipulated that imports would be carried on U.S. ships, thus raising the cost of these items and in many cases making them virtually unaffordable to the majority of the people. Puerto Ricans, earning an average one-fourth to one-tenth the average wages in New York, found themselves paying prices up to 14 percent more than those prices paid for similar items in New York.[37] One would assume that shipping costs would account for the price differential. However, it cost 15 cents to ship 100 pounds of sugar from Puerto Rico to New York, approximately 10.7 cents per 1,000 miles; sugar shipped from the Philippines to New York cost 2.7 cents per 1,000 miles.[38] The aggregate toll of these costs and policies not only affected the physical well-being of the nation but also placed the people in a situation where the urgency to satisfy life's simplest needs became the breeding ground upon which the United States propagated its political and economic stranglehold. The dismal reality facing workers in the garment and needlework industries was vividly presented by Bailey Diffie and Justine Diffie in their book *Puerto Rico: A Broken Pledge* :

The situation of the workers in this important industry is more distressing every day that passes. . . . We are in danger, therefore, of having to face a new social problem, created by thousands of women and children suffering from malnutrition, debility or sickness brought on by this condition of things.[39]

In a predominantly rural country and lacking the encouragement— economic, political, or otherwise— to farm, the vast majority of a growing Puerto Rican population remained in poverty and subject to the changes that the new colonial economy would bring.

In 1900 the population of Puerto Rico was approximately 953,243. By 1930 it was 1,579,413.[40] Approximately 72.3 percent lived in rural areas.[41] The Brookings Institution noted that almost 80 percent of the rural population owned no land and were dependent for their well being upon the benevolence of the colonizer or landowner. [42]

In the same report the Brookings Institution reported that the "condition of the masses of the Island people remains deplorable."[43] During the 1930s resistance to U.S. presence gained more visibility as voices called for independence and workers demanded change as the contradictions that characterized Puerto Rican colonial existence grew worse.   Faced with such a reality, the United States implemented a Puerto Rican variation of Franklin Roosevelt's New Deal.

The New Deal might well fall under the category "planning economy response to laissez-faire failures." Economically, for Puerto Rico this meant the legitimacy of more direct government control in determining the vision of development for the country. Furthermore, this program legitimized the tightening of the economic/ideological net. In other words, the rationality supporting U.S. interests and orthodox development could now, through government direction, seek its legitimacy in carefully constructed appeals to notions of "freedom" and "free enterprise" or "opportunity" and "progress and modernization." From an overall standpoint, this might not have seemed like a bad deal. However, the projects in the program aided little in the development of a Puerto Rican economic base, or of the possibilities for a Puerto Rican voice to contribute to the creation of a development model that would address local needs and aspirations. The New Deal produced little for Puerto Rico. The country's development problem was not grounded in the need to restore an economy; rather, the issue was economic and developmental construction that would respond to Puerto Rican national needs that would generate development. Instead, U.S. investments through the New Deal proved to be temporary and ameliorative, offering little in the way of contributions to long-term structural projects able to address the needs of Puerto Ricans.[44]

During the 1930s, the Nationalist party became stronger and more visible as the demand for independence was taken into the international arena under the presidency of Pedro Albizu Campos. "Perhaps it was coincidental," remarks James Dietz, "that the demise of the New Deal reconstruction program in Puerto Rico occurred at this time, but it seems more likely that it was connected with attempts to suppress the Nationalists."[45] The worsening of conditions for most Puerto Ricans, U.S. failures to deliver on the promise of political and economic self-determination, and a sense that the Puerto Rican nation and culture were the targets of destruction contributed to the rise in Nationalist efforts to challenge the United States through, among other means, direct action. Hence, it seems plausible that the rationale behind the colonial government's infusion of relief was actually part of a strategy to do little more than mitigate the suffering. "They did little permanently," cites Harvey Perloff, "to strengthen the foundation of the economy or to solve the underlying economic problems."[46] The failures of the above policies forced the colonial government to come up with a different strategy, one that would squelch the nationalists by adjusting economic policies while preserving colonial rule.

The 1930s saw the rise of resistance to U.S. economic plans, often resulting in strikes. In 1934 the Agricultural Adjustment Act was implemented in Puerto Rico, encouraging farmers to plant and produce less, with the hope that higher prices in the presence of higher demand and shortages would increase farm prices to what they had been between 1900 and 1914.[47] The rationale and logic for a strategy of government involvement in the development model had been initiated through these U.S.-aided projects in the colonial government, and found a Puerto Rican manifestation under a U.S.-designed local strategy.

The new strategy was known as the Chardón Plan. This plan called for the creation of small-scale local capitalists who would be able to compete in the global arena by exercising local control over capital, production, and economic decision making. There was a sense that through this plan the devastation facing Puerto Rico would be reversed only economically, and that all underdevelopment and colonialism would disappear. The plan called for some rather interesting changes that would have an important impact on schooling. This plan at no time suggested the need for the fundamental change of any institutions, political or other, in the existing colonial relationship. The overarching rationale of the plan was to encourage emigration, relocate farmers, develop "appropriate" industries, and give the government control of one sugar *central*.[48] Generally speaking, the plan proposed that industrial development for export become the focus for addressing the economic ills facing Puerto Rico. Export was the Chardón Plan's generative theme. And so it was that Puerto Rico's economy was characterized by the progressive proliferation of industries built on labor; sugar refining, canneries, bottling companies, shoe and furniture production, ceramic production, and tourism.[49]

Although it was estimated that unemployment would fall by 17,000 persons and that it would create some 50,000 new jobs, the Chardón Plan fell far below the requirements for addressing the needs of over 150,000 heads of households.[50] The solution proposed by the commission was emigration. This had a lasting effect on schooling and the language issue. By promoting emigration to the United States as an alternative that offered the Puerto Rican people a promising option for economic survival and growth, English as the language of instruction would receive needed legitimacy and support.

From the perspective of the orthodox argument, the failures of the program resulted from the Puerto Rican people's inability to develop the processes and institutions that would ensure maximum development under such a model. The political economy paradigm might explain it as a failure of the development model to take into account the dynamics and differences characterizing Puerto Rico. And the fact that the model was under the strict control and articulation of the colonial government constituted a form of domination. The rise of nationalism during the period was, in part, an expression of the dissatisfaction of the Puerto Rican people with the manner in which the country was developing. To ward off any further development of the nationalist struggle, the United States implemented numerous projects under the New Deal as "safety valves" to curtail the rising anti-American sentiment— to some degree, this might help explain part of the logic behind the Chardón Plan. Again, orthodox economics might criticize the actions of those Puerto Rican people in their demands for political and economic self-determination as hasty. Nevertheless, the model was not to be abandoned, only modified in order to keep it intact while granting some concessions.

DEVELOPMENT AS A FORM OF CONTROL

The technological advancements in sugar production and the expansion of the factory system of work, whether in the sugar mills, the manufacturing of cigars, or needlework, introduced a new conception of development and work relations to Puerto Ricans. The rationalization and bureaucratization of work through hierarchies and the development of scientific management contributed to the establishment of a rationale that was to undergird the language of Puerto Rican development under the United States. This was evidenced by the implementation of policies affecting the patterns of migration to the lowland sugar-producing regions, where the United States was investing the greatest part of its capital. The orthodox paradigm of development might reject the view that tight controls are necessary to secure the success of a capitalist project. This seems to contradict the very nature of "free" enterprise or "free" market. Yet these controls were exercised not only for the United States to inculcate the mechanics for its development plans but also to prepare to transform the people so they would respond positively to those plans despite the reality that the behavior patterns transmitted through economic production and the schools would not focus on the national, cultural, and economic development needs of the local population. How would such changes translate into forms of control? For some understanding of the dynamics, I turn to a brief introduction of the concept of rationalization.

Max Weber's treatment of rationalization and the rise of instrumental reason offers an extremely complex yet fundamental analysis of the shaping of all scientific practice according to the model of the natural sciences and the extension of (scientific) rationality to "the conduct of life itself."[51] Thus, the changes experienced in Puerto Rico, in terms of production and the maximization of rationalization through the transformation of industries in the form of an expanding factory system producing sugar, tobacco, and needlework, not only affected the more visible aspects of the society (concentration of population, displacement of workers, birth control and population control initiatives under the auspices of eugenicists and others, and the demand for a work force able and willing to assume work relations under a U.S. capitalist mode of production) but also invaded the consciousness of the Puerto Rican culture. The concentration of land under the U.S. development plans profoundly affected the population's movements and the role of schooling.

The instrumentality of schooling within the rationalization process under the new economic development plan was made apparent by the manner in which accessibility to schools, a highly centralized administration, language policies, municipal abilities to contribute to teachers' salaries and accommodations, the availability of time for schoolwork, and facilities were mediated by changes in the patterns and fluctuations of the developing economic model.

By challenging the legitimacy of the Spanish language in the context of development, by rationalizing behavior where values were conditioned and evaluated on the grounds of the contribution they made to the maximization of a particular behavior, and by subordinating the Puerto Rican culture to all that was "American," the foundations of the culture were threatened. The effects of the rationalization behind the changes in production, coupled with the process of replacing the Puerto Rican culture with that of the United States including the language, placed demands, restrictions, and constraints on the possibilities for a Puerto Rican voice regarding development. Under the United States, the expansion of the public school system contributed significantly to the reproduction and reinforcement of the rationality behind the development plans implemented by the U.S. colonial government.

In his *Introduction to Critical Theory,* David Held remarks:

Weber's concept of rationalization refers to first, the growth in mathematization of experience and knowledge.... Second, the secularization of life leads to a growth of means-end rationality, whereby there is "the methodological attainment of a definitely given and practical end by the use of an increasingly precise calculation of ... means." Third, there is a growth of rationality in terms of the development of "ethics that are systematically and unambiguously oriented to fixed goals."[52]

With the dominance of the sugar industry in the Puerto Rican economy, the development model under the United States encouraged a particular distribution of labor across the country along particular industrial lines characterized by low yet specific skills. Evidence indicates that human efforts played a significant role in the construction of the economically dominant sugar industry in terms of its mathematical composition (i.e., through tariff protection of sugar, allowing coffee to decline output, investments and capital gains, employment profile, and wealth distribution). In so doing, the value of work and knowledge was more intimately linked, by the rationalization of labor as time and money, in an orthodox economic plan under U.S. control.

The poverty characterizing the coffee sector also contributed to the decline of coffee and the subsequent move to the sugar industry by the many workers left unemployed. This, too, contributed to the "mathematization of experience and knowledge." First, labor for the bigger U.S. sugar companies would be easy to find. This kept wages down and workers in competition for employment. Second, control of wages and employment, accompanied by the improved methods of sugar production, gave the United States the wherewithal to define most of the arrangements regarding industrial development, and the legitimacy to further develop the rationalization ("read mathematization") of knowledge and experience— which would prove to be indispensable in the establishment and administration of the public school system as a partner in the development project. Given the poverty and, comparatively speaking, the low level of economic growth in Puerto Rico, the changes the United States brought, though classical to any definition of colonialism, found considerable support among Puerto Ricans. Technology was fast developing, industries were growing, and it seemed at least minimally, that a better life was in the making. This, however, did not detract from the reality that under colonialism, Puerto Rico was progressively entrenching itself in an environment whose very logic would, for nearly a century, accept the colonizer as the vehicle by which and from which development ensued. And this, too, was attributable to the evolution of a rationalized development program that characterized those first decades. Here Held's remarks prove quite revealing.

Further evidence of the evolution of the rationalization of the colonial economy and its maximization was found in the emphasis upon the export, generally to the United States of most Puerto Rican products. Prices and wages were determined by U.S. companies that maintained low wages, considering them merely as costs. In addition, the forces of production that caused the decline of the coffee industry forced many thousands to migrate to the lowlands, where employment on the sugar plantations was possible though seasonal. Here again, able to control the movement of numbers (through wages, output, and employment), an orthodox model of development under the direction of the United States, found its legitimacy. Rational behavior here argued for the proliferation of an export-oriented economy in order to boost revenues, create jobs, and encourage investments— or profits for U.S. firms. How much would return to Puerto Rico was not for Puerto Rico to decide. Even the New Deal projects provided limited contributions for meeting the needs of the local population.

Improving the efficiency of workers through the establishment of a conception of intelligence predicated upon the mathematization of experience and knowledge and through scientific management became the driving force in many of Puerto Rico's social institutions. By responding to the requirements for the maximization of rational behavior, Puerto Ricans also developed a sense of power and influence that was reflected in their loyalty to the "modern" (and, by implication, developed and advanced) colonizer. This may seem a contradiction. Yet by responding to the mechanical requirements in the maximization of rationalization, reaction becomes not only rational but also reasonable. This is thus perceived by workers as empowering because they are in a position to "participate." As Herbert Marcuse put it:

Man does not experience this loss of freedom as the work of some hostile and foreign force; he relinquishes his liberty to the dictum of reason itself. The point is that . . . the apparatus to which the individual is to adjust and adopt himself is so rational that individual protest and liberation appear not only as hopeless but irrational.[53]

For Puerto Rico, then, the growth in the mathematization of knowledge, vis-à-vis changing employment patterns, the maintenance of a monocultural economy, wage labor under the United States, and the concentration of land and populations figured significantly in the secularization of life, the means-end rationality, and the development of an ethics tied to fixed goals. The impetus of this dynamics originated, and was situated, within the "modern" expertise of the United States. From this position development was a matter of complying with the demands, understanding the "need" for certain restrictions, and inculcating loyalty in the Puerto Rican people, who would become desensitized to the constraints, identifying social and economic ills as the manifestations of a people unable to govern and develop on their own. Control was secured, in part, through the developments in the means of production; they introduced a rationale for an economy not necessarily based on the specificity of place and needs, but more generally on the market demands as identified by the United States.

Development was to follow expanded capital investments in Puerto Rico. Intelligence, in the form of a rational response consistent with the economic demands of the development project characterized by the bureaucratization and hierarchical evolution of labor and capital, of knowledge and experience, contributed to a restructuring of identity grounded in these qualities and redefining individuality. The orthodox model called for a focus on an intelligence that would target the elimination of waste in terms of both human resources and capital. Puerto Ricans would learn to reduce individuality to self-preservation through standardization in the form of wage labor; this would affirm the orthodox assertion that a people's values— and this could include culture— might require considerable alteration in order to meet the demands of the market. This U.S. package was to find its legitimacy in the creation of profits that theoretically were to find their way into Puerto Rican hands.

In order to accomplish such a task, the United States continuously reiterated the need for Puerto Ricans to adopt the value system attached to the economic model introduced under U.S. colonialism. That a society's values may change can at times be desirable. The point, however, is that in a colonial relationship the changes are not introduced in response to the development of the values of the colonized people. Both the introduction of changes in values and the responses to competing values are initially generated by the colonizer, internalized through the dialectical dynamics of the objective world acting upon the colonized and the latter's subjective contribution to the reproduction and reinforcement of a value system they did not originate.

It is no small point that the maximization of rational behavior embedded in the U.S. colonial project in Puerto Rico contributed fundamentally to the popularity of rationalizing economic and social ills in ways that focused on the need to improve the economy of the country without threatening U.S. hegemony. Furthermore, such rationalization finds it difficult to appeal to notions of sovereignty, nation, and culture as significant factors in the development project. These notions have historically been viewed as detriments to orthodox development because the emphasis is on the maximization of rational behavior to which sovereignty, or notions of identity, or values superseding orthodox economics might be subordinated, and national-cultural interests are but a hasty and parochial emotional-psychological appeal.

Generally speaking, then, what constitutes the features distinguishing one culture from another— and this includes those features that aim at the preservation of state control through appeals to culture (i.e., nationalism and sovereignty)— is obscured by the orthodox principle to maximize rational behavior. The values of a people remain subordinate to the requirements of maximizing rational behavior for orthodox development. A people's existence is reified; it becomes a "thing" contingent upon the mechanization and movement of "superior forces." The further Puerto Ricans could be drawn from the culture that distinguishes them from the "American" colonizer and enriches their ability to approach the contradictions in the colonial relationship, the greater the ease of controlling them. In one sense the development of orthodox economic programs immersed Puerto Rico in a process not before experienced by colonialism— the arrival of a highly developed colonizer with, comparatively speaking, a highly structured and rationalized bureaucracy accounting for its economic and military stature and political strength. This had an impact that to this day poses concern for assimilationists and those favoring independence alike. Referring to Weber's categories of rationalization and demythification [*Entzauberung*, usually translated as "disenchantment"], Andrew Arato remarks:

Rationalization, the key to all modernization and industrialization, represents the historical penetration of all spheres of life: the economy, culture, technology, law and politics, and everyday life by a single logic of *formal rationality*. This "logic" is defined by the principle of orientation of human action to abstract, quantifiable and calculable, and instrumentally utilizable formal rules and norms. The key to formal rationality is the phrase "without regard to persons."[54]

Weber here argues that the price for such organization, and hence development, was expensive, rendering most of the people captive in a "steel-hard cage" where they were destined to live the rest of their lives. While this seems quite a pessimistic assertion, the strength of such a statement, even in the context of a colonial relationship, gathered much conviction. What seemed to grant legitimacy to a highly rationalized and bureaucratic colonial system was its appeal to rational constructs and not to the rule of overt violent repression, though certainly Puerto Rico has witnessed much bloodshed and continued repression at the hands of the United States. The efforts to silence the people's voice through changes in the economic structures, and the manner in which orthodox economic development manifested itself as a form of control or domination in the colonial context, appeared considerably more benign than traditional forms of colonial oppression. The development of the bureaucracy implied the inevitable transformation of the culture and the country's identity. Though this can be the case whether or not a country is under colonial rule, the restrictions that such rule places on the bureaucratic development of the colony are themselves embedded in such rationalization, making the colony's development constrained by the colonial relationship.

The decisive reason for the advance of bureaucratic organization has always been its purely technical superiority over any other form of organization. The fully developed bureaucratic apparatus compares with the non-mechanical modes of production. Precision, speed, unambiguity, knowledge of the files, continuity, discretion, unity, strict subordination, reduction of friction and of material and personal costs— these are raised to the optimum point in the strictly bureaucratic administration, and especially in its monocratic form.[55]

For Puerto Rico, the development of a public school system under the United States meant the advancement of such a bureaucratic disposition. The public school then became the premier institution for the inculcation of a value system arising not out of Puerto Rican initiative but as a response to a colonial reality cloaked by a conception of development that appealed, in economic terms, to an orthodox notion of rational behavior as a prerequisite to progress— a behavior that would also incorporate its logic into the development of the public school system. The first instance of such a logic in the schools came in the form of policies mandating the use of English as the language of instruction and the need for strict governance of those policies through a highly centralized public school administration.

NOTES

1. Richard Hofstader, *The Paranoid Style in American Politics and Other Essays* (New York: Monthly Review Press, 1965), 176.

2. George W. Davis, *Report of the Military Governor of Porto Rico on Civil Affairs* (Washington, D.C.: U.S. Government Printing Office, 1900), 14.

3. Ibid.

4. *Congressional Record* , March 2, 1900, 2475.

5. *Congressional Record* , April 30, 1900, 4856.

6. Daniel R. Fusfeld, *Principles of Political Economy* (Glenview, Ill.: Scott, Foresman, 1982).

7. Edward J. Berbusse, *The United States in Puerto Rico 1891–1900* (Chapel Hill: University of North Carolina Press, 1966), 103–05.

8. Centro de Estudios Puertorriqueños (CENEP), *Taller de Migración*, New York: CENEP, 1975, 55, Table 3.

9. María Luque de Sánchez, *La ocupación norteamericana y la ley Foraker: La opinión pública puertorriqueña 1898–1904* (Río Piedras, Puerto Rico: Editorial Universitario, 1980), p. 78.

10. James Dietz, *Economic History of Puerto Rico: Institutional Change and Capitalist Development* (Princeton: Princeton University Press, 1986), 100.

11. Jorge Saldaña, *El café en Puerto Rico* (Chicago: Aldine, 1932), 21.

12. Dietz, *Economic History,* 101.

13. *United States Department of Labor Report, 1919* (Washington, D.C.: U.S. Government Printing Office, 1920), 13, and 37.

14. Centro de Estudios Puertorriqueños, *Taller de migración*, 94.

15. Dietz, *Economic History*, 102.

16. Berbusse, *The United States in Puerto Rico*, 154, 157–58.

17. Gordon K. Lewis, *Puerto Rico* (New York: Monthly Review Press, 1963), 87.

18. Dietz, *Economic History*, 104.

19. Ibid.

20. Victor S. Clark et. al., *Porto Rico and Its Problems* (Washington, D.C.: Brookings Institution, 1930), 457.

21. Daniel R. Headrick, *The Tentacles of Progress* (London: Oxford University Press, 1988), 304.

22. Centro de Estudios Puertorriqueños, *Taller de migracion*, 53.

23. Dietz, *Economic History*, 125.

24. Angel G. Quintero Rivera, *Conflicto de clases y política en Puerto Rico* (Río Piedras: Huracán, 1976), 55.

25. James W. Wessman, "The Demographic Structure of Slavery in Puerto Rico: Some Aspects of Agrarian Capitalism in the Late Nineteenth Century," *Journal of Latin American History* 12 (Nov. 1980): 271–89.

26. Centro de Estudios Puertorriqueños (CENEP), History Task Force, *Labor Migration Under Capitalism: The Puerto Rican Experience* (New York: Monthly Review Press, 1979), 98.

27. A. D. Gayer, Paul T. Homan, and Earle K. Jones, *The Sugar Economy of Puerto Rico* (New York: Columbia University Press, 1938), table 45.

28. Esteban Bird, *A Report on the Sugar Industry in Relation to the Social and Economic System of Puerto Rico,* Senate Document no. 1 (San Juan: Bureau of Supplies, Printing, and Transportation, 1941), 40, and 96–97.

29. K. Antonio Santiago, "La concentración y la centralización de las propiedades en Puerto Rico: 1898–1929," *Homines* 8 (Jan. 1984): 155, Table 13.

30. Dietz, *The Economic History*, 110.

31. Bird, *A Report on the Sugar Industry* , 40 and 96–97.

32. Ibid., 12.

33. Yamila Azize, *Lucha de la mujer en Puerto Rico 1878-1919* (San Juan: Litografía Metropolitana, 1979), 6–19.

34. Dietz, *Economic History*, 117.

35. Artemio P. Rodríguez, *A Report on Wages and Working Hours in Various Industries on the Cost of Living, in the Island Puerto Rico, During the Year 1933* (San Juan: Bureau of Supplies, Printing, and Transportation, 1934), 140.

36. Azize, *Lucha de la mujer en Puerto Rico,* 50.

37. Dietz, *Economic History*, 128.

38. Bailey W. Diffie and Justine W. Diffie, *Puerto Rico: A Broken Pledge* (New York: Vanguard Press, 1931), 124-125.

39. Ibid., 182.

40. Juan José Osuna, *A History of Education in Puerto Rico* (Río Piedras: University of Puerto Rico Press, 1975), 620–621.

41. Diffie and Diffie, *A Broken Pledge,* 153.

42. Clark et al., *Porto Rico and Its Problems*, 13.

43. Ibid., xix.

44. Dietz, *Economic History*, 144.

45. Ibid., 161.

46. Harvey Perloff, *Puerto Rico's Economic Future* (Chicago: University of Chicago Press, 1950), 32.

47. Dietz, *Economic History*, 146.

48. Ibid., 151.

49. Ibid.

50. *Chardón Report* , Puerto Rican Policy Commission, (San Juan: PRPC, 1934), 4.

51. David Held, *Introduction to Critical Theory* (Berkeley: University of California Press, 1980), 65.

52. Ibid.

53. Herbert Marcuse, "Some Social Implications of Modern Technology," in *The Essential Frankfurt School Reader,* ed. Andrew Arato and Eike Gebhardt (New York: Continuum, 1982) 145.

54. Andrew Arato, "Esthetic Theory and Cultural Criticism," in *The Essential Frankfurt School Reader*, ed. Andrew Arato and Eike Gebhardt (New York: Continuum, 1982), 191.

55. Max Weber, "Bureaucracy," in *From Max Weber: Essays in Sociology*, ed. H.H. Gerth and C. Wright Mills (New York: Oxford University Press, 1946)

Pledging allegiance to the flag, in a school in Corozal (1946). From *Puerto Rico Mio*, photography by Jack Delano, published by the Smithsonian Institute. Washington, D.C., 1990.

SILENCING THE CULTURE

That for a society to operate efficiently, there must be a great number of words and phrases which will set up immediate responses in the minds of any group which is appealed to act or to refrain from action. Without such rallying words as "Democracy," "The Constitution," "Americanism," it would be impossible to organize masses into sufficiently integrated groups to produce social action. One definite task of the social studies teaching is to build up the tone of certain words, to place them in a series of contexts so that they come to have a fixed stimulus value in the mind of the listener. The tale of the martyr, the patriot, the hero, the narration of events as traitorous or despicable— all of these have this function.[1]

*P*robably nowhere was the U.S. economic development plan for Puerto Rico more consciously promoted than in the public schools. Through a rationalization of the perceived necessary prerequisite of the Americanization of the culture for economic and social development, the grounds were established for the legitimacy of arguments and policies requiring English as the language of instruction and a centralized public school administration. The development of the economy along orthodox lines under a colonial regime meant that other civil institutions would need to respond to, and interact with, the economy through the preparation of workers while re-creating the social values consonant with the economic model. By so doing, the rationalization of the culture under an orthodox economic model of colonialism would find its way into the struggle between the meaning of Puerto Rican identity and some of the asserted requirements for economic development.

Examining the establishment and development of public schooling in Puerto Rico under the United States, this chapter will argue that in order to secure its economic development plans for Puerto Rico, and its colonial hold on the country, the United States needed to expand its sphere of influence into the fabric of the culture through the contributions that English in the schools and a highly centralized public school administration made to the U.S. development aims. By developing a public school system that had English as the language of instruction, which in great part found its rationale in the economic model, and the requisite administrative agency to oversee such a project, the United States would contribute significantly to the silencing of the culture. This chapter will not focus on the economic development during the period, but references will be made. The material on schooling in this chapter reflects the educational developments that arose simultaneously with the economic period examined in Chapter 3.

The first section of this chapter will examine the political-economic and ideological references incorporated by the colonizer in the process of preparing Puerto Ricans for the politicization consistent with the economic development plan. In the process of such preparation, the colonial government was compelled to develop a public school system whose theory and practice, whose philosophy and language, would have to support those values and other aspects conducive to what the United States viewed as important to economic and social development. This will be the topic of the second section, which in turn is composed of three subsections. The first subsection discusses how in order to curtail popular resistance to educational policies, including the language issue, and to ensure that they were disseminated swiftly across Puerto Rico, the administration of the school system would have to come under the tight control of the colonial government. The second subsection looks at the highly centralized public school administration, which, linked directly to the political-economic apparatus, executed its duty in the development of a school system whose language of development and vision of education remained, ideologically and in practice, parallel with the orthodox economic model of development under U.S. colonialism. The third subsection provides a brief account of how the political socialization process took form in the social studies curriculum.

Borrowing from Freire's examination of his notion of "cultural silence," the chapter's final section, offers an analysis of how the English language in Puerto Rico's schools advanced colonialism through its contribution to the subordination and silencing the Puerto Rican culture.

AMERICANIZATION: A RATIONALIZATION FOR DEVELOPMENT

In an assertion of his department's unequivocal commitment to the objective of Americanization, the first commissioner of education under U.S. occupation, Martin G. Brumbaugh asserted:

The spirit of American institutions and the ideals of the American people, strange as they do seem to some in Porto Rico, must be the only spirit and the only ideals incorporated in the school system of Porto Rico.[2]

Prior to the invasion and occupation of Puerto Rico, schooling was generally reserved for either the privileged or those entering the priesthood. The inculcation of values and skills necessary for survival usually fell under the domain of the church and the home. The struggle over free thought contributed to a long and heated debate between civil government and the church regarding the meaning of progress and development. With the invasion and occupation by the United States came the expansion of public schooling and an emphasis on the separation of church and state. Focusing on the need to Americanize the Puerto Rican population, public schooling as defined, practiced, and administered by the United States would, through the Americanization effort, inculcate a secularized version of knowledge consistent with the demands for the maximization of rational behavior necessary for the expansion of U.S. capital interests in the Puerto Rican market. The emphasis upon appeals to religious arguments for education was replaced by the rationalization of needs under a new economic and social development vision. Progress would, in effect, be contingent upon the extent to which Puerto Ricans internalized the values and practices that the United States through public schooling, advanced as necessary for the country's development and "modernization".

Only twelve days after the United States hoisted its flag in San Juan, a first step on behalf of public schooling was taken. At a meeting open to a number of representative citizens it was concluded that

As regards public education, the best means of advancing our people would be kindergartens and normal schools as established in the United States. Our elementary and superior schools should be transformed and graded according to modern pedagogic methods. Universal education should be introduced based on the best models of the United States.[3]

This assembly, which would set the tone for the formation of future school initiatives, was open to "all those inhabitants of Puerto Rico who accepted the citizenship of the United States and identified themselves with the aspirations of this country."[4] Here the decision to participate was left in the hands of each citizen. The requirements for participation however, represented a radical posturing that may have acted to intimidate Puerto Ricans, or at least to confuse them about the meaning of General Nelson Miles's promise to "protect Puerto Rican property and bestow the blessings of the liberal institutions of the U.S. government," which he had asserted when the United States invaded. In a report criticizing the lack of consensus at the assembly, Luis Muñoz Rivera, owner and director of the daily *La Democracia,* stated, "Only eighty or ninety persons attended this 'general' assembly. The majority of the towns were not represented.[5]

Factoring significantly in the Americanization process, the call for kindergartens and normal schools deserves some attention. It was probably no coincidence that the declaration issued by the assembly should, in its first sentence, advocate the fundamental importance of kindergartens and normal schools. Kindergarten represented the child's first school experience. Given the general perception regarding a child's malleability at four or five years of age, it was argued that most children of that age would internalize that behavior appropriate for advancement and, thus, success. By emphasizing cooperative play under the strict supervision of the teacher, kindergarten became the child's first social experience outside of the home where play was strictly structured and directly supervised.

A call for normal schools constituted the second most important feature of the assembly's initial concern. These training institutions would prepare teachers for their role in educating the youth of the country. Again, the influence of the European experiences, particularly in France and Prussia, of Horace Mann, Henry Barnard, and Calvin Stowe proved pivotal in the creation of a U.S. version of the normal school in Puerto Rico. The word "normal," notes Freeman Butts, "came from the Latin word meaning a 'model or rule,' connoting that the object of the institution was to provide teachers with the rules for teaching."[6] Given the centrality of Americanizing the population, particularly the school population, a uniform set of rules and methods was an imperative. The first normal school in Puerto Rico under the U.S. occupation was in Fajardo, an eastern municipality. Only after the director of public instruction issued a call to all the municipalities, offering a bonus to the municipality that established the normal school within its jurisdiction, did Fajardo become the site.[7] The normal school would furnish manual training courses in agriculture, and that there should be connected with it a model school for practice teaching and a department for training teachers.[8] Generally speaking, the school was a failure. Instruction was in English, there was only one teacher at the school, and the school opened one year after Fajardo won its bid. Furthermore, in October, less than four months later, virtually no progress had been made in terms of students advancement toward teaching preparedness.

Puerto Rico's economy had been devastated by the fury of hurricane San Ciriaco in August 1899. The declining economies of the majority of the municipalities were hard pressed to offer bids for the establishment of normal schools. Fajardo's rising importance, due to the growth of its sugar plantations, during this period arguably provided some support for its ability to make and win the bid. In addition, the need for employment was far more important than the "privilege" of attending school or, for many municipalities, financing a normal school. There was also the continued resistance by many Puerto Ricans to the Americanization project.

That an effort should be made to prepare teachers for Puerto Rico's public school system was, quite obviously, a desirable aim. However, instruction was in English, access to Fajardo from other municipalities was difficult (given its easternmost location), and there was resistance to the emphasis placed on U.S. history and civics. It was not clear to many people why and how U.S. civics and history were prerequisites to development, and specifically to technical training. In January 1899, Major General Guy Henry, the military governor of Puerto Rico, issued an authorization requiring that all teachers learn English, that teachers who spoke English receive preferential treatment when seeking appointments, and that all secondary, normal, and collegiate graduates to be examined in English.[9] Resistance to the development of teacher training sites that focused on English as the instructional language posed a political issue for the United States since the English language, the U.S. administration argued, was central to Puerto Rican development.

In October of 1899, Victor Clark, president of the Insular Council on Education, speaking on the problems of Puerto Rico's public school system, stated:

> There exists opposition to American schools. If it is left in the hands of Porto Rico, schools will not be established until the majority of its intelligentsia classes have received their education in the institutions of the United States. This opposition is due to various reasons. In the first place, the principal educators of the island have studied in France or Spain. They are familiar with the systems used in these countries, but not with the American system; their opposition is a natural result of this fact. All of this is evidenced by the fact that since the professors constituted an officially important class, they resented, as all the privileged classes of Porto Ricans, that the Spanish appropriate the best positions on the island for themselves. They do not want this fact to repeat itself with the Americans, and see in the arrival of American teachers . . . another act of monopolizing the positions.[10]

Familiarity with the Spanish or French system hardly seems to explain Puerto Rican resentment of or resistance to the U.S. imposition of English. The argument was one not of systems but of language and, beyond this, of participation in the determination of school development. The argument proposed that, if purged of the old systems, Puerto Rican teachers would see the necessity and desirability of the American way. Furthermore, the United States needed to accommodate the professorial ranks that had gained some autonomy under Spanish rule and now felt threatened by the new policies.

Clark's statement captured the tension between an American model of education, development grounded in the English language, and the resistance of many Puerto Rican educators to compliance with the dictates of yet another colonizer. Surely many Puerto Ricans perceived that learning English might prove beneficial; however, the aggregation of the many experiences under the United States (economic, political, and other civil laws) exacerbated the imposing manner in which English arrived and, hence, contributed to the resistance— not to mention that it was a foreign language that, under new legislation, would become the "official" language of the country. The foundation was laid for what, to this day, is a battleground whose raison d'être was the issue of the language of instruction in schools and, more generally, the official and legitimate language in which the country's affairs would be conducted. Much of the internal debate regarding the language issue would be divided along political party and ideological lines— republicans or assimilationists favoring English; democrats, independentists, and other autonomists, more skeptical and resistant. Nevertheless, the expansion of schooling and the efforts to enroll as many Puerto Ricans as possible were appreciated by all political affiliations.

Before 1900, statistics on school enrollment were virtually unrecorded. However, between 1900 and 1910 enrollment in schools increased by 257 percent. Between 1910 and 1920 it increased 88.06 percent; and for the period between 1920 and 1940, the increase was 28 percent.[11] While the number of urban schools was greater than of those in the rural municipalities, the country was predominantly rural and dotted with schools throughout the countryside. During the first decade of U.S. occupation, rural schools were limited to the first three grades, and in many of them only the simplest labor in the first or first two grades was offered. For the most part, the rural schools emphasized agriculture and music in their curriculum. They often focused on gardening skills, a practice well understood by most rural Puerto Ricans. The prevailing sugar industry and monocrop economy made it important for the schools to prepare students for agriculture. Furthermore, given the importance of subsistence farming to rural families, the development of small gardening programs was fundamental to the well-being of rural workers. Yet the unyielding and all-encompassing requirements placed upon Puerto Ricans to learn English, transportation problems, and consistency regarding school attendance posed difficulty for U.S. educational efforts. In the context of these and other ills that hampered the expansion of schooling and its qualitative potential, the United States, in reaffirming its commitment to "Puerto Rican progress," reasserted the primary relationship of literacy to democratic development through a campaign aimed at the rural schools.

Given that over 70 percent of those living in the rural sectors of the country were illiterate, the need to strengthen the rural schools made the campaign a political must for the United States. In October 1915, Commissioner of Education Paul Miller, in circular letter number 28, stressed the importance of overcoming illiteracy:

We cannot wait to establish democratic institutions on a secure foundation without having first reduced this enormous mass of illiterates. The honor and obligation of reducing illiteracy has fallen upon you. Do you feel capable of undertaking this effort? Can you initiate the struggle for the good of your country?"[12]

The inculcation of an American model of progress, development, and, more generally, of democracy was to be included in this campaign. Politically, the colonial relationship was intact. By holding the people responsible for the eradication of illiteracy and, by inference, for the potential for Puerto Rican development, the commissioner was challenging them to take the initiative or stand back and comply, for "their own good."

In a somewhat classical argument regarding illiteracy and control, we might ask, "Why make the people literate if illiteracy might more easily secure control?" I do not think that here we can responsibly address all of the ramifications of the question. However, the argument in defense of literacy as a requirement for development might be grounded in an appeal to the rationalization of the economy and the society. The rationalization (the mathematization) of knowledge and experience in the changing patterns of a rationalized and bureaucratized society has the effect of restructuring the essence of human identity, of self and others. The impact this will have on a culture will be determined to some degree by the developments within that culture. In other words, politically, economically, and socially, in terms of people's values, as these values responded to external stimuli—here in the form of economic and school policies from without, Puerto Ricans then articulated the relationship of English to development and democracy through appeals to a rationalized frame of thought—one provided by the dialectic of colonialism, that is, the struggle with the meaning of being Puerto Rican and development as articulated by the colonizer.

In a relative sense, control is asserted not by the use of force but by the juxtaposition of English or literacy to progress and development. The outcome is the same. Whether by use of arms or through other, more rationalized appeals to some form of superiority, one group plays the role of leader and the other is subjected to the aims of the colonizer. Again, this is not an attack on rationalization. Surely, some very desirable ends are attained through a process of rationalization. However, the issue here is the subordinate role played by the colonized in the process; as such, their well-being is significantly contingent upon the decisions of the colonizer. The idea of taking the initiative seemed not to be intended to produce autonomy, as evidenced by the proliferation of more stringent policies and laws and increasing U.S. control of the economy and Puerto Rico's institutions. The commissioner's comments appeared to challenge the people, as if the arena within which this challenge was issued was somehow open or free, and from it the Puerto Rican people would determine or construct their future. The challenge elicited participation in the form of agreement on Puerto Rico's future under the United States. The arena within which such a challenge was issued left no room for debates relative on rules of the game or the parameters of development.

Despite improvements in the expansion of rural education, the recruitment of qualified teachers proved extremely difficult since most of the qualified teachers were given the opportunity to teach in urban schools. The displacement of qualified teachers equated learning English and American ways with moving to the urban centers to teach at the better schools, while the less prepared or more resistant teachers were left with virtually no option but to teach wherever and whenever possible in the rural regions. Partial explanation of the limited success of the rural school improvement campaign might be found in the displacement of the rural populations from the coffee, and tobacco-producing countryside to the the sugar-producing regions that were already overflowing with unemployed and underemployed persons. Such displacement forced many Puerto Ricans to move outside the sugar regions, and even off the island.

During World War I, over 13,000 Puerto Ricans were sent to the United States by the government, to relieve labor shortages.[13] This may have provided some incentive or hope of employment for many of those living in some of the rapidly declining rural areas who now could translate learning English and American schooling into the possibility of work abroad. The failing coffee and tobacco industries and the movement of significant populations to the sugar regions might indicate that less attention would be given to schooling in rural areas. From a cost-benefit analysis, the investments in schooling in those areas might be seen as more of a burden than an asset. This is not to say that rural schooling was abandoned.

Rural schools were consolidated during the 1920s. Consolidation became important to the United States for a number of reasons. First, the campaign to eradicate illiteracy could more easily be carried out; this meant the expansion of Americanization beyond the urban centers. Second, consolidation tightened the administration of schools and the control necessary for the implementation of the curriculum. In his *A History of Education in Puerto Rico,* Juan José Osuna states:

Due to the topography of the land, the many streams and rivers which swell into raging torrents during the rainy season, and the lack of more rural roads, the consolidation of rural schools had been limited thus far to the coast districts where better means of communication were available.[14]

Osuna's statement provides us with an important feature of the Puerto Rican reality regarding rural schools. Yet the movement of the rural population to the coasts, where the largest sugar plantations and mills were located (and hence better possibilities for employment), should be taken into account. It was on these sugar plantations that underemployment and unemployment were often most visible and, subsequently, where some of the country's largest labor strikes originated. Between 1899 and 1910 the population of Guánica, the largest sugar municipality, experienced a growth of 121.4 percent, while the other seventeen municipalities with the largest concentrations of sugar production had a growth of 45.4 percent; coffee-producing regions declined in population by 4.2 percent, and the country grew generally by 17.3 percent.[15] Quite obviously there was a pressing need to attend to schooling in the rural areas, particularly in the sugar-producing regions. The high rate of underemployment and unemployment that characterized the sugar industry, coupled with an unpredictable and somewhat tenuous acceptance of the United States by Puerto Ricans, required attention by school policy officials.

Financing a school development project was a virtual impossibility for the vast majority of the districts. Their inability to finance schools in the first few years was exacerbated by the devastation of hurricane San Ciriaco in August 1899. Most of the criticism charged that with the enactment of the laws, the United States was attempting to implant the type of public school system characteristic of the state of Massachusetts. This was perceived as inadequate, given the different reality in Puerto Rico. On the other hand, it would be naive to believe that the United States would educate Puerto Ricans to oppose or challenge its governance. Thus, with the advent of the economic model of development and the arguments for the educated populations to "participate" in such an endeavor, the United States embarked upon the necessary campaign to spread schooling throughout the country. Since most districts found financing difficult, the U.S. colonial government progressively increased its contribution to the effort, on the conditions that English be the language of instruction and that supervisors and directors be Americans.

The second and third decades of the twentieth century witnessed an expanded yet deficient public school system in rural Puerto Rico. In 1925 approximately 93 percent of all teachers were teaching in elementary schools. Of the 3,799 elementary school teachers, 2,219 were in the rural schools. This distribution repeated itself in the years between 1925 and 1930.[16] The rural teachers represented the less prepared and worse paid of their field. Sending the better-prepared teachers to the towns or cities kept the rural schooling poor. As Osuna put it,

By this shifting, the rural schools received constantly the newly certified, poorly prepared, inexperienced teachers; while as soon as they became better prepared or had improved their efficiency as teachers by actual experience in the classroom, moved to town and made room for new inexperienced teachers.[17]

Virtually the entire teaching profession remained unprepared to carryout much of the administration's policy. The course of study in the rural schools during the period focused on the teaching of civics of an instrumental sort, and on health habits.[18] The rationalization of the economy and the bureaucratization of the society focused on the urban centers, where the economic bureaucracy mainly resided— as did the economic administration. Given this, rural schooling suffered. Unlike the traditional urbanization that accompanies the rationalization of an economy and its concurrent bureaucracy, in Puerto Rico, the majority of the population remained in the rural regions, where less money and effort were being spent to develop schooling. Though somewhat an improvement over the rural schools, the urban schools generally fared little better.

In the urban centers there were graded schools that administered a course of study for children from first to eighth grade. According to the Department of Education in Puerto Rico, "urban" included representative populations in each of the seventy-eight towns on the island. Enrollment figures issued by the U.S. Bureau of the Census indicate that the graded school programs suffered from a roller coaster affect during the period, with 1914 as the year of highest enrollment. It was also the "year of the big budget."[19]

Many of the changes experienced in the graded schools reflected some aspect of the language issue, including the ideological force behind the emphasis placed upon English and its correspondence to development. Virtually every town had Puerto Rico's best English-speaking teachers in charge of its schools. Spanish-speaking teachers, or those with a more limited command of English were generally assigned to teach Spanish and perhaps one other subject. Moreover, teachers of English, usually Americans, were given grades five through eight. [20]

As late as 1950, the graded schools still suffered from low attendance and low levels of completion. Reasons for this situation were complex. Resistance to the use of English as the medium of instruction was evidenced throughout the schools; the political debates over the general philosophy and vision of the public school system; the lack of teachers, buildings, and facilities; and the disarticulated relationship that schooling had to the economy as it related to local development needs, help to explain part of the problems. These all contributed to the growing dropout rate. The lack of a meaningful reason for attending school was provoked by the incoherence at the cultural and socioeconomic levels.

The largest number of students dropped out of school between the fourth and eighth grade, an age at which most of them could find some form of work to help support their families. A fraction of those who completed the graded school course continued on to high school; even fewer went on to university.[21] "The school had not prepared them for anything in particular," Osuna says in his book.

The educational expectations and requirements for participation in the development of a highly rationalized economy, in the form of orthodox production, were not being realized by the Puerto Rican people. Though the new economic model brought a relatively sophisticated and scientific character to Puerto Rico, it was not accessible to most Puerto Ricans. To reiterate Daniel Headrick's statement on technology transfer, from Chapter 3,"The transfer involves the spread of activity and knowledge not only from one area to another, but also from one people to another." Access to the complexity of social and economic developments that characterize the rationalization and bureaucratization of a society was, in Puerto Rico, limited. The role of the schools was primarily sociopolitical. The transfer of technical developmental skills was quite limited because the economic plan focused on the monocultural sugar economy. The lack of "anything in particular," as Osuna puts it, attests to the discrepancies between the expectations of the colonized and development limitations under colonialism. That a population was being prepared for nothing in particular, in a country whose economy and society were growing more complex, indicated that something was controlling the development scheme, and it was not focused on local needs.

During the first thirty years of U.S. occupation, mass public schooling in Puerto Rico became a reality. While the numbers reflect improvements in the expansion of facilities and enrollment, generally speaking the period was plagued by fundamental problems that characterized the fragmentation and erratic nature of public schooling. Evidence of the problems was found in the contradiction between the expansion of schooling and enrollments and growing rates of unemployment— if we accept the argument advanced by the colonizer that more schooling translated into more employment possibilities. Without local technical development, Puerto Rico's chances for contributing to its determination of its future development remained minimal. Yet the degree to which the language of development was internalized also meant that Puerto Ricans would play a subjective role in the reproduction of their own limitations.

In this case, then, colonialism is a significant part of a problem that also resides within the colonized people's dynamics of development in general. The point is that the development of the economy under U.S. colonialism was producing an increasing gap between the technical and bureaucratic requirements for the development of the orthodox model and local satisfaction of those requirements. Puerto Ricans had to struggle with the tension between the meaning of their cultural distinctiveness and the expectations of economic well-being that were growing in a society exposed to the logic and mechanizations of a rationalization accompanying development under colonialism. Unable and, in many cases, unwilling to search for the possibility that there could be a connection between development limitations and colonialism, Puerto Ricans struggled between the rationalization of development under the United States and the preservation of culture. In the schools the policies requiring the use of English as the language of instruction mitigated the possibilities for a critical appraisal of development under colonialism.

ENGLISH AS THE INSTRUCTIONAL MEDIUM

School Law and Policies Regarding English

The enactment of laws mandating the use of English in the Puerto Rican public school system was intimately linked with U.S. efforts to purge Puerto Ricans of a culture whose language interfered with U.S. development plans. Without belaboring the point, the learning of the English language surely, in and of itself, was not undesirable. The imposition of the language as a prerequisite for access to the culture and national development posed the greater problem for Puerto Ricans. Not only what was to be spoken, but its determination, fueled the resistance effort. Nevertheless, many Puerto Ricans viewed English as the language of opportunity and the key to upward social mobility. In one of the country's first reports outlining the recommendations for public school instruction in Puerto Rico, Dr. Martin G. Brumbaugh, president of the Insular Board of Education in 1899, concluded that:

the majority of the people of the island do not speak pure Spanish. Their language is a patois almost unintelligible to the natives of Barcelona and Madrid. . . . Only from the very small intellectual minority in Puerto Rico, trained in Europe and imbued with European ideals of education and government, have we to anticipate any active resistance to the introduction of the American school system and the English language.[22]

From this perspective, the Puerto Rican's "imperfect language" which was here called upon to provide evidence consistent with the country's more general economic and socially "uncivilized" condition, could be elicited in manufacturing the legitimacy for favoring English. Puerto Ricans needed to learn how to think since, to this point in their history, Brumbaugh implied, there was little evidence of the "creative principle"[23] of speech, except perhaps in the small number of intellectuals trained in Europe. And the "mechanical principle" of speech itself was an imperfect one. It is interesting how Clark, earlier in this chapter, granted ideological significance to the English language in his explanation of resistance from those intellectuals trained in Europe and their "understanding of government" in juxtaposition to the proposals for English and an "American school system." Victor Clark could not have been more explicit about the U.S. vision of Puerto Rico than when he asserted:

The great mass of Porto Ricans is still passive and plastic. . . . Its ideals are in our hands to be created and molded. If we americanize the schools and inspire the teachers and students with the American spirit . . . the island will become in its sympathies, views and attitudes . . . essentially American.[24]

In addition to the arguments made by Clark regarding the imperfect nature of Puerto Rican Spanish, the Education Commission issued a statement that reiterated the U.S. commitment to Americanize, and so to subordinate, the Puerto Rican identity

through the legitimation of English, on the grounds that the high rate of illiteracy left
Puerto Rico seemingly "languageless," and thus open for English:

We are totally of the opinion that instruction should be given in the English language. Puerto
Rico already is and will remain a part of the United States' possessions, and its population will
be American. At the present time only one of every ten persons knows how to read and write.
We ask ourselves, naturally, why should we teach the remaining nine Spanish instead of
English. Obtaining a good citizenry and a good education is easier when carried out through the
public school system than by any other means.[25]

The commission was cognizant of the political, economic, and ideological
advantages to English as the medium of instruction. The issue was less a matter of
whether Puerto Ricans actually had a language. It was, however, the case that in order
for the United States to facilitate its development plans in Puerto Rico, the culture—
and that meant the language— should be subordinate to the requirements of English as
the language of development. With this in mind, the United States embarked upon the
establishment of mass schooling in Puerto Rico; English would, by law, become the
medium of instruction. The first school law, was enacted on May 1, 1899.

The law was divided into two general parts. The first part encouraged the districts
to organize and establish public schools. This was an authorization, not an order. Each
district was to have a board composed of five elected members. The authority to employ
teachers remained totally in the hands of the boards. Likewise, they were held
accountable for the rent on teachers' living quarters, and the selection, rent, and
equipping of buildings to be utilized as schools. An important provision of this law was
the authorization of coeducational classes, something that, until now, had been
prohibited by law in Puerto Rico.[26]

The second part of the law was composed primarily of three orders. First, the fee
system was abolished, making public schools entirely free and a graded school system
was established in the urban areas. Second, all books and materials used in the public
schools were collected by the local boards and warehoused in an adequate location, at
the disposition of the Office of Education. Last, a system for grading and evaluating
schoolwork was established. By abolishing the fee system, which was common under
Spanish colonialism, schooling was, at least theoretically, available to everyone. The
establishment of graded schools was also a step toward the development of a mass
schooling system in Puerto Rico. The close control of materials was required because
they were hard to come by and expensive, not to mention the need for close supervision
in the inculcation of values. Establishing a grading system meant that Puerto Rican
students would learn to compete individually in the English schools.

The provisions set forth by Puerto Rico's first organic act under the United States,
the Foraker Act, stipulated that public schooling would come under the close jurisdiction and control of the U.S. government. The Foraker Act legitimized the subsequent
policies that centralized the administration of the public school system. Known as the
Act to Establish Public Schools in Puerto Rico, the school laws of January 31, 1901,
centralized the administration of schools and gave virtually all power to the commis-

sioner of education. The most significant section of the laws outlines the duties and powers of the commissioner, a U.S. presidential appointee:

The Commissioner of Education, being required by act of Congress of April 12, 1900, to supervise education in Puerto Rico, . . . shall, to comply with said act, appoint from time to time supervisors, or superintendents of schools, who shall be subject to the Commissioner in all respects; he shall prepare and promulgate all courses of study; conduct all examinations; prepare and issue all licenses or certificates to teachers; select and purchase all school books, supplies and equipment necessary for the proper conduct of education; approve of all plans for public school buildings to be erected in Puerto Rico; require and collect such statistics and reports from all school boards, supervisors or superintendents and teachers as he may require; formulate such rules and regulations as he may from time to time find necessary for the effective administration of his office.[27]

The School Law of 1901 met great resistance. A series of articles appeared in Ponce, Puerto Rico's largest southern city, citing as "despotic" the dispositions presented in the law.[28] The unilateral power enjoyed by the commissioner as a presidential appointee all but definitively assured that Puerto Rico's public school system would respond to U.S. plans. The breadth and depth of the commissioner's power left Puerto Ricans outside the policy-making arena. The people were left to respond according to the policies coming from Washington via the commissioner of education. Taking advantage of the opportunity to impress upon the Puerto Ricans the U.S. commitment to education, Commissioner Martin Brumbaugh stated:

By visiting and . . . opening . . . the schools, our presence will have, as a mission, the effect of adequately exposing the benefits of a free school system under American conditions . . . . The schools have been christened with the names of Washington, Franklin, Lafayette, Jefferson, Jackson, Adams, Lincoln, Grant, McKinley, Longfellow, Webster, Hamilton, Garfield, Mann, and Peabody.[29]

The necessity of inculcating in Puerto Ricans identity with the United States was central to the legitimation of continued U.S. colonial control. On occasion, however, legitimation encounters difficulties. In the case of Puerto Rico, the problem of legitimacy, at least in the beginning, was confronted by issues of language and the coercive character of a centralized school system committed to Americanizing Puerto Ricans. One function of schools, then, was to provide the colonial government with the requisite loyalty and compliance so that its operations and policies could be carried out and subsequently reproduced in the Puerto Rican consciousness. The U.S. economic activity in Puerto Rico, while faced with numerous crises such as the failure of the Chardón Plan, and the ever-present high rate of unemployment and poverty, treated these as rationality crises from an orthodox economic viewpoint; they arose occasionally, and would be dealt with through intensified government involvement in the economy. And here is where some proponents of orthodox economics run into problems. The involvement of the government as a regulating agency becomes necessary in order to secure the political ideological requirements of the development process; yet, others say that the market and the maximization of rational behavior will automatically provide the desired development results.

In any case, the schools were responsible for inculcating values, that is, allegiance to the U.S., that remained consistent with the planning functions of the colonial government whose legitimacy would be secured by the Puerto Ricans' internalization of those values that identified them with the colonial government's activities. This was possible generally through the commitment to the use of English in the school and in one's overall personal life. In order to ensure that the English language demands were implemented consistently across the country, a highly centralized school administration was established.

Centralization of Educational Administration and the Language Issue

The centralization of the public school system as a component of the Americanization effort is a complex issue. However, for the purposes of this volume a brief statement should suffice to present the case as it relates to policy building. In accordance with the congressional act of April 12, 1900, the commissioner was empowered to do the following:

Sec. 4   Order that schools carryout his directions
Sec. 8   Intervene in the placement of teachers
Sec. 14   Dismiss teachers
Sec. 15   Determine teachers' salaries
Sec. 18   Solely determine who would teach English
Sec. 20   Institute disciplinary laws for teachers and students in the schools.[30]

In addition, the commissioner was empowered to serve as a member of the Executive Council, member of the Public Service Commission, president of the board of trustees of the University of Puerto Rico, president of the board of the Carnegie Library, president of the Teachers' Pension Board, and chairman of the chapter school committee of the Puerto Rico Chapter of the American National Red Cross.[31]

Between 1898 and 1940 the issue of English as the medium of instruction remained problematic in the context of the prospects for Puerto Rican development outside the orthodox paradigm. The laws and policies reflecting instruction in English constantly came under criticism, on the grounds that it was not the language of the people and, being enforced through coercive means, made legitimacy a perennial issue. Responsible for the creation and implementation of the laws and policies were the commissioners of education, all presidential appointees. For Martin Brumbaugh, Puerto Rico's first commissioner of education under the United States, Americanization meant the transmission of U.S. spirit and ideals and the inculcation of a patriotism, a devotion to and enthusiasm for the United States. Under Commissioner Samuel M. Lindsay,

Americanization meant the implantation of American institutions in the Hispanic-American understanding. The schools were fundamental instruments of this process. The best English teachers coming from the United States, would serve as a means for extending the American principles of government and ideals of conduct and life to Puerto Rico. Following Lindsay, Commissioner Roland Faulkner[32] evidenced commitment to English in the schools by insisting upon complete fluency in English for all Puerto Rican teachers, to be achieved by the following:

1. English courses for all teachers mediated by American supervisors
2. Summer courses in English of four to eight weeks
3. Monetary rewards for teachers who demonstrated outstanding progress in English
4. An annual exam for teacher certification; teachers would be placed according to proficiency in English. Failure to pass the yearly exam meant suspension until was passed. If after one year the exam was not passed, teachers in question would lose their licenses.[33]

Commissioner Edwin Dexter, Faulkner's successor, took the language question to new frontiers. For the first time schooling in the rural areas would be totally in English, beginning with the first grade. In the past, English instruction had begun in the second or third grade in the rural sectors. Another innovation, intimately tied to the Americanization process, introduced by Dexter was military instruction. In a statement supporting the expansion of military instruction, Dexter remarked, "It has done much to inculcate a steadfast disposition toward the obedience of orders."[34]

Continuing with Dexter's policies, Edward Bainter extended the use of annual English examinations for placement into each successive grade. Confronted by resistance that charged that he and U.S. policies were intent upon destroying the Puerto Rican personality, Bainter allowed the use of Spanish in the first four grades for the study of nature, health, and hygiene. During this time many Puerto Ricans voiced their growing dissatisfaction with the the first organic act, which controlled Puerto Rico's economy, legislature, and judicial institutions. Furthermore, the question of U.S. citizenship was rising to the forefront of political and cultural debates. Occasionally the colonial government would offer some political concession to the people, such as, the limited use of Spanish in the schools, in order to lay to rest any possibility of mass resistance to forthcoming policies and legislation.

Between 1915 and 1921 the Department of Education was headed by Paul Miller, whose policies were characterized by the slogan "conservation of Spanish and acquisition of English."[35] In light of the development vision of the United States, the allowances for Spanish seem related to a few issues present at the time. First, the English-only policies were generally failing to gather wide support in the communities and schools, though among most Puerto Rican republicans, language policies were not an issue. The growth of resistance— nationalist militancy against the policies of the colonizer, labor struggles, and, in education, the founding of the José de Diego Institute, established to counter the proliferation of English instruction— challenged U.S. hegemony. Resistance from those seeking more autonomy and the establishment of an independence party, all of whom drew much of the support for their arguments from the persistence of poverty, unemployment, and the general underdevelopment that prevailed despite nearly twenty-five years of U.S. presence, spread across the country.

Miller's policy change also had an economic side to it. Since many children were leaving school after the fifth grade in order to go to work then perhaps the more prudent thing would be to commence English training in the fifth grade, as children began to prepare for the upper level of grammar school. By doing so, Spanish would be preserved and English expected for those continuing their education. But this would still pose problems since the children's English skills and, for all practical purposes, their, education would remain caught between instruction in English and the preservation of Spanish.

Significantly, then, the model of development in Puerto Rico was indicating that the level of education could not be linked directly to improvements in the economy. That is, if the language of instruction was a matter of introduction at different grades, what developmental purpose did this serve? The ability to understand complex concepts and technology would seem to require the development of basic language skills, yet the economy was not demanding the development of local expertise for local development. The role that language would play appeared more consistent with Puerto Ricans' understanding the language of colonial governance and business, and less with participation in the creation of the technologies and industries of the country. This was also the era of the campaign to improve rural schooling. And, in political-economic terms, during World War I the Puerto Rican people suffered food shortages as a result of the colonizer's involvement in the war.

The provisions made for Spanish instruction were countered by the imposition of U.S. citizenship. Under the Jones Act of March 2, 1917, U.S. citizenship was imposed on Puerto Ricans. Those not accepting U.S. citizenship had to renounce it within six months and would lose many of their civil rights, and all political rights, including the rights to vote and hold office. Regarding this aspect of the Jones Act, José de Diego declared:

Never was anything like this seen before, in international law, in the democratic nations of the world: one million two hundred thousand human beings, who by law of the Congress of a Republic— which seems more like an order from the times of the Low Empire— are deprived of their natural citizenship, but under the threat and coercion of losing their right as electors and of being eligible for all public offices, in a country where they are obliged to carry all the burdens of the state and to render military tribute to the dominating nation, in the country of their birth and their life, where they long to be buried, Puerto Ricans, who for a crime unknown as yet in universal law—love of their own citizenship— are reduced to the condition of foreigners in their own country, are exiled from their land; and so, through terror, and because of the harshness of the punishment, only a very small number of Puerto Ricans have renounced the imposed citizenship, for almost all of them accept it, to present afterwards to the world with this unheard-of deed the fictitious demonstration that the Puerto Ricans voluntarily and joyfully accepted United States citizenship and with it they abandoned the ideal of constituting their country among the free and sovereign nations of America.[36]

The legitimation of English as the means of instruction was articulated by Miller in the following manner: "The children of Puerto Rico have the inalienable right to learn the English language."[37] Commissioner Miller further declared:

Puerto Ricans, now U.S. citizens, had a right to be subjected to Americanization . . . many of the teachers and not a few of the older students have become efficient propagandists, capable and disposed to take part in the molding of public opinion in patriotic terms.[38]

Following Miller, the first Puerto Rican was appointed commissioner of education. Juan B. Huyke's tenure covered the period from 1921 to 1930. Recognized as a good American, in his first statement issued to the teachers of Puerto Rico, Huyke asserted, "Our schools are agencies of Americanism."[39] For Huyke, Americanization meant the study of U.S. problems as if they were Puerto Rican problems, "the creating in our youth [of] a spirit of loyalty and a true love for our American flag and for all American institutions, in order to induce Puerto Ricans to feel, think and act as Americans."[40] Under Huyke all high school graduates had to pass an oral and a written English examination. No school was allowed to publish anything solely in Spanish. He founded the Society for the Promotion and Study of the English Language. Composed of eighth, ninth, and tenth graders, the members wore an American flag on their jackets and were required to speak English always among themselves. Students in grades one through seven were rewarded academically for participating in English clubs throughout the country. All official meetings were conducted in English. And the evaluation of schools and their academic classification was contingent upon the results of the English examinations taken by their students.

A supporter of the importance of Spanish in the schools, yet not challenging the vocational and ideological significance of English, José Padín was Puerto Rico's commissioner of education from 1930 to 1936. During his tenure Padín confronted the language issue by favoring Spanish as the medium of instruction in the elementary schools for the following reasons:

1. The English language is of enormous value to Puerto Rico.
2. It can be taught without discrediting Spanish and without retarding the mental development of students.
3. A delicate equilibrium in the teaching of both can be maintained.
4. English should remain under constant study.[41]

Between 1930 and 1940 the official policy of the colonial government was to study the language issue from the perspective of what policies and practices would facilitate the learning of English. Yet between 1936 and 1940, the government's unclear policies on the language of instruction resulted in a disarticulated school system where some used English, others used Spanish, and still others used both. Part of the explanation for this probably lies in the political-economic climate of the time. The effect of the depression on U.S. business control in Puerto Rico accelerated the forging of new political associations and economic development projects. "For a time it seemed Puerto

Rico would split apart with dissension, yet the 1940s promised a future not yet glimpsed under U.S. colonial control."[42]

Generally speaking, the reason given for the centralization of power relates to the failures of the municipal boards to carryout their duties properly and to the influence of partisan politics in the local boards.[43] This influence has remained in the debates over school development throughout Puerto Rico's colonial history under the United States. Political partisanship was presented as the element in Puerto Rico that prevented progress. Separating issues of status from those of schooling and progress further legitimized the rationale for Americanizing the country.

The ordering of labor for the improvement of efficiency (as articulated by Frederick Winslow Taylor), accompanied by the compatible position of Edward Ross— "Society is always in the presence of the enemy and social control is, in a significant sense, a compilation of the weapons of self-protection in the arsenal of society"[44]— and Charles Eliot's proposal for the superiority of the "experts," all contributed to the U.S. logic for the centralization of Puerto Rico's public school system.

The battle between the expansion of English and of U.S. policies and resistance to the proliferation of U.S. control of schools and the use of English presented itself in different forms and in different camps. For example, on September 14, 1900, the newspaper *Diario de Puerto Rico* was attacked by forces believed linked to the pro-assimilationist republican party. The reason for the attack was related to a series of articles criticizing the Republican leadership for its staunch support of U.S. policies. In February 1901 the Department of War established a telegraph service in Puerto Rico. Although it cost more than it was making, the U.S. government insisted the service was necessary to expand the development of rapid communications in the country. At the political level, the primary battles over U.S. policies and for power were fought between the Republicans and the Unionists. Between 1900 and 1904, the Republicans controlled the Chamber of Delegates.

Sensing a lack of progress and blind compliance with the United States, between 1904 and 1928, Puerto Ricans voters gave the Union Party control of the Chamber. The Union Party was composed of people committed to some form of self-governance, to independence under U.S. protection, and to statehood. This coalition of positions was organized in an attempt to arrive at a consensus that could confront some U.S. policies regarding the resolution of many of the problems facing the island. However, none of the positions challenged U.S. presence in Puerto Rico or its development model. Contributing to the limitation of broad political participation was the implementation of a new electoral law in 1906. It stated that only parties winning at least 20 percent of the previous election's votes could have observers at the polling sites. This meant that the regulation and registration of voters was in the hands of the Republican and the Unionist parties, both supportive of U.S. policies in Puerto Rico.

Within the first forty years of U.S. control, Puerto Rico witnessed the founding of the Independence of Puerto Rico and Socialist parties. Adding to the rising tide of discontent were two revealing incidents. On May 6, 1936, the Puerto Rican flag was flown at Ponce High School. It was illegal to fly the Puerto Rican flag over public buildings; only the U.S. flag could be flown. Nevertheless, the students at Ponce High School flew their national flag. This act initiated other similar acts. On May 7, the same occurred at city hall in San Juan. The police took the flag down and raised the U.S. flag. The administrator of the city, Jesús Castaño, requested that the Puerto Rican flag be returned to him. He said that he respected the law regarding the flag in public places, but that he was going to exhibit the flag in his office.[45] In another incident, on February 23, 1936, Colonel Francis E. Riggs, chief of police in Puerto Rico, was assassinated by two nationalists as an act of "revolutionary justice." His death, according to nationalists, was in response to the massacre of four nationalist youths in Río Piedras on their way to a meeting at the University of Puerto Rico. Colonel Riggs was the Chief of Police responsible for their deaths. This event brought changes in U.S. policy in Puerto Rico. Gradually, Puerto Ricans replaced Americans in certain positions, with the understanding that the Puerto Ricans were committed to strict punitive actions against the nationalists.

Probably the most tragic example of Puerto Rican resistance to U.S. presence and policies came on Sunday, March 21, 1937. With the permission of and clearance by the mayor of Ponce for a peaceful demonstration, the Cadets of the Republic members of the Nationalist ranks, set out to march down the streets of Ponce, Puerto Rico's largest southern city. Only two hours before the event, the mayor rescinded his decision to allow the demonstration. The police brought in reinforcements from all parts of Puerto Rico. The nationalists commenced their march. As the men, women, and children began to sing the Puerto Rican national anthem, the police opened fire, killing twenty one and injuring hundreds, including spectators. The incident would go down in history as the Masacre de Ponce (the Ponce Massacre). An investigation by the American Civil Liberties Union reported that the police were responsible for the deaths and injuries and that the civil rights of Puerto Ricans had been violated. A new page was being written in the history of Puerto Rican resistance.[46] The option of armed struggle against the United States had become a reality; this would have a lasting impact on U.S. policies and activities in Puerto Rico.

U.S. legitimacy was faced with potential mass uprising in Puerto Rico. The country's public school system would need to make concessions while not sacrificing its ideological and social instrumentality as the premier agency for "proper political socialization." The ideological strength of the school curriculum, and the values asserted, would need to be turned up a notch in the presence of the rising discontent.

Americanization in the Classroom

The Americanization effort was overtly carried out in the classroom lessons. Let us take a look at some examples of this and how they contributed to the promotion of loyalty to and compliance with U.S. conceptions of development.

Regarding patriotism in the schools, the first commissioner of education, Dr. Martin G. Brumbaugh, stated:

In almost every city of the island and in many rural schools, the children meet and salute the flag. The raising of the flag is the signal that school has commenced. The pupils then sing America, Hail Columbia, Star Spangled Banner, and other patriotic songs at various times during the school day.[47]

The exercises and symbols of Americanism as embodied in the songs and salute of the U.S. flag, even the use of the flag to signal the commencement of the school day, served as expressions of the allegiance to superiority of the American culture that was to be reproduced by the Puerto Rican students. The relationship that this had to English instruction and the Americanization process demonstrated the productive capacity of language and symbols.

In civic and moral studies, which were a primary focus of the curriculum in the first through eighth grades, patriotism was a priority.[48] Virtually every detail of children's behavior fell under the careful scrutiny of the teacher for correction. There were lessons that taught the children the proper facial expressions for the different emotions, so that there would be consistency and recognition. Also available to the younger children were classes on the proper arm angle for eating with a knife and fork, standing, brushing teeth, and all other elements of human hygiene. Later in elementary school the children studied patriotism as embodied in respect for and allegiance to the police, the teacher and the supervisor, the commissioner, and all that stood for America. An interesting example is provided in the book for fifth grade civic and moral studies. Under "Patriotism," in the first category of the curriculum, point 1 reads:

What our ancestors have achieved for us— Make a rapid study and in a very simple manner of the history of the Island of Porto Rico, showing the progress that has been made, focusing on the benefits and advantages of the improved conditions today.[49]

In social studies, the students in the fifth grade would learn to develop an interest in the country's economy and understand and appreciate the commercial, industrial, and military developments of the United States and of the United States in Puerto Rico.[50] By the eighth grade the students would be studying nationalism, imperialism, and capitalism. The course was carefully designed to inculcate an appreciation for the U.S. occupation of Puerto Rico. Nationalism and capitalism were treated in the same manner. Thus, rather than avoiding the concepts, the school system implemented lessons dedicated to their study but imbued them with an ideological twist minimizing the controversy that a critical study of such concepts might raise for Puerto Rico-United States colonial relations. The potential for a critical approach to the study of nationalism and capitalism, among other subjects, was swiftly undermined.

The intensification of government involvement in the economy in the following decades provided further legitimacy for the inculcation of a U.S. conception of development and schooling as U.S. policies continued to struggle with Puerto Rican identity. The language of educational reform became a captive of the maximization of rationalization efforts, as evidenced through the industrialization campaign under Operation Bootstrap. Curriculum practices during the first four decades of U.S. colonial occupation reflected intense immersion in the U.S. culture. Libraries were overwhelmingly stocked with English books. Virtually all texts were in English. Teachers and students were rewarded for demonstrating their preference for English and allegiance to the United States. "Language," says Paulo Freire, "is also culture. It is the mediating force of knowledge; but it is also knowledge itself."[51] In Puerto Rico, then, the very essence of knowledge was to be discovered in the English language, and the U.S. culture.

By replacing the Spanish language with English, the United States was in a position to predict and determine the outcome of school developments more easily. Regardless of the possibility that some of the people committed to English were well intentioned, the impact that English as the replacement for Spanish had upon the identity of the country transcended every aspect of the culture. The acquisition of a new language, English, on the basis of its impact upon the culture, does not seem a sufficient ground for launching an attack upon it as the language of instruction. However, acquisition of English as a vehicle for incorporating a development plan that for the most part, left Puerto Ricans outside the decision-making or policy-making arena became a silencing experience. The logic and values to which any development scheme would appeal would have to be articulated in English. By depending upon the colonizer's language as the language of development and progress, the colonized internalized the implicit superiority of the colonizer. Freire says, "As long as they live in the duality in which to be is to be like, and to be like is to be like the oppressor, this contribution is impossible."[52] In his statement "this contribution refers to the possibility of the oppressed to see themselves as the hosts of the oppressor, at which point the oppressed would begin to participate in the pedagogy of their liberation.

For Freire, then, English in and of itself as a newly acquired language does not seem to represent an issue. The issue arises as the identity of the colonized is replaced by an attempt to be like someone else. At this point development not only is contingent upon others but also, according to Freire, impossible because development here hinges upon purging the subject from the dialectic between subject and objective reality as the two interact in a development process. In this case, the subject is determined by the objective reality, required only to respond to that reality and not to participate in its conceptualization and actualization. Identity is molded by the product of the response of the colonized to an objective reality of which the colonized is an object.

We are reminded of Clark's remarks cited earlier in the chapter: "If we American-ize the schools and inspire the students with the American spirit . . . the island will become in its sympathies, points of view and attitudes . . . essentially American." Representative of some of the earliest comments on the importance of acculturation and identity substitution, Clark's statement encapsulated the implicit political, ideological, and economic significance of such a project. This meant that the evolution of the Puerto Rican culture was not to be a Puerto Rican initiative but a response to a colonial plan.

In essence Puerto Rican perceptions of the Puerto Rican reality and a Puerto Rican vision of the future would be silenced.

CULTURAL SILENCE

Freire's work in liberation pedagogy, and in particular his introduction and elaboration of the notion of a "culture of silence," provides an interesting tool for an examination of the manner in which development, and in this case the requisite language arguments asserted by the colonizer for development, can represent a form of control. To avoid an oversimplification of what I believe is a complex relationship between the colonizer and the colonized, especially in the context of contemporary colonialism in Puerto Rico, Freire reminds us that "It is not the dominator who constructs a culture and imposes it on the dominated. This culture is the result of the structural relations between the dominated and the dominators."[53]

In the case of Puerto Rico, the imposition of English in the schools was viewed by the colonizer as a necessary component in the process of Puerto Rican development. The structural demands informing such a position and the relations that evolved engendered the silencing of the culture. That is, the geopolitical and economic dispositions that motivated the United States to colonize the country after the Spanish American War played a significant role in the decision to Americanize Puerto Rico. The necessity of English as the language of instruction in the schools, in order to facilitate development plans as articulated by the structures which existed, was perceived as consistent with development generally. Freire would not say that this makes the structures any less problematic or oppressive. However, the decision to inculcate American ideals and to do so through the use of the English language need to be considered in the context of the structural relations that arise under colonialism.

Initially, part of the defense for English-language instruction stated that nine of ten Puerto Ricans were illiterate. The implementation of English, then, would not constitute the subordination of one language to another. However, such an argument does not take into account the importance that spoken language has to the development of culture and identity, or the possibility that writing and reading are not necessarily the only legitimate means of communicating and developing culture. Language in this case is not to be understood as only a vehicle for the appropriation of or access to the development of a society's rationalization of production. Language is also a fundamental means by which a complete system of values is transmitted and through which a culture's identity evolves not solely but significantly.

The assertion that Puerto Ricans should "become Americans," concurrent with economic development arguments, was to fuel the issue of identity and development. On this Freire said:

Without a sense of identity, there is no need for struggle. I will only fight you if I am very sure of myself, I am definitely not you. The reasoning process is similar for groups, even at a subconscious level. In this subconscious process, which the very nature of conflict involves, we do not even recognize the significance of our elaborating a particular language while we are consciously defending ourselves in the struggle for liberation. This is why colonized people need to preserve their native language. And the more sophisticated they make their language, the better it will be that the colonizer not understand it, and in this way they can use their language to defend themselves against the colonizer.[54]

If the value of language is to be found, among other places, in the contribution that it makes to the preservation and development of a culture, then that culture needs to be aware of such a value.

In Puerto Rico, if the definition of development was couched (rationalized) in the value of learning English, and if the Puerto Rican people did not grant fundamental importance to their language as a requirement for development, then the potential of language to provide a defense against the encroachment of colonialism was minimized. We have seen that the economic and political structures supporting English arguments, though resisted throughout Puerto Rico, remained subordinated by pressing economic demands. Part of the power of the English language in Puerto Rico resided in the role that it played as a vehicle through which the rationalization of development was articulated. Constituting such a significant aspect of how and why orthodox economics would be promulgated, English left little for Spanish to challenge in Puerto Rico. If development depended on the English language, then to what would defenders of the Spanish language in Puerto Rico appeal? The developmental force of identity, as manifested in language preservation on a mass scale, had not yet, "recognized the significance of our elaborating a particular language while . . . defending ourselves in the struggle for liberation."

The silencing of the culture is not the same as saying that Puerto Rico had no cultural voice. Freire reminds us that we must "guard against idealizing the superstructure, dichotomizing it from the infrastructure." Understanding the complexity of the issue in Puerto Rico is simplified if we approach colonialism from either an objectivist or an idealist perspective. "Social structure exists as a dialectic between superstructure and infrastructure."[55] Unable to understand this dialectic, Freire states, "We will not understand the dialectic of change and permanence as the expression of the social structure."[56] In the case of Puerto Rico this means that we must approach the colonial issue of development and English language as actions of the colonizer's society upon the colony; the colony is meant to respond to the directives of the colonizer, and even in the context of initiatives coming from the colony, the basic character is one of dependence and pending approval. An interesting example of local initiative can be witnessed in the character, logic, and outcome of the Chardón Plan for economic development (see Chapter 3).

At the level of classroom instruction, cultural silencing manifested itself in many ways, for example, as evidenced in the social studies curriculum presented above. Allegiance to the United States, the repeated singing of U.S. patriotic hymns and songs throughout the school day, the connection made between "being educated and being an American" through a specific understanding of personal hygiene and etiquette, and the emphasis placed upon the growth and improvements in Puerto Rico since the arrival of the United States had the effect of introjecting the values and lifestyle of the colonizer upon the colonized. Freire asserts, "This results in the duality of the dependent society, its ambiguity, its being and not being itself, and the ambivalence characteristic of its long experience of dependency, both attracted by and rejecting the metropolitan society."[57]

For Puerto Rico, being itself meant that there was a Puerto Rican identity, a Puerto Rican self, that though suppressed by centuries of colonialism, was also developing through that dialectic between what it identified as self and what would be resisted. The dynamics of cultural identity, then, are not defined simply in terms of what is preserved or rejected, but also in terms of the resultant configuration of the culture rising out of the struggle between the preserved and the rejected. One such instance was the flag–flying issue. Though some were supportive of U.S. development plans or presence, many of that same group strongly identified themselves as Puerto Rican. In the debates over language, while English was viewed as fundamental to development, Spanish remained the overall language of the culture.

The ensuing struggle between orthodox development and cultural affirmation and preservation presented itself in many ways. Whether through the establishment of local newspapers in Spanish, demonstrations, political sabotage in the schools, marches, or even armed guerrilla warfare, Puerto Ricans sent a message to the United States that the social and economic situation under colonialism, even in its "better" days, was unacceptable. The United States was constantly having to legitimize its colonial grip on the island country.

Whereas the metropolis [colonizer] can absorb its ideological crises through mechanisms of economic power and a highly developed technology, the dependent [colonized] structure is too weak to support the slightest popular manifestation. This accounts for the frequent rigidity of the dependent structure."[58]

The development of the Chardón Plan sheds light on this aspect of the colonizer's situation. The need to develop programs and a rationalization for each activity of its development plan made the United States acutely aware of its economic and political policies and of local resistance. In the schools, by inculcating an appreciation for the improvements in lifestyle under the United States, and through appeals to the technological language of development brought to Puerto Rico by the colonizer, the needed legitimacy for a continued colonial presence was affirmed. Despite the many strengths attributed to the nationalist struggle, the forces against the colonial regime lacked structural alternatives to which they could appeal in formalizing and universalizing their efforts against the United States. Each act of resistance was answered by the military and police forces of the United States. Each ideological and political economic argument, it was expected, would be neutralized and coopted by the rationalization of the orthodox economic plan and development project in which the Puerto Rican economy and Puerto Ricans were being progressively entrenched.

Throughout the first forty years of colonialism under the United States, Puerto Rican education wrestled with the issue of English-language instruction. Although, from a rationalization grounded in orthodox economics, the arguments seemed to favor the English initiatives of the United States, much of Puerto Rico remained skeptical regarding the requirement of English as the vehicle for development. If English was required for social and economic development, then Puerto Ricans would have been acknowledging, albeit in a somewhat fragmented manner, the contribution that language makes cultural development. If development was not contingent upon language, then English might have been more easily challenged— or more easily promoted. The tension between the prescriptions under orthodox economics and the struggle to preserve the culture posed formidable challenges to the colonizer and the colonized. The issue of the language of instruction in the schools would someday have to be resolved. Whether this would overcome the silencing of the culture would depend upon whether Puerto Ricans could consciously articulate a Puerto Rican meaning of the dialectic between a voice of their own and a culture of silence.

NOTES

1. Margaret Mead, *Report to the Committee of the Social Studies Commission on the Secondary School Curriculum,* (Washington, D.C.: Report published by the Committee on Secondary School Curriculum, 1935).

2. Martin Brumbaugh, *Annual Report of the Commissioner of Education* (Washington, D.C.: U.S. Government Printing Office, 1901), 8.

3. Henry K. Carroll, *Report on the Island of Porto Rico* (Washington, D.C.: U.S. Department of the Treasury, U.S. Government Printing Office, 1899), 789.

4. Ibid., 56.

5. Luis Muñoz Rivera, *La Democracia,* San Juan, Nov.3, 1898, 2.

6. Freeman R. Butts and Lawrence A. Cremin, *A History of Education in American Culture* (New York: Henry Holt,1953), 286.

7. Juan José Osuna, *A History of Education in Puerto Rico* (Río Piedras:University of Puerto Rico Press, 1975), 155.

8. Ibid., 156.

9. U.S. Department of War, *Report of the United States Insular Commission to the Secretary of War upon Investigations Made into Civil Affairs of the Island of Porto Rico with Recommendations* (Washington, D.C.: U.S. Government Printing Office, 1899), 21.

10. George W. Davis, *Report of the Military Governor of Porto Rico on Civil; Affairs* (Washington, D.C.: U.S. Government Printing Office, 1900), 179.

11. Osuna, *History of Education,* 626.

12. Paul Miller, *Annual Report of the Commissioner of Education for Porto Rico 1916* (Washington, D.C.: U.S. Government Printing Office, 1917), 354.

13. Dietz, *Economic History of Puerto Rico: Institutional Change and Capitalist Development* (Princeton University Press 1986, 202.

14. Osuna, *History of Education,* 213.

15. Centro de Estudios Puertorriqueños (CENEP), *Taller de Migracion* (New York: CENEP, 1975), 53.

16. Osuna, *History of Education,* 303.

17. Ibid., 304.

18. Ibid., 360.

19. Ibid., 215.

20. Ibid., 217.

21. Ibid., 218.

22. Brumbaugh, *Report of the Commissioner,* 65.

23. For an explanation of the notions of the "creative principles" and "mechanical principles" of speech, see, Noam Chomsky, *The Chomsky Reader,* ed. James Peck (New York: Pantheon Books, 1987), 147. Chomsky refers to the species-specific characteristic of language, a Cartesian point he examines in his book. The "mechanical principle," according to Decartes, governs the primitive aspects of animals, while the "creative principle" governs higher forms of speech.

24. In Aida Montilla de Negrón, *La americanización de Puerto Rico y el sistema de instrucción pública 1900–1930* (Río Piedras: Editorial Universitario, 1977), 250.

25. U.S. Department of War, *Report of the United States Insular Commission,* 53.

26. Davis, *Report of the Military Governor,* 2.

27. *Report of the Commissioner of Education of Porto Rico, 1901* (Washington, D.C.: U.S. Government Printing Office, 1901), 168.

28. Rafael Cordero Matos, *La instrucción pública en Puerto Rico* (Ponce: Imprenta Manuel C. López,1901), 14–20.

29. *Report of the Commissioner, 1901,* 52.

30. Montilla de Negrón, *La americanización,* 46–47.

31. Osuna, *A History of Education,* 141.

32. Montilla de Negrón, *La americanización,* 254.

33. Ibid., 258.

34. Ibid., 261.

35. Ibid., 265.

36. José de Diego, in Manuel Maldonado Denis, *Puerto Rico: A Socio-Historic Interpretation* (New York: Vintage Books, 1972), 75-76.

37. Montilla de Negrón, *La americanización,* 265.

38. Ibid., 266.

39. Ibid., 268.

40. Ibid.

41. Adalberto López and James Petras, eds., *Puerto Rico and Puerto Ricans: Studies in History and Society* (New York: Halsted Press, 1974), 175.

42. Dietz, *Economic History,* 181.

43. Osuna, *History of Education,* 132.

44. E. A. Ross, *Social Control: A Survey of the Foundations of Order* (New York: Macmillan, 1901), 190.

45. Maldonado Denis, *Puerto Rico,* 117–29.

46. Ibid., 117–31.

47. Osuna, *History of Education,* 135.

48. Susan D. Huntington,*Curso de estudios en la educación moral y cívica para las escuelas públicas de Puerto Rico,* 2 Vols. (San Juan: Bureau of Supplies, Printing, and Transportation, 1917).

49. Ibid., vol. 2, 11.

50. *Outline for the Teaching of Social Science in the Fifth Grade,* (San Juan: Dept. of Education, 1936).

51. Paulo Freire and Donaldo Macedo, *Literacy: Reading the Word and the World* (New York: Bergin and Garvey, 1987), 53.

52. Paulo Freire, *Pedagogy of the Oppressed* (New York: Continuum, 1990), p. 33.

53. Paulo Freire, *The Politics of Education* (New York: Bergin and Garvey, 1985), 72.

54. Ibid., 186.

55. Ibid., 72.

56. Ibid.

57. Ibid., 73.

58. Ibid.

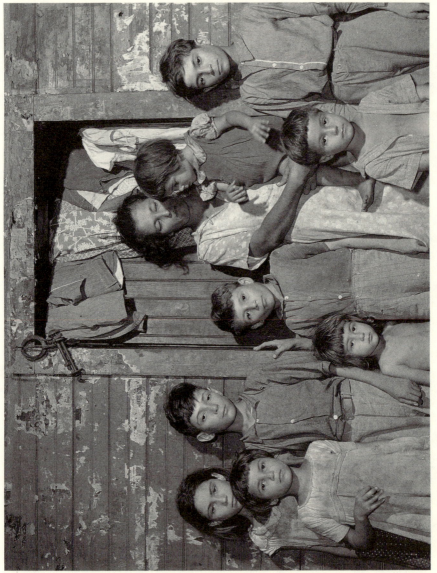

Family of a farm laborer in Barceloneta (1941). From *Puerto Rico Mio*, photography by Jack Delano, published by the Smithsonian Institute. Washington, D.C., 1990.

ECONOMIC GROWTH AND UNDERDEVELOPMENT

When action is informed by a technical interest (techne), it is constituted by a number of elements. These are the eidos (the guiding idea) and the techne (the guiding disposition) that together provide the basis for poietike ("making" action) . . . . Technical interests will not facilitate autonomy because it is an interest in control. An interest in control will certainly facilitate independence for some, but this is false autonomy, for it is an "autonomy" that entails regarding humans and/or the environment as objects.[1]

*T*he title of this chapter may, to some, seem contradictory since one of the paradigms treated in Chapter 2, equates growth with development. Yet how much of development is growth? We have seen that a country's economic growth can improve while the quality of life or the standard of living for the majority of the population remains poor or worsens. These concerns constitute part of the second paradigm (political economy) examined in Chapter 2. If we agree that there is more to development than economic growth, and that in Puerto Rico the establishment and expansion of a U.S.-controlled school system was a central feature of a U.S. economic growth project, then development would require more than merely reacting to the demands of the market as evidenced through the maximization of rational behavior.

In Puerto Rico, the first forty years of U.S. occupation witnessed broad-based conflict in schooling and school reform. From the social-political perspective, the debates over the language of instruction were a central feature of the conflict. This, however, does not mean that other factors did not contribute significantly to the hardships faced by Puerto Ricans in the development and expansion of schooling on the island (teacher shortages, limited facilities, U.S. centralized control, etc.). Chapter

3 examined how an orthodox model of development was engendered by the United States in Puerto Rico and how this conception provided for the maximization of rational behavior as advanced in an orthodox economy. The role that public schooling played in that development project, primarily through the ideological power residing in the use of English as the language of instruction for the purpose of politically socializing the Puerto Rican people, was articulated in Chapter 4.

Autonomists, independentists, and even some assimilationists regularly criticized the U.S. administration of Puerto Rico's public school system. This posture was also affected by the economic distress in that the vast majority of Puerto Ricans found themselves. The need to place some checks on the economic development project became the focus of the new period of industrialization. Satisfying these needs became possible, in part, as a result of the weakened U.S. economic hold following the depression and the U.S. war buildup. Operation Bootstrap intensified the problems of national development and the ability of Puerto Ricans to improve their condition. Those who held the controlling interests in Puerto Rico had interests other than the development of Puerto Rico in mind.[2]

The legitimation of the control enjoyed by U.S. firms was found, among other places, in the language of schooling and in school reform as these articulated a consistency with colonial development plans. Efforts to increase the number of schools and an emphasis on vocational training presented problems for the development of a schooling program and an economic project whose primary purpose was to satisfy Puerto Rico's development needs. School expansion generally took the form of vocational training schools, while the already established schools focused on the intensification of a vocational curriculum. Expenditures on schooling in 1929 were estimated at $22,659 for junior high schools and $351,081 for high schools; they increased to $1.4 million and $4.2 million, respectively by 1947, with the initiation of Operation Bootstrap, the leading industrialization program (that continued in force, for all practical purposes, through the 1980s).[3]

Although Spanish became the language of school instruction in 1949, English remained an ideological instrument connoting a superior education. Taught as a subject, English was equated with notions of modernization, development, and, more generally, a progressive vision of the future. The more advanced the level of education, the more English was required. Thus, secondary school texts contained more English than those for elementary or junior high schools, and at the university level texts in English predominated. This had definite implications for the majority of Puerto Ricans, who found themselves living in poverty and receiving little if any schooling— usually less than six years. Furthermore, the value placed on English was reinforced by the domination of U.S. firms in Puerto Rico because they conducted business primarily in English. The English language was promoted as a vehicle for opportunity and advancement. In arguing that the orthodox model of development continued to envelop the Puerto Rican political-economic environment and culture while truncating the possibilities for the legitimacy of alternative conceptions of development in the language of progress and school reform, this chapter will examine some of the changes during the period from 1940 through the 1980s.

The chapter is divided into four sections. The first, that examines the 1940s, will look at the political, economic, and social conditions that characterized Puerto Rico during the 1940s. This decade is important to highlight for various reasons. First, World War II had a significant effect upon the development projects and upon schooling (in particular, vocational education). Second, the Puerto Rican economy experienced a drastic transformation during the war and the immediate postwar years. Puerto Rico experimented with state capitalism during the war yet rapidly returned to the predominance of privately owned industries in the period immediately following the war. Also, the projects and effects of state capitalism brought the Puerto Rican government under tighter control by U.S. interests; this had a lasting effect on Puerto Rico's public school system. The second section will briefly examine the decade of the 1940s.

The commitment of the United States to develop Puerto Rico in a manner consistent with orthodox economics meant that forces would be called upon to maximize the rational behavior of Puerto Ricans. In this respect, the 1940s provided a transitional period from the earlier monocultural model to one on the brink of mass industrialization. In order to present a wider picture of the Puerto Rican situation, the section will include two brief subsections that outline an overview of various aspects of Puerto Rican life during the period.

The third section of the chapter treats the period from roughly 1950 to the 1980s. It outlines the developments rising out of the transitions from the state capitalism of the early 1940s through the call for private investments and the ensuing industrialization campaign called Operation Bootstrap. Drawing on the work of Herbert Marcuse, the final section of the chapter presents a brief analysis of some of the potential repressive implications of technological development, specifically as related to a colonial reality.

INDUSTRIALIZATION: THE POLITICAL ECONOMY OF THE 1940s

Food Consumption

Life for Puerto Ricans during the 1940s was extremely difficult, even when some progress was made. With the U.S. involvement in World War II, basic food imports to Puerto Rico were severely constrained by the attacks of German submarines on U.S. ships en route to Puerto Rico. While the option of growing food to make up for the loss was available, it was met with considerable resistance. Rexford Tugwell, governor of Puerto Rico in 1941, explains:

The Farmers' Association (front for the sugar producers and roughly corresponding to that better-known American phenomenon, the California Farmers' Association) would never accept the suggestion of conversion from cane to food. It was their feeling that it was dangerous for it to get abroad that food could be raised in Puerto Rico. Cane was more profitable for them and their most earnest attention had always been given to lobbying for higher quotas on the ground that no other crop could be grown.[4]

The rationalization of behavior patterns consistent with the development model was important insofar as it contributed not only to the development of "a dependence upon the 'objective order of things' . . . to be sure, itself the result of domination,"[5] but also to domination as carried out in the colonial relationship. Thus, the synthesis resulting from a U.S.-introduced and Puerto Rican–re-created rationalization of the message that agricultural development for local consumption was unviable from a cost-benefit analysis perspective in orthodox economics, influenced the decline of local agriculture. The developments in the evolution of the rationalization of the economy and society did contribute to the advancement of the economy throughout the industrialization period. However, the grounding of such advancements in a colonial relationship restricted the possibilities for Puerto Rico to exercise its own creative and developmental powers, leaving the people with the role of respondents to the initiatives or rules of another.

The strategy here was then to convince Puerto Ricans, through appeals to the logic of orthodox economics, that agriculture for local consumption was not a rational alternative, given the geography of the country, population growth, unpredictability of crop yields, and so on. While agriculture alone could not provide the base for long-term economic development in Puerto Rico, the U.S. control of the Puerto Rican economy, including the emphasis placed on sugar as the only viable agricultural product, troubled the U.S. development program. The total substitution of industrialization for agriculture would remain a problem for Puerto Rico. The fixation with industrialization as the solution to development, at the expense of and general disregard for agriculture, proved significantly detrimental to Puerto Rico. Agriculture and industrialization need not have been placed in an either/or situation. Together they could have contributed to a broad and more solid developmental foundation for the country.[6]

Rather than impose such a policy against food growing in Puerto Rico, the strategic move by the colonial government and U.S. firms was to assure Puerto Ricans that local food agriculture was significantly limited as a way of providing Puerto Rico with a viable alternative to alleviate the shortage or contribute to development.[7] The focus was to define and control the industrialization of the Puerto Rican economy and society. In this way any changes arising in Puerto Rico were tied to and dependent upon the United States. The land that was devoted to food production concentrated on a few of the starchy crops such as *yautía* (a root food) and sweet potato. Having to rely so heavily on imports, Puerto Ricans faced enormous increases in the price of food. During the first years of the 1940s, prices on imported foods increased twofold over those of locally produced goods.[8]

Two points should be noted here. First, throughout the war period, Puerto Ricans were facing the real possibility of starvation. Also, price regulators like the federal Office of Price Administration were ineffective in controlling price abuses in Puerto Rico. The colonial government's initiatives to curtail the suffering through programs aimed at the procurement and distribution of food encountered virtually total opposition from private interests (importers, business and legal [lawyers] representatives).[9] The proper behavior expected of Puerto Ricans was to not disturb the construct of an economy that was centrally controlled and determined by the combination of private interests from the United States, local business interests tied to the United States, and the U.S. Congress.

The Puerto Rican Chamber of Commerce went so far as to accuse the insular government of "communism" for having undertaken emergency measures to prevent hunger.[10] These measures included activities such as, "setting up price guidelines or the procurement and distribution of food from other than the usual U.S. sources."[11]

Thus, Puerto Rico's problem of satisfying food needs was not so much a matter of the country's available agricultural resources as of controlling interests that perceived such a project to be detrimental.

Poverty and Wages

Adding to the problem of food availability was the general poverty, as evidenced in the real per capita income on the island. One of the most important industries predicated on poverty was needlework.

As Daniel Ross remarks:

Needlework was without any foundation except misery. It could exist only on desperation wages. No one could make a living at it; but a woman whose husband is unemployed and whose children are starving will go to great lengths for the price of a few pounds of rice.[12]

Mostly women, the 44,731 persons working in the home needlework industry made up more than 44 percent of the manufacturing labor force. By 1948, the number of needleworkers increased by 16 percent, accounting for two-thirds of the increase in manufacturing employment between 1940 and 1950.[13] Despite minimum wage legislation, an amendment in 1940 to the Fair Labor Standards Act of 1938 allowed industries to set lower standards, though the target of 25 cents per hour remained. In 1949 the actual hourly wage for needlework was still 15 cents an hour. In 1955, it was 17.5 cents. At the time the minimum wage in the United States was $1.00 per hour. Weekly earnings in the needlework industry represented one-tenth the weekly earnings of government workers in Puerto Rico.[14] Dependent upon cheap labor yet confronted by the Puerto Rican government's commitment to reasonable wage practices due to the high cost of living, the needlework industry declined rapidly, from 54,000 workers in 1950 to 15,000 in 1957.[15] Schooling was appealed to as a "way out and up" for the tens of thousands of workers displaced from this industry. Given the changes in wage standards and the huge gap between the earnings of needleworkers and that earned by government employees, part of the reason for the decline in the needlework industry is made apparent. Labor costs had to be kept down while labor needed to be employed. In order to support the rationale for the changes facing production in Puerto Rico, schools would be called upon to prepare a labor force for work in the newly arriving factories. Much of this shift contributed fundamentally to the urbanization of Puerto Rico.

Many workers sought employment in the cities. Throughout the 1940s, Puerto Rico witnessed a demographic shift from the rural regions to the cities. While this is usually the case for industrializing societies, Puerto Rico offers us some revealing evidence for the arguments of underdevelopment. Emigration took the form of movement from the rural regions to the United States. During that period when Puerto Rico was experiencing its most rapid GNP growth, the country was also witnessing the greatest flight of its workers.[16] The high cost of living, that compelled many to emigrate, was made more evident by the numbers that reflected the wages earned in Puerto Rico.

In 1940 the real annual per capita income in Puerto Rico was $122, in Mississippi it was $203, in Alabama $207, and in Georgia $317. Nationally, the United States had a real annual per capita income some five times greater than Puerto Rico. For other countries in the region, in 1942, the figures indicate: $20 in Haiti, $104 in Jamaica, and $102 in Barbados. Even by 1950 Puerto Rico's real per capita net income was only $181.[17]

Puerto Rico became a welfare society whose determinations originated externally. The requisite local institutions and control in the development of the structure were missing. U.S. control of the capital initiatives focused on the contribution that the welfare structure made to the long-term benefits of U.S. orthodox economics in Puerto Rico. Furthermore, the means to support such a structure locally required the development of local institutions whose efforts would not be subverted by the impending capital-intensive projects residing in the plans of the colonizer.

Though many U.S. private firms struggled with the Puerto Rican insular government's involvement in the economy during the early 1940s, World War II compelled the U.S. government to extend some local, albeit temporary, economic control to Puerto Rico's government through such measures as the creation of the Puerto Rican Development Company and its component firms: Puerto Rico Glass, Puerto Rico Paper and Pulp, Puerto Rico Shoe and Leather, and Puerto Rico Clay. This extension of power however, did not lessen the impact of popular resistance, as evidenced in the many strikes on the sugar plantations and elsewhere, following the political decision to allow for these local firms (45 strikes in 1939 and the formation of the Confederación General de Trabajadores, with over 159 unions and 150,000 workers).

The combination of popular discontent, persistent poverty, and the U.S. predicament brought difficulties for the orthodox projects that formerly had enjoyed unchallenged predominance in the economy. Extending some control to the insular government had an important impact upon schooling. The active and direct role of the insular government in the economic function and development of the society kept public schooling under the close supervision and direction of the government. In this way, instead of expanding the possibilities for educating Puerto Ricans beyond vocational preparation, the new arrangement under the insular government only replicated the former; in both cases school reform initiatives generally responded to the economic demands of the colonial relationship, severely constraining the possibilities for an expanded language of school reform and for seeking alternative conceptions of development. The short-term gains of participating in the development projects under the United States offered some immediate relief for many Puerto Ricans in poverty. The role that schools played in this effort was significant. The long-term effect was a bit more difficult to address. Under the conditions mentioned above, the reality of acute poverty (in many cases near starvation) and the immediate need for alleviation made the short-term government projects more tolerable to many Puerto Ricans than any struggle to overcome the system that in part accounted for their condition.

The Early 1940s: An Experiment in State Capitalism

Leading the promotion of industrialization was the Puerto Rico Development Company, the result of legislation initiated by Governor Tugwell. The company, as a state enterprise, worked on various projects, including research leading to an increase in the uses of land for industrial purposes, marketing for exports, the establishment of Puerto Rican firms for local production of goods manufactured from domestic materials, and the promotion of industrial participation by local fims— in hopes of avoiding the problems generated by absentee capitalism.[18] Ideologically, the Development Company posed no threat to the colonial relationship. At this point, the company was actually a local extension of U.S. interests. The presence of import-substitution programs, like those characterizing the Development Company, should not be understood as expressions of hostility toward at the United States, private capital, or capitalism.[19]

Thus, much of the Puerto Rican government's resources that were to contribute to local development actually paved the way for more capital-intensive projects. Linked primarily to construction and trade, the effect that these loans had upon the development of technical requirements for Puerto Rico's development was slight. The loans did not find their way into development projects for the expansion of local industries or of the demand for a more technologically advanced work force requiring advanced schooling; thus, while contributing to some aspects of growth, these changes provided scant evidence of development.

Although in conflict with some private firms over the involvement of government in the economy, the Development Company nevertheless reinforced capitalist production while preserving the political-ideological configuration of colonialism. Generally, then, debates over the island's economy concerned not the nature of the process by that development is ascertained, as is the case for the political-economic analysis, but the degree to that government involvement in the colonial relationship (orthodox capitalist production) did or did not meet the demands of the market. This is not to say that the Development Company did not have serious problems with the private firms.

At the core of the problems facing the Development Company was the issue of creating publicly owned firms. Such ownership was perceived by many as nothing short of socialism. The key term here is "public." These companies were not owned by the workers, as some socialist arguments assert. The "public" nature of the firms resided in the insular government's control of the companies. Though there may have been government officials who believed that the long term might best be served by addressing immediate needs through activities such as state capitalist projects, the insular government itself did not challenge U.S. colonial presence. It was probably more likely that those officials involved in the Development Company were compelled to establish such an entity. Members of private firms saw this as a threat to their interests. Yet from the beginning, the Development Company made it clear that "Any subsidiaries of the Company would not be in already existing industries, nor would they operate in competition with private capital."[20]

Thus, the Development Company did not depart from the orthodox scheme; it only acted as a first-aid effort that might, or might not offer long-term opportunities for Puerto Rican development. Capital development under the Company, then was an extension of the dependency relationship under colonialism that did not translate into capital development as a means of self-sufficiency providing for national development. The Development Company was responsible for the creation of four new enterprises: glass, shoes, paperboard, and clay building materials. Representing attempts to meet local demands for products that otherwise were imported from the United States, these enterprises were essentially import-substitution projects whose productive lives were short-lived.

Internally, Puerto Ricans were struggling to define the role that the Development Company and its firms would play in Puerto Rico's development. Political struggles ensued across and within the different parties and ideologies taking part in, or resisting, the effort. From economic and cultural perspectives contradictions were perceived in the Development Company's initiatives. The Company was not interested in challenging the firms already established in Puerto Rico.

The ongoing struggle between the government corporations and private firms needs to be analyzed, in part, within the context of political party loyalties. Much of Puerto Rico's local private firms were owned or controlled by the wealthier republican elements who opposed many of the colonial government's programs, that they perceived as benefiting the government of the Popular Democratic Party (PPD). In this way, private firms retained an advantage and the power to block the government's plans to import-substitute and to stimulate greater integration within the economy. The parameters for the planning and execution of development projects were defined not by the colonial government of the PPD but by the U.S. private capitalist interests.[21]

Many of the island's local private firms had close ties with the United States, or at least with U.S. capital and political interests, while the colonial government was, throughout this period, controlled by the PPD. The PPD favored some semblance of a more expanded autonomy for Puerto Rico, whereas the republican position sought more integration into the U.S. economy and polity through annexation. The PPD's economic vision of autonomy withered away as government firms and capital grew ever more dependent upon private firms (primarily from the United States); and as the party in control throughout the 1940s and 1950s the PPD continued to emphasize the view that matters of economic development were different from matters of political status.

The persistence of the view that economic development and political status were different aspects of the Puerto Rican experience, in that status was subordinate to economic development, gave schooling an ideological bent consistent with this view. While providing school reform with the political legitimacy for a reform language responsive to economic development under the United States, such reasoning gave additional importance and justification to the values and behavioral changes consonant with an orthodox economic model in Puerto Rico. The results of the Development Company set the climate for a more entrenched colonial relationship rather than the extension of autonomy and Puerto Rican determination in articulating a satisfactory development program.[22] Charged by the new programs for industrialization and supported by the efforts of school reforms to meet the new industrial demands, the U.S. and Puerto Rican governments initiated Operation Bootstrap (Operación Manos a la Obra) "an industrial program aimed at stimulating the growth of output, based on orthodox economic principles of behavior."[23]

THE LATE 1940s AND OPERATION BOOTSTRAP

The failure of many local government enterprises to accumulate profits and promote more cost-effective projects, and the attacks launched by many private firms over the government's involvement in the economy, motivated the decision by the insular government to reduce government ownership of many firms. Government ownership was reduced to those areas where it is usual that government be engaged, even in capitalist economies: municipal bus services, electric power, water supplies, and sewage.[24] In 1948 the government sold the five subsidiaries controlled by the Puerto Rico Industrial Development Company.[25] This of course meant that the government-controlled public school system would be called upon to respond to the need for an industrial discipline in the workers. The emphasis placed upon vocational schooling was intimately linked to that need.

By 1945 efforts were made to make Puerto Rico attractive to expanded U.S. industrial capital investment. With offices in New York, the Puerto Rico Industrial Development Company, under the aegis of the Aid to Industrial Development (AID) program, sought out investors. Not sufficiently impressed by the offer of rental subsidies, only 3 of 726 firms contacted relocated in Puerto Rico.[26] These were Red Cape Leather, Río Grande Artificial Flowers, and Ponce Candy. Exactly why these companies moved is not known, though companies were being offered incentives to relocate on the island, such as, tax exempt status and low rents. Quite possibly some of the companies had experienced hard times in the United States and the incentives offered them some time and an opportunity to recover or rebuild. Again, the low skills needed by workers in the companies may have contributed to the move. The tasks were simple; the investments in production may have been worth the risk.

Cognizant of the shortcomings of the AID, the government embarked on a massive campaign to convince the Puerto Rican people that their interests would be served by catering to the profit-oriented interests represented by increased U.S. investment. This was not entirely false, since possibly some of the immediate needs might at least be met in this way. Here we are reminded of the role that planning can play within the orthodox paradigm of economic development.

On the side of nonrational behavior, the government can attempt to convince its citizens of the need for "modernization" while at the same time substituting its own entrepreneurial ability and knowledge to fill that vacuum .... By developing a coherent overview of the economy and by forcing this on the actors in the economy through the various means at its disposal .[27]

Even with the proliferation of U.S. firms investing in Puerto Rico during the late 1940s under Operation Bootstrap, sugar refining and needlework accounted for approximately 60 percent of income from manufacturing.[28] With their low or semi-skilled requirements, these jobs signaled the concurrent projections for the development and expansion of vocational education programs that would prepare a work force with minimal skills for employment in industries whose contributions to Puerto Rico's national development remained problematic.[29]

Along with the exemptions provided to the firms relocating in Puerto Rico, the Puerto Rican government provided training programs that included an emphasis on the expansion and focus of vocational education. Commenting on the relationship between national income and the vocational role of schools, the commissioner of education, José Gallardo, remarked:

It is an established fact, that school expenditures aid considerably in the maintenance of a high level of national income. Education not only increases production by improving the skill of the worker, but through technological progress increases production by improving the productive process and by lowering its costs. As regards consumption, education changes the patterns of consumer spending and helps to create a demand for new products.[30]

The commissioner's remarks had yet to be realized in Puerto Rico. The relationship of school expenditures to a high level of national income implies that investments in schooling yield an improved national income. While schooling was expanding during the period of rapid industrialization and some economic growth was occurring, this was not necessarily due to school expenditures. None of what was said by Gallardo should necessarily to be perceived as a plan for Puerto Rican development. After all, education may improve production and may lower costs, yet the benefits of lower costs and increased production are of little import if they result in the repatriation of profits abroad. Finally, the changes in consumption patterns and the creation of the demand for new products generated by education would, among other things during this period, make it difficult for local products to find substantial support and growth, and would advance the perception that a preference for imported goods connoted a commitment to modernization and progress. And the more Puerto Ricans viewed imported goods as "better" or more "efficient" than local goods, the less likely it was that local goods would flourish. In this way, the element of an ideology consistent with orthodox economics was factored into the schooling process as "efficiency" and "better" become defined and evaluated on the basis of criteria residing in the rationalization favoring such an economic model.

From a long-term perspective, what was to have been an insular government's program for local development became an extension of U.S. control in Puerto Rico, and actually contributed to the preservation of dependency and a sustained orthodox model of development whose movements were determined by the United States. On a short-term account, the changes, as adverse as they may have been, provided some immediate legitimacy for the capital-intensive projects under Operation Bootstrap.

Support for the government's program was not difficult to gather. This consent, however, was not the result of the workings of the market. Instead, the improvements in living standards were the result of government intervention programs and colonial political interests that allowed for some improvement in the absence of any long-term development of institutions that might contribute more permanently to Puerto Rico's national well-being.[31] In other words, the colonial relation secured the legitimacy of the insular government's directives in determining Puerto Rico's disposition. The federal government appeared to have a project outlined for Puerto Rico that did not take into account some of the country's vital needs. For example, Washington did not make available money for the land reform projects of the mid-to-late 1940s because Congress opposed the reform, thereby forcing the program to seek other sources of funding.[32] Thus the possibility of developing a viable local agriculture industry was constrained, and the blueprint for Puerto Rican development under U.S. control remained intact.

Again the drive toward industrialization turned attention away from agriculture— perceiving it as a detriment to growth from a cost-benefit calculus. With the advent of social efficiency as articulated in the growth-first arguments, and of Operation Bootstrap, Puerto Rico turned away from the earlier government-generated programs, that generally characterize the initial stage of state capitalism,[33] and emphasized private investments. Such a turn had a marked impact on schooling and school reform. Having improved in some important ways, though temporarily and in a limited fashion, the relationship established between the expansion of schooling, the development of vocational education, and some economic growth tended to legitimize a continuation of the call for schools and the language of school reform to meet the demands for economic development. This reliance upon schools for development created a kind of mirage in Puerto Rico— one in which schools appear to be the answer to development while actually contributing to the preservation of an economic model of development sustained by Puerto Rico's colonial status. As an agency of the insular government, the public school system gave students the proper skills and dispositions necessary for employment in predominantly U.S. firms, such as assembly-line work in textile, chemical, and clothing factories, that were arriving with the trend toward private investments. Of the incentives used to lure investment in Puerto Rico, none was more enticing than the tax exemption programs.

This section has presented evidence that during the 1940s Puerto Rico's living standard improved. Nevertheless, the immediate gains realized by the economic programs under state capital initiatives and the subsequent private investments of Operation Bootstrap, did little to secure the well-being of most Puerto Ricans. The possibility of forging a local development project remained constrained by the economic requirements under a colonial relationship and the internalization of such requirements in the everyday values of the people. In sum, Operation Bootstrap and the development programs that arose in the late 1940s remained loyal to the colonial relationship and the restrictions on Puerto Rican power to institutionalize national change. Puerto Rico had become encarcerated by a set of invisible limitations that actually further entrenched it in colonialism by introducing reforms that were issued from the top down, from the colonizer to the colonized. And it was these reforms that answered the call during the crises of the 1930s.

Not venturing beyond the invisible limitations, Puerto Rican development remained safely within acceptable boundaries that did not threaten the colonial configuration. The people's values, as expressed in their daily lives, attested to the existence of the tension from these limitations. The extension of a Puerto Rican-originated expectation was tempered by the limitations. This contributed to much social-political tension throughout Puerto Rico's colonial history. Additionally, in order to maximize a conforming response to the limitations, all of Puerto Rico's civil institutions had to contribute. In this, the law and schools played a major role.

Of fundamental significance was the passage of Law Num. 53 (approved as Project Num. 24, passed on May 24, 1948). Commonly referred to as the Ley de la Mordaza (the Muzzle Law), this new law, a product of the U.S. cold war initiative, was enacted in order to criminalize any revolutionary national liberation effort in Puerto Rico. The law stated that:

To foment, advocate, advise, preach, voluntarily or through knowledge, the necessity, desireability or convenience of dismantling, destroying or paralizing of the Insular government, or any of its political subdivisions, by means of violence; that printing, publishing, editing, circulating, selling, distribution or public exhibition with the intent to dismantle . . . (etc.) as well as organizing or helping to organize any such society, group or assembly of persons that foment, advocate, advise or preacvh such a thing . . . will be considered a felony.[34]

The law clearly put a muzzle on any, speech, or action aimed at liberating Puerto Rico from the colonial grip of the United States. With such a law in place, the types of repression Puerto Rican independentists would since then experience has acquired new meaning. The field of inquiry regarding development and school reform also became more restricted. Any talk of development was restricted to that language legitimized by the colonial government of Puerto Rico and the U.S. Congress. Resistence to U.S. initiatives was legal only within the framework established U.S. law. This exacerbated the obvious limitations of Puerto Ricans to conceptualize and construct alternative conceptions of development.

The invisible limitations became part of what might be called the hidden curriculum in school and in the language of school reform and political and social development. The language arising from the limitations set the standard for determining the legitimacy of certain alternatives in school and political economic reform initiatives. As long as the language of school reform respected the boundaries (acceptable colonial behavior), the legitimacy of reform programs was preserved.

RECAPITULATION AND INDUSTRIALIZATION: THE POLITICAL ECONOMY FROM THE 1950s TO THE 1980s

Fundamentally speaking, there were no changes in the direction and model of development in Puerto Rico between 1950 and the 1980s, "only variations on the theme of industrialization," notes James Dietz, "dependent on U.S. markets, inputs, technology, financing, and ownership."[35] This basic arrangement of social existence had a profound impact on virtually every institution in Puerto Rico. While portrayed as a planned economy within the constructs of orthodox economics, the insular government through its planning boards, including Fomento, concentrated on strategies that would appeal to U.S. investors rather than on Puerto Rico's domestic needs. Puerto Rico's needs and interests and the interests of industrial capitalists had been viewed as synonymous, raising serious questions of national development for the country. To many, then, the responsibility for rising incomes and modernization in Puerto Rico was to be attributed to the presence of investment by international firms. However, the import of this investment to the life of the Puerto Rican society needs to be carefully considered.

Operation Bootstrap: Tightening the Knot

Roughly speaking, Operation Bootstrap can be divided into two stages. The first, dating from 1947 to the 1960s, was characterized by primarily labor-intensive projects. The second stage, the stage of capital-intensive projects, has been dominant from the 1960s to the present. By 1967, during the first stage, textiles and clothing accounted for approximately 20 percent of all manufacturing firms.[36] Some arguments state that low wages were more important than were the tax incentives for attracting U.S. firms to Puerto Rico. Low wages provided a larger subsidy than did the tax holiday under the

Industrial Incentives Law. They remained the key to profitability for firms arriving through Operation Bootstrap, leading one observer to refer to this as the "sweatshop" phase of the operation.[37]

Throughout this period, the importance of developing and expanding a public school system conducive to the continuation of the development model in Puerto Rico called upon schools to advance Puerto Rican development by preparing students for productive life in the colonial economic environment.

Adding to the problem of schooling, and of incorporating the products of the school system into the economy and society generally, was the persistence of high rates of unemployment. It would be reasonable to state that unemployment remains Puerto Rico's most persistent economic issue.[38] Labor force participation declined steadily from 1950, regaining its 1950 level only around 1965.[39] Paradoxically, such a decline in worker participation occurred at the same time that Puerto Rico was experiencing its greatest industrial growth under the initiatives of Fomento, that had as an objective the reduction of unemployment.[40]

Unemployment was viewed as the result of an untrained work force— essentially the same argument raised earlier in the country's educational and economic history. The improvement of unemployment rates in Puerto Rico during a short period of the 1950s and the 1960s has been explained as the result of "increased migration and lower labor-force participation particularly among male workers of the prime labor-force age."[41] The definition of "unemployed" is significant. Those not working at all represent one group, while those not working ful-time need to be accounted for in some way. Puerto Rico, as an economic and political colony, has long had a history of many underemployed or less-than-full-time employed persons. For example, "In 1953 approximately 40 percent of all workers worked less than thirty-five hours per week; in 1960, it was 33 percent."[42]

Under the U.S. economic development plans, unemployment and underemployment in Puerto Rico served as an incentive for the emigration of huge numbers of Puerto Ricans to the United States during the first stage of Operation Bootstrap. Net out migration between 1950 and 1960 averaged approximately 50,000 every two years. For nearly twenty years Puerto Rico witnessed mass emigration, generally to the United States. Emigration totals during these decades represented approximately 28 percent of the country's total population in 1950.[43] The fact that considerable numbers of workers schooled in Puerto Rico, were leaving the country indicated that the country was now facing the out flow of its educated sectors.

The industrialization of Puerto Rico under Operation Bootstrap was meant to turn around Puerto Rico's ailing economy. Yet the shift to manufacturing "has done nothing," cites Dietz, "to alter Puerto Rico's long-standing dependence on external trade."[44] He noted that Operation Bootstrap concentrated on export-oriented firms, that the verticality of companies locating in Puerto Rico made it extremely difficult for Puerto Rico to develop internally, and that the unnecessary sacrifice of agriculture brought about by the emphasis upon industrialization increased Puerto Rico's reliance on imported goods and foods.[45] Given the establishment and expansion of hundreds of factories (as many as 300 by 1952), there remained the need for a trained labor force. The skills needed for virtually all of the positions were little more than a basic understanding of simple tools and some English. More important through vocational education, schools would help create the disposition conducive to factory labor. The presence of so many foreign factories and Puerto Rico's growing population became instruments in the language of educational reform that constantly focused on the ascendance of vocational education during the period.

These changes in the Puerto Rican character were perceived as natural aspects of modernization and development under industrialization. While this may be the case, school reform did not address the relationship that these changes had to Puerto Rico's political-economic situation. The reform initiatives were informed by and articulated a language that constrained the meaning of development from including anything more than growth under colonialism. A host of references were made to such ideals as "progress," "democracy," "modernization," "human development," and "order," yet these ideals were not addressed except within the context of a conventional language unable or unwilling to expand the parameters of legitimacy to other conceptions of these ideals. And this, in significant ways, constrained the possibility for a school reform language grounded in an expanded conception of development. In other words, the language of school reform, by appealing to the importance of vocational education as evidenced by the urbanization of Puerto Rico, its industrialization, and its population growth, without examining the relationship that these changes had within the Puerto Rican political-economic reality, remained bound by a conception of development consistent with the colonial relationship.

In the 1950s and 1960s Puerto Rico's output and income increased dramatically. Many of the country's basic needs were improved as a result of the developments under Operation Bootstrap. Schooling expanded, life expectancy lengthened, and per capita income rose, among other improvements. Yet the 1950s and 1960s also contributed markedly to a sustained colonial political-economic relationship. It goes without saying that this kind of relationship becomes a powerful incentive for advancing schooling based upon a particular conception of development, given the improvements in many areas. Nevertheless, the connection between Puerto Rico's growth and schooling needs to be critically addressed. For example, it has been noted that the insular government's contribution to growth during this period was second only to that of manufacturing. As a service-oriented sector, after manufacturing's contribution is accounted for, that of the government is closer to occupying the top spot as a contributor to the country's GNP. The improvements in wages, due primarily to government employment, were actually responsible for the massive infusion of U.S. investments through the establishment of hundreds of private firms. In neither case was the expansion of schooling necessarily responsible for the experienced growth. While schooling could meet the need to prepare workers, the level of schooling needed remained minimal. Concentrating on vocational education, schools trained Puerto Rico's industrial labor force, that was to learn to live with low wages lest Puerto Rico risk losing its preferential treatment by investors.

By the 1960s, manufacturing was the largest employment sector in the economy. However, schooling was to provide a minimally educated work force. Through the 1960s manufacturing accounted for approximately 15 percent of employment. Most of those employed in manufacturing worked in the apparel industry and virtually all of them worked at sewing machines or on an assembly line. José Madera, at one time the director of Fomento, stated:

The industries attracted here by means of that [early] strategy had a common profile: Firms that needed only a modest investment (labor-intensive and of a relatively low technological know-how) that produced consumer goods for unstable markets; and, moreover, industries that did not need each other, nor link themselves into a chain of economic development.[46]

School reform was to respond to those needs. The continued focus on vocational education would prepare Puerto Ricans for employment in those firms. By so doing, Puerto Rico's public school system reproduced the colonial ideology within a conception of development in Puerto Rico's political-economic relationship with the United States. This had the affect of not allowing for the expansion of the meaning of development and the contribution that schooling has to that project.

This chapter has examined the relationship of GNP to Puerto Rico's development between the 1950s and the 1980s. While Puerto Rico's GNP was at some of its highest levels some of the greatest numbers of Puerto Ricans were emigrating. Thus, the claim that the expansion of schooling is as closely linked to improvements as reformers would like us to believe remains problematic; and the persistence of high rates of unemployment and underemployment only aggravates the problem. Beginning in 1950, the level of participation in the labor force declined and did not return to the 1950 level until 1965. There was also a marked decline in the willingness of workers to enter the labor market. Thus, while schooling expanded and the language of school reform alluded to the contribution that the public school system made to Puerto Rico's immediate growth, such an argument remains problematic when considering development as more than the satisfaction of growth requirements.

In other words, Puerto Rico's growth was more closely defined by its ability to school workers for low-paying positions in firms aimed at exports than by the contribution schooling made to local development. The growth experienced in Puerto Rico, while contributing to the improvement of the society in some significant ways, was not the result of a Puerto Rican development (in the sense that the country had experienced local development or even locally originating growth). Instead, the improvements were determined by and dependent upon the presence of U.S. firms that controlled and directed the country's political-economic environment. Concurrently, the public school system, through reform initiatives and their language, was expanded in a manner that provided the economic program with an institution responsive to Puerto Rico's political economy under the United States.

The language of the school reforms during the 1950s and 1960s aided in the rationalization of an economic program based upon dependency. The logic was that Puerto Rico's development was on a course toward modernization. This was certainly the case, yet the relationship of such modernization to divergent conceptions of development was not closely scrutinized by the reform language. That is, Puerto Rico's modernization was less the result of developments in schooling and the growth in local technologies and know-how that characterize the evolution of rationalization in a society, than it was based upon the growth of investment by U.S. firms. Fortifying the political economy under U.S. control and the maximization of rational behavior within this context provided U.S. firms with a captive market of consumers. The predominance of capital-intensive firms presented Puerto Rico with a problem that would make schooling less attractive to a population whose record of staying in school was, generally speaking, quite poor.

Somehow the government, through the public school system, had to reassure the people that schooling was the ticket out of poverty. Yet under a capital-intensive program of development, the employment pool was drastically reduced; fewer high-skilled workers, and more less-skilled workers were needed. What benefit Puerto Rico has derived since the 1950s from the expansion of capital-intensive projects under Operation Bootstrap has for the most part contributed to a continued decline in the local economy and most social institutions. The result has been the proliferation of U.S. private firms in the island's social, economic, and cultural life. And they continue to demand the expansion of policies for preferred treatment and increased incentives for investments in the country— at the expense of local development potential.

The transition to capital-intensive industries demanded a semiskilled and skilled labor force.[47] Leading in the change to capital-intensive industries was the petrochemical sector. Capital-intensive petrochemical firms had been doing business since the 1950s, accounting for 27 percent of total investment in manufacturing in 1958.[48] It seemed logical to encourage such an attractive industry, given the potential for employment and the allowances for the Caribbean Oil Refining Company (CORCO) to capture at least a portion of the value added in the production process, thus contributing to the creation of local jobs and income.[49] Yet by 1979, roughly two years before its complete closure, the refining company had only about 1,450 workers. Additionally, though the chemical, machine, and metal industries accounted for approximately 33 percent of the gross output of all industries in 1982, they provided only 10 percent of manufacturing employment.[50] Last, in Puerto Rico some eighty-four pharmaceutical companies tested new products with fewer restrictions on testing and production than in the United States, and produced 50 percent of their worldwide profits on the island.

While it is often alleged that capital-intensive firms tend pay better, they also employ fewer workers. This has fundamental implications for employment and for schooling as an agency in the production of the labor force. For example, between 1947 and 1961, an average of seventy workers was employed by Fomento firms, declining steadily to about 28.7 percent of the employment projections they had made.[51] Although optimistic that these firms had some backward linkages into the development of the local economy, what Puerto Rico faced was quite the contrary. These firms made no attempts to forge linkages within the island economy, nor were they motivated to do so by the government or its incentive package.[52]

The shift to capital-intensive firms exacerbated the problem of foreign ownership in Puerto Rico. For the entire group of core industries (metals, petrochemical, chemical, machine, electrical, petroleum, etc.), which produced 57 percent of total manufacturing output by 1977, foreign ownership averaged 98.3 percent.[53] This had a definite effect on the development of schooling in Puerto Rico as a response to the employment needs in the country. By 1978, there were more than 2,000 Fomento-promoted factories in operation. Included on the list were Westinghouse, General Electric, Gulf & Western, Firestone, Ford, General Foods, Gillette, Colgate-Palmolive, DuPont, and Johnson and Johnson.[54] The U.S. Department of Commerce has noted:

These subsidiaries have primarily used the island as a production point, bringing in raw materials and intermediate goods while shipping the output directly to their mainland parent companies for distribution . . . . Corporate investment and production decisions, materials supply, and product distribution systems are almost entirely related to policies, practices, and financial and tax considerations of mainland parent corporations with little influence from Puerto Rican economic forces.[55]

In the wake of the oil crisis of the mid-1970s, the Puerto Rican economy was transformed from export-based to an international finance center for U.S. transnational capital operating under the auspices of the Caribbean Basin Initiative, first introduced under the presidential adfministration of Ronald Reagan. In the first place, U.S. corporations in Puerto Rico under Section 936 of the U.S. Internal Revenue Code receive tax incentives which amount to a tax-holiday. These corporations are free to repatriate profits free of federal taxes to parent companies in the United States.

With such a tax haven available to these corporations, Puerto Rico becomes a premier player in the development of the Caribbean Basin Initiative (CBI) through its role as a finance center for the "twin plant" or *maquiladora* projects. Puerto Rico then contributes fundamentally to the CBI by affording 936 corporations the financial breaks otherwise not available in matters of international Caribbean trade.

The twin plant concept was first introduced by the Agency for International Development in Puerto Rico. The idea being the to locate labor-intensive projects in different Caribbean nations where low-wages could be exploited, while finishing and packaging the products in Puerto Rico. In this way, costs to labor are reduced, and the less labor-intesive (read less employment-intensive) stages of production are reserved for Puerto Rico, where the exportation and repatriation of final products and their capital are protected by the Internal Revenue Service's 936 code. The strength of the *maquiladoras* is then to be found not in generating the creation of development projects, but in generating foreign exchange needed for debt financing. Again, Puerto Rican development is not necessarily the goal of U.S. interests. The interest is rather that Puerto Rico become the homebase for the profits of U.S. interests in the Caribbean region through tax code 936 under the twin-plant program of the CBI.

Foreign ownership and control of the production process have only contributed to the reliance upon outside forces to determine Puerto Rico's future development or underdevelopment. This has had a detrimental effect on employment. In 1971 approximately 20 percent of males between 16 to 34 years of age were unemployed or not seeking employment; in 1984 the percentage was approximately 30 percent for the same age group.[56] For females the average was 51 percent in 1971 and 49 percent in 1984.[57]

The problems of unemployment and underemployment continue to plague Puerto Rico's prospects for development. In June 1989, a Labor Department report, cited in the periodical *Claridad*, stated that only 37 percent of Puerto Ricans were working. That is, of 2.359 million Puerto Ricans between the ages of sixteen and sixty five who were able to work, 867,000 were employed, 173,000 were seeking work, and 1.452 million were unemployed or not actively seeking employment.[58] In 1989, manufacturing was second to government and services as a leading employer; it accounted for only 18 percent of employment, while government and services accounted for approximately 45 percent.[59] This demonstrates the degree to that certain core productive industries, or those that could contribute to Puerto Rico's local development, disappear, while the increase in services and government as major employers gives some indication of the manner in that the management of such a political economy is sustained to some degree at the bureaucratic level by local agencies— by Puerto Ricans themselves. Thus, the rationalization of the society remains defined not by its own development or modernization but, rather, by the way in that it acts as a bureaucrat legitimizing the political-economic control by the United States. In this way, Puerto Rico's working population oversees itself in the interest of another— silencing itself and being silenced. In other words, Puerto Ricans continue to rationalize corporate interests and those of Puerto Rico as one and the same, yet now from the perspective of more active players in the regulation of themselves, even though their interests may conflict fundamentally with those of U.S. corporations in the country.

In order to deal with the endemic problem of unemployment, the U.S. government has had to infuse Puerto Rico with massive amounts of federal dollars. In 1950, at the beginning of Operation Bootstrap, transfer payments from the federal and Puerto Rican governments accounted for 12 percent of personal income; by 1970, they had increased to 20 percent, and by 1980 to 30 percent (by comparison, in the United States, federal and state transfer payments account for approximately 13 percent of personal income). Of these transfers to individuals, federal transfers— primarily social security and food stamps— have constituted 75 and 80, respectively, percent of the total; for 1982, this meant that federal transfers were the equivalent of nearly $900 per person, and it is certain that without them, there would have been a marked decline in the standard of living.[60] In this manner, unemployment has become institutionalized,[61] through maintenance of an economy and spending in an otherwise collapsing situation. Today nearly 60 percent of families receive food stamps, and approximately 80 percent of the population is eligible to receive them by virtue of their low incomes.[62] With the introduction of food stamps in Puerto Rico in 1974, the spending power of many Puerto

Ricans increased significantly. While some 30 percent of the population earned incomes of $60 per month or less, families making $200 per month rose from 20 percent to over 60 percent; food stamps added approximately $125 of monthly income, nearly doubling their spending power. Merrill-Ramírez note that, "with one-eighth the population of California, Puerto Rico was receiving twice as much in food stamps."

In the midst of so much direct federal involvement in the form of transfer payments, Puerto Ricans are led to believe that the country's existence and possibilities for development are contingent upon federal dollars and continued dominant U.S. presence. In 1988 net federal dollars totaling $2.959 billion were paid to Puerto Rico, while U.S. investments yielded profits and interest exceeding $8.869 billion. Additionally, in 1988 Puerto Rico imported $7.8 billion— the sixth largest importer of U.S. goods.[63] This being the case, the role of public schooling in contributing to development and the inculcation of a disposition consistent with this model of development presents some rather dramatic ramifications. Puerto Ricans are constantly reminded that Puerto Rico represents a burden for the United States, and that only strict social and economic (read ideological) compliance (as manifested in the political-economic programs articulated through the colonial relationship under the United States) will make possible the persistence of a life at least twice as poor as the poorest state in the United States, yet considerably better than in most other Latin American countries. In other words, if colonialism is such a burden for the United States, it is because it is favorable to Puerto Rico; and this has the effect of disengaging the people— and this includes schooling— from challenging the myth that under colonialism the colonizer loses as the colonized gains. Through the language of reform, changes in the public school system remain within the framework of the ideological myth confining the parameters of legitimate alternatives within a conception of development growing out of that myth.

TECHNOLOGICAL DEVELOPMENT AND RATIONALIZATION: IMPLICATIONS OF AUTHORITARIAN CONTROL

Earlier in this volume space was devoted to the argument that development rationalized in terms of the orthodox paradigm can manifest itself as a form of control. Additionally, the maximization of rational behavior was synonymous with a necessary pattern of behavior concurrent with the dynamics of a market-driven economy in that the measure of development was determined by growth (e.g., per capita growth and consumption patterns). While the reconstitution of the Puerto Rican economy under the United States in the first decades of colonialism provided some dramatic changes in the island's dynamics, the rationalization that grew out of those changes represented the embryonic phase of the evolution of rationalization that would characterize the country in the decades to come. With the advent of industrialization, new social and economic constructs were forged. On the one hand, the changes offered possibilities for expanding the technical base of the Puerto Rican society. On the other hand, such changes seemed to do little more than strengthen colonial dependency. Technological developments, then, were not benign products of economic growth, but simply the child of natural progress. These developments were both the product and the perpetrator of a rationalized system of production and its concurrent values. Writing on technological rationality in 1941, Herbert Marcuse, examined the social process of technology or technics and the potential for technological rationality to be either liberating or authoritarian: "Technology is taken as a social process in that technics proper (that is, the technical apparatus of industry, transportation, communication) is but a partial factor."[64]

Though Puerto Rico's colonial situation was central to whatever changes occurred under industrialization, Puerto Ricans were also central to the proliferation of those changes in terms of all the positive and negative outcomes. This idea reinforces Paulo Freire's work on the "culture of silence" mentioned earlier. The silenced are not without a voice. The voice has been silenced by the domination from without and the internalization of that domination from within. Technical development, then, can be as liberating as it can be authoritarian; it can contribute to the abolition of toil as well as to enslavement.

New Individualism and the New Rationalization: On Marcuse and Freire

The rise of a new individualism and a new rationality evolves in the course of the technological process—different, yet rising out of what initiated the march of technology.[65] The value attached to the individualism and the requirements for the development of that rationality were important to the United States in Puerto Rico, developmentally, both economically and in schooling. The individual to whom Marcuse refers, however, is the one who originated in the middle-class revolutions that were perceived as the "ultimate unit as well as the end of society."

In colonial Puerto Rico, the individual remained under the jurisdiction of the colonial power. Hence, the ultimate unit was the colonizer, and the end of society was colonial. This is not to say that all Puerto Ricans viewed themselves in such a manner. The expansion of schooling, developments in the relationship that school training had to employment, and an emphasis on English as the vehicle for advancement played a significant role, similar to Marcuse's explanation, in developing an individual. Where Freire states that the culture under domination is silenced, Marcuse asserts that "rationality itself has been transformed into technological rationality." Throughout the industrialization process Puerto Ricans were expected to respond to the mechanization of the development project. As the project became definitive in terms of the dominant perceptions and language of Puerto Rican economic and social developmental viability, the rationality representative of Marcuse's authoritarian technological environment gained the upper hand. So strong was the tendency to comply that often even elements considered in opposition were incorporated into the apparatus.

In retrospect, during Puerto Rico's experiment with state capitalism, there was no intention of challenging the presence or influence of the United States. The belief that matters of development were separate from matters of status was significant in this rationality. The incorporation of many of the country's autonomy-seeking interests into the technical apparatus served well the short-term interests of the island while securing U.S. domination.

Considering Freire's notion of a culture of silence as manifested in the "new individualistic rationality" that Marcuse affirms rises out of the development of modern technological society, some insight is gained into the manner in that identity is reconstituted in the image of the new rational individual. Such an individual finds identity not in relationship to others but in the coordination and organization of individual achievement transformed through standardized efficiency.[66] That that constituted the relationship to others— the culture with that and in that they coexisted, understood, and struggled collectively—is slowly replaced by the characterization of individuals and their performances, guided and measured by standards external to them—"by standards pertaining to predetermined tasks and functions."[67] For Freire, the individual and the emancipatory potential are not missing but dormant; what is needed is the consciousness of such silence to commence the struggle out of that despair. Yet precisely within that despair lies the world of possibilities for liberation. But arriving at such a consciousness may entail dramatic changes in behavior and challenges to conforming patterns of obedience—both difficult to come to terms with when one's livelihood is, in essence, dependent upon compliance with those external standards.

The advancement of the "new individual," then, is accompanied by the evolution of a rationalized pattern of behavior and obedience. Humans learn that obedience to directions is the only way to obtain desired results.[68] Part of the reason for the failures of Puerto Rico's polity and school system to address the relationship of development to status is related to this point. The mathematization of knowledge and experience that Max Weber raises in his treatment of rationalization here finds a way to rationalize the immediacy of growth requirements and development within the context of those requirements. To address the issue of status as related to development is to introduce a factor into the equation that is not easily quantified. Marcuse, in explaining the propensity of the colonized toward standardized behavior, remarks: "The mechanics of conformity spread from the technological to the social order; they govern performance not only in the factories and shops, but also in the offices, schools, assemblies, and finally, in the realm of relaxation and entertainment."[69] In Puerto Rico, as the economy came under the tighter control of a U.S. development model, the values concurring with the colonizer's presence and dominance, while embedded in the rationalization of the society under colonialism, were also reproduced by Puerto Ricans themselves as they perceived the colonizer and development synonymous. The conforming behavior of the machine in the industrialized society became the example for the colonized. Though harboring the potential for liberation, the colonized nevertheless lived in the struggle where "to be is to be like." For Freire, then:

The only data the dominated consciousness grasps are the data that lie within the orbit of its lived experience . . . . This mode of life cannot objectify the facts and problematic situations of daily life. Lacking structural perception, men attribute the sources of such facts and situations in their lives either to some superreality or to something within themselves; in either case to some objective reality.[70]

The possibilities that the culture, through the schools and other civil institutions, can articulate alternative conceptions of development and gather support remain truncated by the developments of the new rationalized being. Furthermore, the very perception of culture becomes distorted or fragmented. We are reminded of those cases when students and administrators of Puerto Rico's public schools flew the Puerto Rican flag though they knew it was against the law and, in some instances, were quite supportive of U.S. law in Puerto Rico. The meaning of identity, of what it is to be Puerto Rican, was subjected to the same rationalization principles of observation or "matter-of-factness" as the mechanics of production. The colonized asserted a clear distinction between being Puerto Rican and development— between development and colonialism. What liberating power resided in rationality was reduced to a logic for conforming behavior.

The critical force of rationality is transformed into "one of adjustment and compliance."[71] The potential for autonomous development at the individual and social levels is, under colonial rule, replaced by requirements for compliance with technological rationality, and the subordination of the uniqueness of the culture and its contribution to its development. In Puerto Rico, the persistence of high rates of unemployment has been posed as the result of failures by the insular government to comply with the policies requisite for further development. Likewise, the public school system historically responded by emphasizing the need to expand the role of vocational education. In both instances, the critical potential embedded in the reality of high unemployment is subordinated to the efficiency and expediency requirements of technological rationality. Thought and truth were reduced to a set of preordained technical standards outside the realm of cultural development— that is, rather than being the product of the culture's struggle with itself, with development and identity, decisions of development, of technological significance, appeal to a set of technics for decision making predicated on efficiency.

The unconditional compliance with rationality subjects thought to pregiven external standards. Truth then becomes technological, in that it is seen as an instrument of expediency and not an end in itself, and also in that it follows a particular pattern of technological behavior. However, the contribution that efficiency can make to the liberating potential of technical rationality will depend upon whether critical truths translate into technological truths. Marcuse asserts that critical truth and technological truth are not simply opposite ends of a rationality scheme. In fact, they may complement one another, that demonstrates the complexity of the relationship. For example, the notion that all Puerto Ricans had an inalienable right to an education was a critical proposition. However, that such an experience fortified rather than attenuated the colonial relationship, or the silence of the culture, proved to be a consequence of an efficiency determination of the relationship between technological and critical truths. In this way, technological truths can be transformed or preserved in critical rationality.

Furthermore, the distinction between the two sets is not rigid. "The content of each set changes in the social process so that what were once critical truths become technological truths."[72] The critical truth of Puerto Rico's poverty in the 1940s was addressed by technological changes (state capitalism, then Operation Bootstrap). Persisting through recent decades, the country's poverty in the 1970s was technically addressed through the introduction of food stamps. Providing much–needed immediate assistance, the liberating potential of such legislation was reduced to a mechanism whose instrumentality was found in its ability to exacerbate dependency. In both periods school policy responses were consistent with the technological truth interpretation.

Today, the push is for increased privatization both in the economy and in the schools. The liberating potential that technical rationality can provide is laid aside as the more immediate, expedient, and efficient responses provide some satisfaction in the midst of an otherwise dismal and volatile situation. The replacement of critical rationality by technological rationality has made it difficult for Puerto Ricans to address alternative conceptions of development. Different influences account for this social impotence. Industrial growth has transcended all spheres of Puerto Rican life. The rationality attended to by those who subscribe strictly to this conception of development has "transformed numerous modes of self-discipline and self-control. Safety and order are guaranteed by the fact that people have learned to adjust their behavior to the other fellow's down to the most minute detail."[73]

In the case of the colony, the "other fellow" is the colonizer and the rules and values that govern the participation of the colonized in colonial development. In such a situation, the responses to issues arising in the history of the colony will be ascertained according to the technological rationality reinforced by the colonial environment and reproduced by the colonized. These potentially liberating issues are then viewed through a technical lens; any external compulsion will be rejected as irrational—unless the critical aspect, its liberating potential, offers a desirable alternative that a strictly technical response is no longer able to govern. However, the technological rationality is also reproduced by the colonized. This rationality is as much the result of the colonizer's imposition as it is sustained by the colonized's identification with the colonizer and technological rationality. Such an identification has the affect of undermining the critical potential within the colonized population.

Viewed by many as the model for development and democracy in the world, the U.S. position as colonizer in Puerto Rico was strengthened by its global power and appeal. The development of a technological rationality in Puerto Rico easily permeated the very fabric of the culture. In many cases, the once-assertive opposition, as in the case of the autonomists, grew closer to the colonizer without losing the title of opposition.

The PPD, once concerned with the growth of autonomy, actually reinforced the technological rationality of the colonizer, and yet maintained some semblance of opposition by affirming its commitment to the Puerto Rican culture. Though not mentioned in this volume specifically, the development of the labor movement in Puerto Rico under the leadership of Santiago Iglesias, like much of the history of the American Federation of Labor in the United States, resulted in a similar "incorporated opposition"; as a matter of fact, Santiago Iglesias was closely associated with the A.F.L.

Being incorporated while not ceasing to be of opposition, critical truth is transformed. Those values once characterized as liberating now become part of the authoritarian potential of technological rationality. The experiment with state capitalism in Puerto Rico and its subsequent transformation under Operation Bootstrap provide interesting evidence for an explanation of how social movements and "ideas, such as liberty, productive industry, planned economy, and satisfaction of needs"[74] are fused into the colonial apparatus— into a technological rationality. If at the higher levels of industrial production work is reduced to standardization, the lower levels of production, usually reserved for the colonized, represent the crudest form of standardization and the pursuit of self-interests along the most primitive lines of prearranged functions. Vocational training and schooling essentially become experiences in the training for various psychological and physiological adaptations to the "job."The creators of the job also create the character of that job and the kind of disposition and personality they feel appropriate for carrying it out. In this way, a worker's personality is dictated by the instrumentality of the job, and is replaceable by any similarly trained personality with similar skill. Human agency is here divorced from the individual and reduced to its simplest mathematical, rational, and instrumental genre.[75]

Between the 1940s and the present, low-skilled factory jobs have constituted the majority of employment. Little education was required, yet the proper psychological and physiological disposition was necessary. The characterization of Puerto Rican workers as instruments figured prominently in their reluctance and inability to elicit the critical side of technical rationality. As the Puerto Ricans' lives became more regimented within the colonial configuration, the procurability of their critical potential was progressively replaced by the technological rationality of a development project under the United States. Rather than requiring the input of a critical individual human being, or of a distinct culture, development was reduced to an instrumental conception of technological rationality grounded in an orthodox paradigm. The various intellectual activities constituting the realm of thought became a kind of technique, a matter of training rather than uniqueness, "requiring the expert rather than the complete human being."[76] Perceptions of society and of culture were standardized within the rationality of technical requirements. The Puerto Rican culture became a mass culture under colonialism; the quantification of the qualitative features of the people were standardized. While this might seem to engender the potential for collectivity, in actuality individualism was retained, though in a standardized form, one not easily viewed critically since the potential for such critical appraisal was embedded in the very logic of the new individualism residing in technological rationality. This standardization of society, of the culture, transformed the relationship between the colonized and their culture.

The transformed relationship was the result of the dialectic between superstructure and infrastructure. The existence of one is dependent upon the other. Without the transformation of the culture into its technological, rational personification, standardization is weakened. Freire asserts that if we "fail to understand this dialectic, we will not understand the dialectic of change and permanence as the expression of social structure."[77] Thus, Puerto Rico, as a culture whose level of development was the result of its internalization and local reproduction of the technological rationality, concurrently encouraged the experience of culture as an "objective embodiment of the collectivity." The transformation, then, of the relationship between individuals and their culture is one of exacerbated objectification. Society is viewed as a composite of things, places, and agencies. "It is virtually everything that one is not, yet it affects one's habits, behavior patterns, and values from the outside."[78]

In this instance, society can be taken as synonymous with culture since the society of the colonized is ostensibly the outcome of a silencing of its unique culture combined with the evolution of that objective entity arising from the proliferation of the colonizer's technological rationality in the colony's development model. The expansion of vocational schooling in Puerto Rico, beginning in the 1940s and continuing up to the present, has contributed significantly to such objectification. The potential for critical reflection arising out of technical rationality has been obscured under a veil of colonial relations and their requisite economic and social demands. The language of development and school reform remains consonant with the orthodox paradigm of development and the further rationalization of the culture's critical potential along technical lines.

NOTES

1. Shirley Grundy, *Curriculum: Product or Praxis?* (New York: Falmer Press, 1987), 23.

2. James Dietz, *Economic History of Puerto Rico : Institutional Change and Capitalist Development* (Princeton: Princeton University Press, 1986), 238-239.

3. Juan José Osuna, *A History of Education in Puerto Rico* (Río Piedras: University of Puerto Rico Press, 1975), 622-623.

4. Rexford Guy Tugwell, *The Puerto Rico Public Papers* (San Juan: Services Office, Government of Puerto Rico, 1945), 215.

5. Herbert Marcuse, "Some Social Implications of Modern Technology," in *The Essential Frankfurt School Reader*, ed. Andrew Arato and Eike Gebhardt (New York: Continuum, 1982), 119.

6. Dietz, *Economic History*, 274.

7. See, for example, the recommendations for agriculture or the lack of such recommendations in Osuna, *A History of Education*, 1975; *Teachers College Curriculum Guide for Schools in Puerto Rico, 1950* ; Osvaldo Pacheco, *A Land of Hope in Schools: A Reader in the*

History of Public Education in Puerto Rico,1940–1965 (Río Piedras:Editorial Edil, 1976). In the dominant cases, agriculture was sacrificed in favor of what was perceived as the more advantageous industrial development.

8. Harvey Perloff, *Puerto Rico's Economic Future* (Chicago: University of Chicago Press, 1950), 157.

9. Dietz, *Economic History*, 202–203.

10. Tugwell, *The Puerto Rico Public Papers*, 386–390.

11. Dietz, *Economic History*, 202.

12. Daniel F. Ross, *The Long Uphill Path—A Historical Study of Puerto Rico's Program of Economic Development* (Río Piedras: Editorial Edil, 1969), 17.

13. Puerto Rico Planning Board, *Economic Development of Puerto Rico, 1951–1960* (San Juan: Puerto Rico Planning Board, 1961), 5.

14. A. J. Jaffe, *People Jobs and Economic Development* (Glencoe, Ill. : Free Press, 1959), 127-130.

15. Dietz, *Economic History*, 224.

16. Ibid., 227.

17. Ibid., 205.

18. Agustín Cueva, *El Desarrollo del Capitalismo en América Latina* (Mexico City: Siglo XXI, 1977), 208; Ross, *The Long Uphill Path,* 62-63.

19. Dietz, *The Economic History,* 207.

20. Ibid., 190.

21. Ibid., 193.

22. Ibid., 194.

23. Ibid., 210.

24. Ibid., 215.

25. Ibid.

26. Ross, *The Long Uphill Path*, 84–95.

27. Charles Wilber and Kenneth Jameson, "Paradigms of Economic Development and Beyond," in *The Political Economy of Development and Underdevelopment*, ed. Charles Wilber (New York: Random House, Business Div., 1988), 9.

28. Dietz, *Economic History*, 209.

29. Puerto Rico Planning Board, *Economic Development of Puerto Rico, 1951–1960*, 32.

30. José Gallardo, *Annual Report of the Commissioner of Education 1945–46* (San Juan: Bureau of Supplies, Printing, and Transportation, 1946).

31. Dietz, *Economic History*, 209.

32. Mathew D. Edel, "Land Reform in Puerto Rico." *Caribbean Studies num. 2*, (January 1963): 28–50.

33. Dietz, *Economic History*, 199.

34. Yvonne Acosta, *La Mordaza*, (Río Piedras: Editorial Edil, 1989) 233.

35. Dietz, *Economic History*, 200.

36. María Merrill-Ramírez, "Operation Bootstrap" (Master's Thesis, University of Texas, 1979), 87, Table I.

37. Dietz, *Economic History*, 248.

38. Ibid., 274.

39. Ibid.

40. Ibid.

41. Ibid., 275.

42. Junta de Planificación, *Compendio de Estadísticas Sociales,* (San Juan: Junta de Planificación, 1979), 21–68.

43. Dietz, *Economic History*, p. 286.

44. Ibid., 287.

45. Ibid., 288–289.

46. José R. Madera, "The Strategy of Development," *Industrial Newsletter* (Puerto Rico Economic Development Administration) 22 (1982): 1–2.

47. " El Desarrollo económico de Puerto Rico durante los últimos veinte años" (mimeograph) (San Juan: Administración de Fomento Económico, 1971), 1–10.

48. Jorge F. Freyre, *External and Domestic Financing in the Economic Development of Puerto Rico* (Río Piedras: University of Puerto Rico Press, 1969), p. 89.

49. Dietz, *Economic History*, 253.

50. Ibid.

51. Ibid., 255.

52. Ibid., 254.

53. Ibid.

54. Ibid.

55. U.S. Department of Commerce,*Economic Study of Puerto Rico* vol. 1(Washington, DC: U.S. Government Printing Office, 1979), 44.

56. Junta de Planificación de Puerto Rico, *Informe económico al gobernador 1982-83,* (San Juan: Junta de Planificación, 1984), tables 3–24.

57. Ibid.

58.*Claridad,* 31, no. 1915 (June 24–30, 1989).

59. Ibid., 3.

60. Dietz, *Economic History* . 298.

61. Merrill-Ramírez, "Operation Bootstrap," 12.

62. Dietz, *Economic History* , 299.

63. *Claridad*, 31, no. 1920 (Nov. 3–9, 1989).

64. Marcuse, "Some Social Implications of Modern Technology," 138.

65. Ibid., 139.

66. Ibid.

67. Ibid., 142.

68. Ibid., 144

69. Ibid., 145

70. Paulo Freire, *The Politics of Education* (New York: Bergin and Garvey, 1985), 73–74.

71. Marcuse, "Some Social Implications of Modern Technology," 146.

72. Ibid.

73. Ibid., 147.

74. Ibid., 148.

75. Ibid., 149.

76. Ibid., 150–153

77. Freire, *The Politics of Education*, 72.

78. Marcuse, "Some Social Implications of Modern Technology," 159.

Changing Schools in a Changing Economy: The Response of Vocational Education Initiatives

It follows that hegemony is the predominance obtained by consent rather than force of one class or group over other classes or groups. And whereas "domination" is realized, essentially, through the coercive machinery of the state, "intellectual and moral leadership" is objectified in, and mainly exercised through, "civil society," the ensemble of educational, religious, and associational institutions.[1]

*T*his chapter examines how school reform initiatives, as articulated through the calls for an expansion of vocational education (roughly between 1940 and the present) responded to the changes in the orthodox economic model.

EXPANDING SCHOOLS AND VOCATIONAL EDUCATION

Following a September 4, 1939, approval of an amendment to the Insular Board of Vocational Education, a campaign was launched to achieve objectives pertinent to the establishment and expansion of vocational education in Puerto Rico's public schools. The amendment represented a change in the directives regarding vocational education in Puerto Rico that had not addressed the massification of vocational education as the new amendament would now do. Vocational education would be emphasized by teachers in their classrooms; superintendents were to organize vocational education programs in all of their junior high and high schools; the government would provide money and other support (field trips, office consultations, conferences, etc.); schools would keep abreast of advances in the field, expand the study of occupational and social trends so as to respond appropriately, and so on.[2] Additionally, much emphasis was given to vocational education counseling. In 1942 and again in 1944, policies arising from insular legislation made available huge appropriations for vocational education counseling throughout the public school system.

Vocational education was fast becoming the focus of schooling in Puerto Rico. Prior to 1940, attempts at extending vocational education in the territories of the United States had been made. In 1901 Senator Knute Nelson of Minnesota proposed the extension of vocational education across the curriculum. In 1923, the resident commissioner of Puerto Rico introduced a bill to amend the Smith-Hughes Act, that provided for U.S. federal aid to vocational education programs. Neither of these was successful. Part of the problem lay in the fact that the Smith-Hughes Act stipulated a minimum age of fourteen for vocational education assistance. Due to Puerto Rico's plans for extending a substantial vocational education curriculum into the elementary and junior high schools, as evidenced in the Second Unit schools (schools whose main function was to prepare rural workers for employment in the changing economy), successful implementation of the act was stifled.

The Wright-Cushman Report

In the mid-1930s, despite some initial difficulties with the plans to launch an extended vocational education program, Frank Cushman, chief of the Industrial Education Service, and Dr. J. C. Wright, director of the Service, conducted a study on the viability of vocational education programs for Puerto Rico. Following their study, Wright and Cushman reported:

We are of the opinion that an efficient program of vocational education, if properly organized and extended so as to cover the principal occupations and pursuits carried on in the Island with facilities for offering it to the majority of those who need it would contribute materially to improving the economic conditions of Puerto Rico and the welfare of its people . . . the need for vocational education in Puerto Rico is urgent since the people living there are U.S. citizens and can seek outside help from no other source.[3]

In other words, a vocational program would, it was hoped, contribute to alleviating some of Puerto Rico's immediate development needs by preparing those who needed skills in order to secure employment. Yet part of the reality was that a considerable number of Puerto Ricans already needed employment, a number that continued to grow throughout the period; and to focus on vocational education was, in some rather essential ways, adding to the development problem. Without the creation of a local technological base and institutions that would generate capital internally, the future of workers remained in the hands of firms whose capital was repatriated to the United

States. Vocational education alone could not address the problem of unemployment and underdevelopment.

Initially, agriculture was the focus of vocational education efforts. Yet the changes in the economy that faced Puerto Ricans presented agricultural vocational education with a substantial problem. Throughout the history of U.S. occupation, Puerto Ricans have been told that agriculture is not a viable component of development. Yet for some time, sugar remained an important product and producer of revenue. Of course this had less to do with Puerto Rico's development than with the profits for absentee owners of sugar companies. As land for agriculture production became scarcer, the options available through agriculture dwindled. Nevertheless, some provisions were made for agriculture in the vocational education projects. The Wright-Cushman report hoped to implement an agricultural vocational education program that would apply theoretical and practical teachings to local conditions, assist in the application of more scientific approaches to subsistence farming, instill pride of home ownership and improve living conditions, and increase the wealth of farmers on the island by developing successful and more intelligent farmers.[4]

The report did not offer a detailed explanation of how those results would materialize. Regardless, the above expected results tell us something about the importance of scientific management and the scientific method for the development of efficient land use. This in itself could have engendered a positive trend in the development of agriculture. Yet the downside to such provisions and expectations was found in the ever-decreasing importance of agriculture as a contributor to the country's overall industrial development. Thus, the best agriculture could do, or was encouraged to do, was to offer individual families some technical skills in subsistence farming. In the decades to follow, mass consumption of imported foodstuffs, primarily from the United States, further discouraged farming on the island, even at the family level. Regardless, agriculture initially proved important as a vehicle for promoting participation in vocational education programs.

The highest enrollments in vocational agriculture education were during the year 1941–42. Following the 1941–42 school year there was a drastic decline in enrollment and in centers offering agricultural vocational education. The difficulties in receiving shipments of food from the United States were related to costs during the war years and German submarine attacks on U.S. vessels. Puerto Rico's response was to increase its agricultural production. Yet pressure from various major farmers' associations in the U.S. placed constraints upon the government forcing restrictions on the expansion of agriculture in Puerto Rico, lest U.S. agricultural domination be challenged. The immediacy of fulfilling basic food needs in Puerto Rico encouraged at least those vocational agricultural programs concentrating on family farming.

Drawing from Puerto Rico's predominantly rural population, the Vocational Agriculture and World War II Training for Out-of-School Youth Program was organized and implemented. The program was arranged and administered under the National Defense Training Program. One of the major divisions of the program, National Defense Training for Out-of-School Youth, trained out-of-school youth in occupations essential to the national defense and to agriculture.[5] Courses offered included operation, care, and repair of automobiles and trucks; metalwork; woodworking; and elementary electricity. This project was part of President Franklin D. Roosevelt's New Deal.

The programs tended, on the one hand, to prepare Puerto Ricans for positions requiring manual labor and, on the other hand, inculcated an ideological allegiance to the United States by combining the (minimal) exposure to U.S. technology with U.S. national defense, including patriotic motives. During this period the insular government was creating public corporations. Thus, it would seem that for any long-term development plans, any program offering rural youth experience with electric drills, bench grinders, forges, and woodworking machines would be expanded and incorporated concurrently in order to advance local technology. This not being the case, by 1942 these programs were terminated. Agriculture was being replaced by other industries and programs that would contribute to the development of these other industries.

To cope better with the virtual starvation facing Puerto Rico due to the scant availability of food, the federal government extended the Food Production War Training Program to Puerto Rico in late 1942. One of its primary objectives included the promotion of vocational education programs in agriculture.[6] This program targeted out-of-school youth, thus attempting to alleviate one aspect of Puerto Rico's dismal condition—poverty due to unemployment. Having youth return to school was one way of addressing the unemployment issue without revealing the relationship of unemployment to underdevelopment. Attending school, these youths were not counted as unemployed. By the 1944–45 school year, two years from the time it was introduced, the Food Production War Training Program's enrollment had decreased from 8,641 in 1942–43 to 2,320; course offerings were also reduced from 500 in 1942–43 to 134 in 1944–45.[7]

The constitution of the vocational education program included trades and industries and home economics. Some of the expected results of the trades and industries component included youth skills training, cooperation between workplaces and schools, Puerto Rican development advancement, increased economic wealth of Puerto Rico through the development of human resources, assistance in reducing unemployment with the new capital that would be attracted to the country for the development of new industries, and the development of local industrial leadership.[8]

For the most part, the expectations seemed desirable, given the provisions for some local control of the economy during the early 1940s. However, the political economy of Puerto Rico as a colony made such local development difficult. Furthermore, local control was actually a response to the war and depression, which both the United States and Puerto Rico had to face. In a way, then, the period of state capitalism in Puerto Rico bought the United States time while its capital-intensive projects, recovering from the war and the depression, gathered strength. The control of the economy exercised by the United States forced Puerto Rico to develop not according to locally generated needs and aspirations but in response to the requirements and limitations of an economy whose primary role was to provide the colonial power with profits or access to profit accumulation. For orthodox economics, this is not necessarily a problem, since the accumulation of profits should yield new jobs, encourage investments, and motivate production. The problem lies in where and how those profits are distributed.

Thus, in the trades and industries training, as in the agricultural training, what was proposed and what was actually practiced offered somewhat conflicting results. It appeared that the language of school reform and development, while seemingly progressive, nevertheless remained discordant with the more general reality of colonial existence. In other words, it was the colonial relationship that would mediate the extent of Puerto Rico's local development; and school reforms that offered more far-reaching proposals would continue to collide with that reality. As difficult as the reality was, the private lives of Puerto Ricans were also impacted by the vocational projects, this time in the form of home economics programs. Like the trades and industries programs, this program aimed at improving local farming practices and living conditions for individual farmers, with hopes of improving the living conditions and social life for families generally.[9]

The problems facing the development of the home economics programs were also tied to Puerto Rico's economic problems. Though the program was well received in Puerto Rico, as a course of study focusing on out-of-school women, it required the attention of teachers able and willing to work with girls and adult women. This proved difficult for some teachers.[10] The employment patterns of women in needlework added to the proposed viability of such a program. Importance was given to sewing projects related to the manufacturing of uniforms for the Red Cross and Boy Scouts, and of military apparel.[11] As in the agriculture and the trade programs, enrollment soon fell. By 1944, the enrollment figures for home economics had decreased by more than 50 percent.[12] However, in 1946, under the auspices of the University of Puerto Rico, the home economics curriculum at the university level was revitalized and expanded. Thus, the teaching force needed for the program's expansion in the island's schools received a new breath of life. The influence of technological rationality was intensified in the development of the vocational programs during the war years. Additionally, reducing the problem of development to individual discipline in the face of institutional barriers constraining development possibilities worsened the situation for Puerto Ricans.

In each case above vocational education played an important role in preparing individuals for participation in an efficient production process by equipping them with the necessary technological rationality. In its final comment on a proposed vocational education program, the Wright-Cushman report remarks, "All of these desirable results would tend to improve the social attitude of the people as well as their physical well-being."[13] The "improved social attitude" referred, among other things, to the maximization of rational behavior, including control, punctuality, loyalty, and respect for authority, as well as the all-important element of having a healthy labor force. The issue was not one of desirability, however, but one of definition. What and whose values would enjoy overriding influence in the improvement of the people's social attitudes remained ill defined. The overall result of the vocational education programs during the war years was little gain in the development and improvement of Puerto Rican lives. Through assistance granted by the federal government, school reform and the language of development reiterated capitalist relations and production under U.S. colonialism in Puerto Rico. The importance of vocationalism in the schools increased significantly. In agriculture and trades and industries, as in virtually every other aspect of colonial life, the parameters of legitimate development under colonialism were determined not by Puerto Rico but by those interests identified by the U.S.-Puerto Rican relationship.

The Educational Reform of 1942

In order to establish a consensus regarding schooling and to fortify the language of the vocational projects, the commissioner of education and some of his Puerto Rican subordinates introduced the Educational Reform of 1942. The reform represented Puerto Rico's first grand attempt to formulate a philosophy of education. Subsequent policy initiatives were (or at least appear) more coherent and convincing by being grounded in general principles such as the following:

• The school is a social agency and is responsible for the realization of those duties expressly assigned to it by the society that supports it.
• Society uses the school, among other institutions, to ensure its survival and progressive betterment. Therefore, it is only right to expect that the school will contribute to maintaining those standards sanctioned by society, for as long as they may be sanctioned.
• Education should be continued until there has been developed in the student the greatest possible capacity and disposition for contributing to the betterment of society.
• The golden rule of education should be to teach young people to carryout with more efficiency those duties that they will have to perform in life.
• Education should be organized and carried on according to the philosophic and scientific principles that govern the learning process.
• The cultural environment of the Puerto Rican child must be the point of departure for all teaching.
• The schools of Puerto Rico should develop a true comprehension of the culture of the United States.[14]

None of these necessarily challenges the practical and ideological control that the United States exercised over Puerto Rico. Furthermore, the compulsion to pose such a challenge in a philosophical statement on education might not be the best developmental strategy for contributing to the satisfaction the country's needs. Nevertheless, let us take a brief look at how each of the above allowed, or encouraged, the toleration and persistence of some of the problems facing Puerto Rico.

First, the schools were to respond to those "duties assigned . . . by society." The space for a proactive critical voice remained abbreviated by the duties identified in terms of technological demands. Furthermore, the meaning and possibilities for a developmental conception of "progress and betterment," as articulated in the second point, thus remained considerably muted, since both the definition and the implementation of progress and betterment remained fixed to a very specific language.

In the third point, the philosophical statement alludes to the development of the child. Yet determining the capacity of the child and the child's limits, for the betterment of society, juxtaposed to the addendum on rural schooling in the reform statement, reflects some rather underdevelopment practices— at least at the individual level, and arguably at the societal level as well. In the addendum to the School Reform of 1942, part of the section on attendance stated:

The rural school programs in this area [attendance] should be adjusted in a way that would make it possible for students to obtain the highest degree of profit from school offerings during their relatively limited time of school attendance. The differentiation of rural and urban school programs seems thus advisable. The rural school program of grades one, two, and three should be reorganized in terms of the needs of a school population that is expected to drop school before grade four. At least, this seems to be the most realistic approach if there are no means to increase the holding power of the school to an appreciable extent, not to mention that an increased holding power would conflict with present facilities.[15]

A number of proposals were implicated in this kind of language. First, rural schools would be reformed not necessarily to meet the educational needs or aspirations of the rural populations, but to make efficient use of them and to promote adjustment to the changing political-economic and social environment, with minimal attention to rectifying the low attendance across all years of schooling. In other words, the perceived need was to get as much return as possible from the limited time investment of many rural students— a return that would provide some profit for the political-economic relationship. The issue, then, was how to increase a perceived view of efficiency. This is consistent with a cost-benefit analysis of schooling in that part of the measure of school reform success is determined by the degree to which investment costs for schooling are less than the return gained from such investments. Second, the statement from the reform report alludes to the importance of a differentiated curriculum in the rural and urban regions. Rural schools would be reformed in order to reach a specific objective for rural students who, for the most part, dropped out by grade four. This had numerous implications for the type of schooling that rural students would receive. In the first place, the rural schools evolved into vocational education sites. Second, this had a lasting affect on the composition of the rural regions— that is, on the production side, the view that progress means more industrialization at the expense of local agriculture, accompanied by the decline in agriculture for local food consumption, contributed to the massive migration from the rural regions to the cities and out of the country.

According to the addendum, the rural child's capacity reached its peak by the fourth grade, at that point, it was stated, most rural children dropped our of school. With this in mind, rural schooling would concentrate on inculcating what was necessary for productive participation in the society as a laborer and, in a limited way as a participant at the level of concrete and ideological consumption and reproduction. Here the child's development was predetermined by the understanding of development and betterment articulated by the society— one controlled by the condition of colonialism. Furthermore, faced by the economic and social problems of the early 1940s, Puerto Rican reform initiatives, such as the Wright-Cushman report, appealed to the functional and instrumental potential that schooling, as an agency under the highly centralized control of the government, had for dealing with the persisting problems in the colonial economy.

The fourth expectation, regarding the efficiency with which duties would be carried out offers an interesting parallel between the reform initiatives and the principle of scientific management in labor that Frederick W. Taylor advanced in Scientific Management, published in 1912.

Overall, the orthodox paradigm of development in the colony gave one particular meaning of efficiency; and this had the affect of limiting or disallowing the legitimacy of other possibilities from being raised and debated. While obviously insufficient for a critical treatment of efficiency, scientific management does imply that forms of learning, conceptions of knowing, and the practice of vocations will generally accept the above-mentioned notion of efficiency. In this case, to be efficient, we have to be able to determine, to some extent, the outcome of an investment such that the outcome will prove profitable. Our capacity to predict allows us to anticipate what our environment (probably) will be like tomorrow based upon our experiences of today.[16] The element of predictability provides for a kind of control. In the case of schooling, this control establishes the parameters for the language of development, at the individual level and contributes to a restrictive and constrained forum for the possibilities of an expanded language of alternative conceptions of development, including that of school reform policy.

While in the final two points schools are asked to consider the Puerto Rican culture as the point of departure, the points do not specify what this means for the preservation and development of the culture. Furthermore, the meaning of the uniqueness of Puerto Rican culture was not explicitly outlined or implied. In fact, given the colonial relationship, one can defend the position that the schooling process retained all of the political socialization characteristics of Americanization advanced during the previous forty-four years under colonialism. The identification and persistence of problems in Puerto Rico remained articulated within the general political-economic framework. The Reform of 1942 recognized the presence of major problems facing education in Puerto Rico: the need to adjust the schools to development, failures of the Department of Education to address Puerto Rico's social and economic goals, the persistence of conditions that limit Puerto Rico's capacity to adjust educational goals and practices to national conditions, needs, and aspirations.[17] The limitations set by the lack of a Puerto Rican voice were not easily overcome in the years to follow. Though problems were recognized, their solutions remained informed by the political relationship between the United States and Puerto Rico, and exacerbated by the concurrent technological rationality that placed limitations on what was to be identified as a problem and what would be avoided.

The expansion and development of vocational education during the 1940s, it was hoped, would provide Puerto Rico's public school system with a much-needed boost in enrollment and retention. The war years offered manual training for many Puerto Ricans. Success in these programs continued to be measured, for the most part, by the use of English as the medium of instruction, the commitment to learn more English, and the use of texts and workbooks in English. In July 1948, Spanish became the language of instruction from the first through the ninth grades, leaving English for the last three years. The problems this posed for learning and achievement, and the ideological and political statement that such a policy made by placing English as the language of instruction for the more advanced studies, remained central to Puerto Rico's school reform efforts.

In November 1948, Puerto Rico held its first gubernatorial elections. Facilitated by the repression against nationalist and other independentist factions under the Muzzle Law and the implementation of new economic projects and policies under Operation Bootstrap, the Partido Popular Democrático (PPD; Popular Democratic Party), under the leadership of Luis Muñoz Marín, a staunch advocate and supporter of U.S. presence in Puerto Rico, won the election. On January 4, 1949, an administrative act decreed teaching in the vernacular at all levels of public schools, beginning in the school year 1949–50. Though no longer the language of instruction, English in some ways retained much of its importance. The vehicle of technological rationality in Puerto Rico was still the English language. Thus, while Spanish became the medium of instruction, it remained subordinated as a language of development, economically and educationally, ideologically and culturally.

In terms of retention and enrollment, schooling in Puerto Rico remained troubled during the early 1940s. The prescription for alleviation of this situation generally cited the need for the expansion of adequate facilities and a modified curriculum able to balance local educational aspirations with U.S. policy expectations. Only 59.1 percent of the school population of Puerto Rico between the ages of six and fourteen was attending school in 1940; in the urban areas 70 percent of the same age group was in school. In the rural areas the numbers were about 55 percent.[18] With little more than half of the school-age population attending school, an important goal of the process— the political socialization of the student body— was not reaching nearly half of the target population. In the wake of a depression and with the onslaught of a world war, not to mention the more local aspect of worker dissatisfaction evidenced in the many strikes during the late 1930s, other labor unrest, and growing resistance, the U.S. plan for Puerto Rico's schooling would have to make some significant policy changes. In order to contribute to the maintenance of its prospects for an extended United States economic development program, the U.S. education reforms in Puerto Rico would need to devise a policy able to elicit local satisfaction with the schools, through increased attendance, among other ways.

Poverty, limited access, and unemployment kept many Puerto Ricans from receiving an education. In Herbert Marcuse's words:

The social position of the individual and his relation to others appear not only to be determined by objective qualities and laws, but these qualities and laws seem to lose their mysterious and uncontrollable character; they appear as calculable manifestations of (scientific) rationality. The world tends to become the stuff of total administration, that absorbs even the administrators. The web of domination has become the web of reason itself.[19]

Aside from the ideologically constrained education of the population in U.S.-controlled schools, the problems with attendance and uniformity in schools brought some important changes in the attitudes and focus on how to rectify such a situation. First, there was the growing influence that industrial production and organization had on schooling. The impact affected every aspect of schooling, from the administration to the curriculum and classroom behavior. Administratively, education became more centralized. Burdened by the lack of basic consumer goods during the period following the depression and throughout the war, and also in part due to the general feeling of discontent with the school system and the persisting debates over the language of instruction, the insular government's role as state capitalist provided the legitimacy for a more tightly knit relationship between capitalist production (as articulated by the government's policies) and school reforms. Thus, the proposals for school reform advanced by the insular government increasingly responded to the economic plans for Puerto Rican development under U.S. control.

THE COLUMBIA UNIVERSITY'S TEACHERS COLLEGE STUDY

Following the 1940s, the connection between the economic program, its employment problems, and schooling remained at the forefront of many debates and policy proposals, this time in a 1950 Columbia University study, *Public Education and the Future of Puerto Rico*. The "purpose of the study was to examine the teaching plan with a look towards recommending means to more strongly connect the function of the public school with the economic and social development of the country."[20] The study, by Teachers College of Columbia University, reiterated the historical call for the development of vocational education. According to Osvaldo Pacheco, "The committee of educators in both studies recognize the great potentiality of the new Division of Education . . . . It recognizes the convenience of accentuating the tendency towards an increase of the means for vocational teaching."[21]

The importance of industrial vocational education in Puerto Rico remained motivated by numerous factors. Related to the changing socioeconomic dynamics, some of these factors included the growth of the urban sectors; the decline of agriculture; the expansion of government programs creating incentives that would expand private U.S. investment; the mechanization of society; the need to have a labor force attractive, in terms of degree of skill, to potential investors and employers on the island; and the fact that participation in the labor force during the 1950s was declining.

Puerto Rico's rapid industrial growth made vocational education projects quite appealing. During the 1950s and 1960s, Puerto Rico experienced some of its most rapid and dramatic GNP growth, in part as a result of the labor-intensive programs under Operation Bootstrap. As we have seen, much of the growth was mistakenly presented as evidence of Puerto Rico's development. The study by Teachers College of Columbia University was instrumental in promoting the language of vocational education, and more generally reproducing a school reform language compatible with an orthodox conception of development in Puerto Rico. The impact of this study was considerable. Its contents "brought out great interest for the adaptation of educational programs in harmony with the tendencies of economic and socio-cultural development."[22] The language of the study was repeated by some of Puerto Rico's most influential educational leaders.[23] While this is not an extensive review of the study, an introduction to its findings will contribute to the overall thesis of this volume.

Recommendations of the Teachers College Report

The study was divided into twenty-one chapters that focused on three concerns related to the Puerto Rican society in transition: (1) socioeconomic problems, (2) a changing value system, (3) the nature of resources. Here we are reminded that under the orthodox paradigm of development, it is purported that a society's value system should adjust to market demands in order for orthodox development to take place. Throughout the study, the Puerto Rican situation is argued. Such arguments culminate by proposing prescriptions for development. This rationalization is significant because it becomes instrumental in forging the character of the language of school reform in such a way that the legitimacy of any conceptions of school reform and development remains determined by their consistency with such rationalization.

The first section addresses Puerto Rico's socioeconomic potential. Each subheading in this section concludes with a negative statement regarding Puerto Rico's limitations on agricultural production. For example, under the topic of topography, "It has been estimated that more than 25 percent of the country's topsoil has already been washed away" (p. 8); under climate, "Crop damage by storms becomes one of the Island's permanent risks" (p. 8); under natural resources, "The lack of energy-producing resources takes on profound significance as a determinant of the Island's industrial future" (p. 9); under mineral deposits, "On the other hand, such amounts of copper, lead, gold, zinc, and other minerals as have been discovered seem so negligible or scattered as to render these materials as a commercial scale a venture of dubious merit" (pp. 9–10); under fishing, "Informed authorities . . . assert that it is wholly beyond the possibilities of the waters immediately adjacent to the island to supply local requirements in fish" (p. 10). In each instance the topic becomes the incentive for motivating changes in the behavior patterns of Puerto Rican workers and the values that accompany such patterns.[24] Furthermore, the emphasis is on a negation of any possibilities for Puerto Rican national development of its resources through the use of language that tells Puerto Ricans what they do and do not have. At the time each of these points could have been debated, and they continued to frame development possibilities within the construct of a U.S. orthodox model.

Though recommendations were made for the improvement of local agriculture, the 1950s and 1960s witnessed a sharp decline in the productivity of agriculture in Puerto Rico— a 50 percent drop between 1959 and 1969. The drastic decline in the productivity and attention given to agriculture was not seriously addressed until the 1970s. Thus, the revitalization of agriculture as proposed by the study faced a rather dismal future. Exacerbating the ominous situation facing agriculture was the number of people employed in agriculture. In 1950 agriculture accounted for nearly 36 percent of the country's employment; in 1960 it was approximately 23 percent.[25] During both periods, agriculture remained the largest employer in Puerto Rico while cultivated land decreased drastically, creating large numbers of unemployed and underemployed.

Relating the educational needs to the economy, the study dedicates a few chapters to education and economic efficiency. Regarding this, the study asserts: "A people with limited resources and with resources that are rapidly being depleted must . . . use every means at its command to conserve the resources it has and to develop new ones."[26] The rationalization for this statement lay in the study's proposals for changing the curriculum in Puerto Rico's public school system. For example, the study proposes that schools embark upon a program for manpower development and skills that can be exported, and by so doing Puerto Ricans would contribute to reducing the population through emigration to the U.S. and improving life in Puerto Rico while possessing the required marketable skills.[27] Another argument for the need to educate for economic efficiency related to Puerto Rico's requirement to establish some semblance of parity between exports and imports. In this way, the study called for the expansion of schooling for employment in sectors of the economy whose focus was on exports.

The role of the schools was to prepare workers for efficient methods of production. "By improving efficiency," states the report, "other types of constructive work could be attended to for additional revenue."[28] The study goes on to remark, "Once the primitive methods were abandoned, the society was ready to experiment with new uses of manpower."[29] Given the affects that declining agriculture had upon a majority of the employed work force in the 1950s and 1960s, the logic for experimenting with efficiency and improving the imbalance between exports and imports resulted in a school reform language that asserted the expansion of vocational education with a focus on training for employment in sectors of the economy whose business nucleus was exports. Educating for economic efficiency included the expansion of vocational education programs, development of an understanding of the contributions that all fields of study could make to economic efficiency, the integration of vocational education programs into Second Unit schools and junior high schools, and making study of arithmetic and community problems synonymous with the study of consumer habits.[30]

Regarding education and economic efficiency, then, school reform was articulated by a language growing out of a conception of development consistent with the maintenance of Puerto Rico's political-economic situation under an orthodox model of development. By improving efficiency, it was believed that Puerto Ricans would be in a better position to improve their standard of living and prospects for employment. On the surface these recommendations appear desirable. Yet interestingly, the study makes clear that these recommendations are not to be carried out with a focus on Puerto Rico:

There is no implication here that the educational program should be focused solely on an internal look at Puerto Rico's problems. Rather, it is believed that these problems must be worked on in their world setting. If these problems are faced realistically, a world view will be demanded.[31]

Again, the implication is that any "realistic" approach to these problems in Puerto Rico is to not consider Puerto Rico's political-economic status as a condition for dealing with these recommendations. By so stating, this study, which became the hallmark for educational and curriculum reform in the 1950s and 1960s, defined the legitimacy of the language of school reform and continued to preclude any alternatives whose conceptions of development lay outside the prescribed parameters set forth by the study.

MORE SCHOOLING FEWER JOBS

The 1960s fell into both periods characterizing Operation Bootstrap. The early years of the decade belonged to the labor-intensive efforts while the later years responded more to the desirability of attracting capital-intensive firms.

During the 1960s, the concern over the situation in Puerto Rico's public schools compelled the insular government to draft another report that would identify problems and provide recommendations for the improvement of Puerto Rico's public school system. Spearheading the effort was the Division of Pedagogical Research of the Superior Council of the University of Puerto Rico. It published *The Study of the Educational System*, a report that identified various aspects of the public school system that, it perceived as problematic, and hence as disallowing for the implementation and practice of a "sound" public school policy. Though school expansion, in terms of enrollment, grew dramatically throughout the 1950s, numerous concurrent issues facing such expansion had yet to be resolved. Among these were problems of overcoming double enrollment, retention, pedagogical research, curriculum reform, improvement of teaching materials, the reorganization of the administration, and the use of new media of communication for education.[32]

The Study of the Educational System made recommendations with respect to Puerto Rico's philosophy of education, organization and administration of schools, financial resources, school buildings, school supervision, and the teaching of English. Regarding each of these areas, the study recognized that despite some gains in the expansion of schooling (i.e., enrollment), the prospects for success faced difficult problems. For example, many schools lacked a water supply, science facilities for a majority of classrooms, an adequate number of classrooms and sizes of classrooms, overcrowding, shortages of texts and classroom materials, and building facilities in compliance with minimum governmental safety requirements.[33] Emphasizing these problems made the possibility of addressing other, more fundamental, issues distant. The above concerns for the most part represented symptoms of a larger problem. Shortages of many sorts are easier to talk about, or at least less threatening when publicized, than issues of structural failures.

Vocational Education: Notes on the Recent Years

While vocational education played a central role in the expansion of schooling between the late 1940s and the 1960s, the developments in the second stage of Operation Bootstrap under capital-intensive firms, with its need for fewer employees with higher education, propelled the vocationalization of schooling. The federal government's investment of funds for schooling, that created a greater demand for postsecondary education, was not absorbed by the University of Puerto Rico, and thus led to the rapid growth of many private postsecondary institutions. Private postsecondary schooling concentrated on preparing students for the market by identifying market needs and constructing curricula consistent with those requirements. This, coupled with the expansion of private capital-intensive firms, provided the language of school reform with the necessary rationale for complying with orthodox development while making it more difficult for the creation and legitimacy of alternative conceptions of development to be accepted.

An indication of the vocationalization of schooling is the fact that the fastest-growing departments in postsecondary institutions have been those of the occupational careers. For example, in the University of Puerto Rico, enrollment through 1988 remained frozen at 52,000 students. However, its regional colleges, that are primarily oriented toward programs for occupational careers at the bachelor's degree level, experienced a growth of over 4,000 students between 1979 and 1983.[34] Other departments—such as the natural sciences, social sciences, education, and the humanities—registered marked declines in enrollment. Thus, though an economy requires a productive base for the satisfaction of autonomous development needs, the trend in Puerto Rico's public school system has been to reproduce a value system detrimental to the possibilities for autonomous expression. In recent years, this has, given way to a third sector consumer economy and the continued growth of the occupational careers fields in schooling. The tertiary sector here refers to the increment in the services sector of the economy. In Puerto Rico this sector focuses on exports and the financial services which facilitate an export-oriented economy advancing the support of internal consumption.

Some Contradictions of Educational Expansion in Puerto Rico

In 1970, fiscal resources invested in public schooling represented 6.4 percent of the gross national product (this does not include U.S. federal aid to schooling). In that year it was the second highest rate in the world— Canada was first, with 6.5 percent, and the United States was third, with 5.1 percent.[35] U.S. federal dollars in public schooling in Puerto Rico represents the overwhelming percentage of dollars available for public schooling. Rafael Irizarry states, "For the year 1985–86 there were $274 million in federal funds assigned to the Department of Public Instruction. This amount represents 34 percent of the total $818 million in the budget for that agency."[36] Such school expansion has created some rather notable contradictions.

In addition to the above funds, the United States has transferred $125 million annually for Pell grants (basic educational opportunity grants). As of 1987 these grants were helping finance the schooling of over 100,000 postsecondary students. Postsecondary schooling has grown dramatically since the 1970s, in part because of the availability of these grants in times of high unemployment and rising expectations for social and economic improvement. Federal grants have increased the demand for a higher education that has not been absorbed by the University of Puerto Rico, and thus has provided space for growth in the private sector of higher education.[37]

The most rapid expansion of schooling occurred in the private sector during the 1970s, a period when Puerto Rico's high rate of growth was accompanied by a serious fiscal crisis. The private sector of schooling had a tuition rate approximately nine times higher than that of public schooling during the period. By 1983 the private sector enrolled approximately 65 percent of postsecondary students.[38] Exacerbating the contradiction, is the reality that this expansion has occurred in the absence of adequate employment opportunities.

As people compete for a limited number of jobs, they increasingly press for higher levels of education. Educational expansion is fueled by the combination of popular pressure and the use of educational credentials as a criterion for employment. A lack of congruence results between growing levels of schooling and the limited availability of high level jobs.[39]

Another contradiction arises between the expansion of schooling in Puerto Rico and credentialism. "There persists a continued devaluation of the credentials acquired through higher education as evidenced in the requirements of the labor market for a major number of prospective employees."[40] For example, a study by the Division of Research of Interamerican University (a private postsecondary institution) determined that 47.9 percent of its 19,200 graduates with a bachelor's degree and those with associate degrees were unemployed. Of those working, 59.6 percent of those with bachelor' degrees were employed full-time with salaries of $500 to $600 per month— less than a typist earns.[41] Thus, though less schooling might technically be necessary for a particular job, the more schooled are placed.[42]

While these contradictions have a definite effect on the relationship of Puerto Rican development to schooling, the importance of attending school remains high, as we would generally assume. Yet the impact upon low levels of schooling and retention tends to reveal part of the problems associated with schooling, expectations, and the lack of visible results that would act as a motivation for continuing. In recent years, it is estimated that 50 percent of the children enrolled in the first grade will not complete high school. The majority, more than 90 percent, complete the first cycle— elementary school. At the intermediate and high school level approximately half drop-out.[43]

Thus, while schooling has expanded considerably, such developments have not yielded an improvement in Puerto Rico's political economy. The growth of the private sector at all levels of schooling, particularly at the postsecondary levels, has contributed to a language of reform responsive to the increased privatization of the economy and schooling due in part to the fiscal burden confronting the insular government as it remains subject to the fluctuations of administrations in Washington whose policies regarding transfers can and do change, forcing the insular government to cut back or freeze its contribution to schooling. The gains experienced in the 1970s and 1980s by the private education sector while the public sector suffered, had a significant impact upon the fields of study in which postsecondary students were enrolling.

CONCLUSION

Schooling as the "great equalizer" remains a powerful political and ideological institution that has, for the most part, succeeded in tempering the expectations of a people. The more schooling is required for personal economic improvement and political participation, as access to more schooling becomes progressively difficult, and as its results contribute less to the improvement of the human condition, the easier it is to legitimize levels of poverty and the loss of power, both economic and political. This in part contributes to an explanation of the expansion of schooling in Puerto Rico and the investment of fiscal resources despite poor results in the country's attempts to overcome unemployment and poverty under the erratic, and in the past two decades the continuous, decline of GNP. If Puerto Ricans accept that more schooling is the answer to the problems facing the country's development, then the low levels of schooling explain underdevelopment. Here again, public school reform, while making an important claim in supporting the advancement of higher levels of academic training, fails to take into account the correlation between that training, the expectations of those receiving it, and the ability of the Puerto Rican national economy to absorb and develop the products of the training.

Widespread at one point in the history of education in Puerto Rico was the provision for expanding vocational education as a means to access cultural capital. We witnessed not only the transformation of the location of populations in Puerto Rico but also the rationalization that legitimized such changes and the role that public school reform initiatives played in carrying out and sustaining that legitimacy. This fundamental change, resulting in the near death of agriculture, had a profound effect on the value patterns of the people. Such a transformation of the economy and values needs to be juxtaposed to the relationship that Puerto Rico has with the United States.

The pattern of meanings and values through which people conduct their whole lives can be seen for a time as autonomous, and as evolving within its own terms, but it is quite unreal, ultimately, to separate this pattern from a precise political and economic system, that can extend its influence into the most unexpected regions of feeling and behavior. The common prescription of education, as the key to change, ignores the fact that the form and content of education are affected, and in some cases determined, by the actual system of [political] decision and [economic] maintenance.[44]

More recently, Puerto Rico's school system has focused on the changes in a predominantly service economy, requiring more schooling for its employed but fewer employees. The literature on credentialism offers important insight into this issue. If we can argue that more schooling is needed despite the availability of fewer jobs, the criteria for filling the limited spaces in the labor market are more easily justified. Thus, even if a job actually requires high school education only, the person with higher education credentials will be the likely candidate for employment. The discrepancies resulting from these changes in Puerto Rico have encouraged more and more students to seek postsecondary schooling in occupational careers, for the most part in private institutions whose curricula tend to be significantly linked to the private sector of the economy, which claims that a large high-tech work force will be necessary in the future.

Though schooling in Puerto Rico throughout the 1970s and to some degree in the 1980s received huge amounts of insular and federal dollars, throughout the period there remained a consistent ideological argument affirming the role of schools as providers of socioeconomic opportunity. In other words, it was necessary to continue to subsidize the "great equalizer" in order to maintain that schools remained the country's first and best hope for upward social mobility and development, despite a colonial relationship.

NOTES

1. Joseph Femia, *Gramsci's Political Thought* (Oxford: Clarendon Press, 1982), 24.
2. Juan José Osuna, *A History of Education in Puerto Rico* (Río Piedras: University of Puerto Rico Press, 1975), 481–82.
3. Ibid., 420–421.
4. Ibid., 421.
5. Ibid., 430.
6. Ibid., 431.
7. Ibid., 431.
8. Ibid., 421–422.

9. Ibid., 422.

10. Ibid., 435.

11. Ibid., 434–450.

12. Ibid., 435.

13. Ibid., 422.

14. Osvaldo Pacheco *A Land of Hope in Schools: A Reader in the History of Public Education in Puerto Rico, 1940–1965* (San Juan: Editorial Edil, 1976), 172.

15. Ibid., 54.

16. Ibid. 11

17. Ibid., 52–53.

18. Ibid., 54.

19. Herbert Marcuse, *One Dimensional Man* (London: Abacus, 1972), 138.

20. Pacheco, *Land of Hopes*, 165.

21. Ibid., 166.

22. Ibid., 166.

23. Pacheco, *Land of Hopes* ; the leaders included the dean of the College of Education at the University of Puerto Rico; the commissioner of education and Enrique Laguerre of Catholic University.

24. Institute of Field Studies, Teachers College Columbia University, *Public Education and the Future of Puerto Rico* (New York: Columbia University Press, 1950), 8–20.

25. Junta de Planificación. *Informe económico al gobernador: 1980* (San Juan: La Junta de Planificación, 1980), A-27, Table 24.

26. Institute of Field Studies, *Public Education*, 127.

27. Ibid., 127.

28. Ibid., 128.

29. Ibid., 128.

30. Ibid., 164–166.

31. Ibid., 610-611.

32. Pacheco, *Land of Hopes* , 209.

33. See Pacheco, *Land of Hopes* ; Rafael Cartagena, *Puerto Rico Enfermo.* (Río Piedras: El Roble 51, 1983).

34. Rafael Irizarry "El desempleo de la población joven y la espiral inflacionaria de la educación en Puerto Rico," unpublished paper (Río Piedras: University of Puerto Rico, 1987), 16.

35. Ibid., 8.

36. Ibid., 10.

37. Ibid., 8.

38. Janice Petrovich "Some Contradictions of Educational Expansion in Puerto Rico," *Homines* 7, no.1–2, (1983): 141–146.

39. Ibid., 143.

40. Ibid.

41. Irizarry, "Desempleo de la población joven," 15.

42. Petrovich, "Contradictions of Educational Expansion," 143.

43. Ibid., 145.

44. Raymond Williams, *The Long Revolution* (London: Chatto and Windus, 1961),119–20.

LOOKING AHEAD: CURRENT SCHOOL REFORM INITIATIVES

Liberated hope is not the cold rational calculus of probability à la Herman Kahn or Henry Kissinger, but a daring calculus of possibility that reverses the past, shatters the present, and creates a new future.[1]

*T*he rapid economic developments that characterized Puerto Rico under Operation Bootstrap and the concurrent changes experienced in the public school system examined in the last two chapters, significantly impacted the colonial relationship between Puerto Rico and the United States. Rather than expanding the possibilities for alternatives favoring local development, public schooling since the 1940s, though providing for some marked growth in Puerto Rico, has been characterized by some of the same contradictions faced by Puerto Rico throughout its colonial life. In the country's economic history, colonialism has been sustained through a host of policies and practices that fundamentally limit the potential for a Puerto Rican determination of development. This is not to say that many external and internal factors in the economic and social life of a country need not inform the dynamics of a development program aspired to by that country; this goes without saying. However, exactly when and how the blueprint for a particular country's development is to be drawn does indeed raise the issue of self-determination.

In the case of Puerto Rico's public school system, we have seen that, through the language of its policies, the institution has been unable to create the space needed to address some fundamental issues related to education and development inasmuch as these are tied to Puerto Rico's colonial reality. However, the expansion of the school system was both a necessary and a desirable outcome in a country whose means of production and economy generally were rapidly entering the world of high industrialization. The development and emphasis given to vocational education were also a response to the new realities facing the movement of the society into the ranks of the industrialized world. However, the primary issue remained the same as it does today. The expansion of schooling and the development of vocational education often raise many significant concerns among educational policymakers and theorists, regardless of the country or its political status. Yet any preoccupation with these two is exacerbated by the reality of colonialism. The fact that a people remains under the domination of another surely raises serious questions regarding the possibilities for the development of the colonized and the role that their schools play in contributing to a continued colonial relationship or to the promotion of their development.

This chapter will examine the relationship that current high tech demands in the economy have to the language of school reform initiatives today in Puerto Rico. Here I will investigate how high technology is being viewed as the high-status knowledge of today in Puerto Rico's school reform. Generally, this chapter will look at some of the language from which current reform projects have been established and then look at some of the problems confronting the role of high tech in the reform initiatives. The chapter is divided into three sections. The first will examine some of the arguments and language promoting educational reform in the past few years. In order to ground the arguments in policy, the section is divided into two sub sections. The first will look at the language embedded in some of the articles that make up the body of the School Reform Pre-Project report submitted by the 11th legislative assembly of Puerto Rico in 1989 which laid the groundwork for the passage of Law Num. 68, The Organic Law of the Department of Education of the Free Associated State of Puerto Rico, passed on August 28, 1990. The second subsection will examine some of the arguments advanced by officials of the education system and university officials in response to the initiatives.

The second section of the chapter will highlight some of the most recent debates on public school reform as manifested in the passage of Law Num. 68. Here we are reminded that in November of 1992, Pedro Roselló, the gubernatorial candidate for the Partido Nuevo Progresista (PNP; New Progressive Party), the pro-statehood party of Puerto Rico won a landslide victory becoming Puerto Rico's most recent governor. This was a shift from Rafael Hernández Colón of the Partido Popular Democrático (PPD; Popular Democratic Party) the governor since 1988 and proponent of the Estado Libre Asociado (ELA), the Free Associated State. The shift in administrations has been accompanied by some interesting changes in the initiatives to reform public schooling in Puerto Rico. The relationship that such changes have to development and public schooling will be examined briefly through an introductory examination of Senate Project Num. 227, presented by Governor Roselló as a seven point project to establish community schools and as such initiate broad reforms in the public school system of Puerto Rico.

The chapter will then turn its attention to some of the political-economic implications in the appeals to an expanded focus on high technology in the schools. The third and final section outlines some of the economic concerns with the assertions that high-tech proponents affirm will contribute to education and the economy.

One point should be raised here before continuing. Much of the language today regarding development and growth employs terms such as "interdependency" or "dependency." Given the political, psychological, and cultural force of language, I find these terms problematic as references to both the world economic dynamics and to its social and cultural breadth. First, "interdependency" implies that the distribution of power, economic and otherwise, in the world is somehow mutually responsive in any country; and yet, the economic and social issues facing many so called Third World nations appear not to be interdependent.

This brings us to what might seem the next logical explanation— dependency. While it is certainly the case that many countries rely upon the United States, the use of the term "dependency" as a characterization needs to be carefully articulated. My primary issue with the term "dependence" is its political and ideological force. It seems to imply that dependent countries are at the mercy of the metropolis; that their only hope for survival is compliance with the policies that for the most part, originate in the metropolis. If we take a more careful look at how the sequence of events evolve, there is good reason to consider that economic dependency might more accurately be described as exploitation. However, the term dependence is more passive—and the relationship, though complex, is projected moreso by the language used to describe it—and this certainly has an impact on the education of dispositions. The dependent country receives, and the more powerful extends, benefits. Politically and culturally the term "dependency" supports the economic exploitation taking place, again by pacifying and objectifying the potential of the exploited country. Thus, though many nations have become independent states, many of the issues regarding development, modernization, and democracy remain problematic. It is not enough that a nation become an independent sovereign state. Nor is it sufficient that a nation unreflectively attempt to duplicate the propensities of others.

EDUCATION AND TECHNOLOGY: THE NEW REASON IN PUERTO RICO'S PUBLIC SCHOOL REFORM INITIATIVE

In Puerto Rico the 1980s experienced a continued decline of the economy. The manufacturing sector, for example, "was in much better shape in 1970 than in the 1980s," according to Dr. Edwin Irizarry Mora, coordinator of economic research at the University of Puerto Rico. Manufacturing was responsible for approximately 18 percent of all employment in 1988. Moreover, foreign firms in manufacturing earned over sixteen times what locally owned firms earned.[2] This reality had a definite impact on the movements in employment and production in the manufacturing sector. In Chapter 6 we saw how Puerto Rico, during the late 1940s, was left with little control of its economy. Except for its utilities, Puerto Rico's contribution to development was quite restricted. Exacerbating the economic situation upon which the school reform initiatives of the 1980s were built was a call to privatize some of the utilities. Targeted were the Puerto Rico Telephone Company, the Aqueducts and Sewage Authority, and the Metropolitan Bus Authority. With the rise in the Puerto Rican debt, such moves toward a more concentrated privatized economy, accompanied by a work force of which nearly three-quarters is employed in the service sectors, provide the language of development and school reform with a formidable challenge.

The 1989 reform initiatives in Puerto Rico, now over four years old, are still being debated. One of the first calls to reform the school system came, as they often do, during the period of intense political campaigning for the governorship in 1987. Miguel Hernández Agosto, the president of the Senate under the Popular Democratic Party's (PPD) administration, noted that the school reform initiative needs to focus on decentralizing the school system and better coordination of the life of the public and private schools in Puerto Rico.[3] In the same article, the Secretary of Public Instruction, Awilda Aponte Roque, asserted the need to place more power in the hands of the districts. In the last chapter the problem of the declining public school sector, during the expansion of schooling during the 1970s and 1980s, demonstrated that there were some fundamental problems with public school enrollment while private school enrollment was growing. Additionally, at the level of postsecondary schooling, the University of Puerto Rico grew by 36.2 percent between 1970 and 1985, while private institutions grew some 338.4 percent— unprecedented in Puerto Rico's history. These dynamics have led many to believe that the answer lies in seeking to replicate the aims and processes of the private schools. In this climate, members of the Puerto Rican economic community articulated their positions.

The president of Banco Popular of Puerto Rico, Richard Carrión, voiced his concern over the burden that private enterprises have had to undertake in the preparation of the specialized personnel needed in a changing technological economic arena. He asserted that "The educational system is not responding adequately to those needs."[4] On the other hand, there was the voice of a seemingly alternative position. Doctor Angel Quintero Alfaro, former secretary of public instruction and member of the Council on Higher Education, declared: "Puerto Rico needs to better integrate the school process with the process of the socializer . . . and that the Puerto Rican society in that transition was unbalanced, hierarchical, with the majority of the population separated from its history."[5]

In addition to the debates over the role that pubic schooling should play in answering the new technological needs was the impact of the U.S. federal government on public schooling in Puerto Rico. The director of the Commission of Higher Education of the Middle States Association of Colleges and Schools, Dr. Howard L. Simmons, advised the Puerto Rican public school system to seek financial resources from private foundations and the corporate community. He suggested that Puerto Rico institute higher education, through contracts with private laboratories and other facilities in the industrial sector, as a means to develop technologies. Regarding the need to prepare students for the world of high technology, Simmons suggested, "That Puerto

Rico consider implementing certain specialized programs, like computer sciences, in educational institutions located in particular regions of the island, instead of trying to include that learning in all of the country's schools."[6]

Puerto Rico's legislative bodies and Governor, Rafael Hernández Colón were being told, in essence, that Puerto Rico would have to assume much more of the responsibility for the costs of schooling its people— among other ways, by soliciting the contributions of (mainly U.S.) corporations— during a period of serious economic decline. In light of the deteriorating economic and social conditions facing Puerto Rico, and having potentially much to gain from such a move, the private post secondary schools provided expedient arguments in defense of privatization. With Governor Pedro Roselló, privatization has become the new *modus vivendi* in matters related to Puerto Rico's development, including schooling. Economically, the tendency in Puerto Rico has been toward the expansion of private enterprises. This tendency is both a response to and affiliated with Puerto Rico's role in the Caribbean Basin Initiative and the 936 corporations. The growth of finance capital-intensive projects, accompanied by the marked expansion of private school enrollment, offered private schooling an opportunity to address reform from a position of power. Private schools, in addition to their growth in enrollment, were responding more effectively to the demands of the employment market and U.S.-controlled interests. Though ideological lines between the government and private industry would not be severed, the failures of public schooling and the success of the private schools gave the latter sector some room to demand more support.[7]

In some important ways, then, the meaning of schooling and reform were coming under the growing control of the private sector, in part because of its apparent success in addressing some of Puerto Rico's most immediate and most obvious social and economic problems. The challenge for public schooling was found, on the one hand, in its ability to address the economic climate of the country and the many indicators of public school failure. On the other hand, the challenge could be found in the system's commitment to an education predicated on the right of all Puerto Ricans to receive an education without dregard to economic status. Before an examination of the relationship that high tech as high-status knowledge has to Puerto Rico's development, and specifically to the language of school reform as it reinforces an orthodox conception of development under a colonial relationship, the following offers a cursory view of some of the principal contents of the 1989 Puerto Rican Senate Pre-Project Report for the reform of public schooling, Law Num. 68, the Organic Law of the Department of Education of the Free Associated State of Puerto Rico, and Senate Project Num. 227.

Puerto Rico's 1989 School Reform Pre-Project

From the outset, the reform initiatives posed numerous political and economic concerns for many of the players. For example, the insular government was blamed for dragging its feet. The schools were accused of not providing a coherent plan that the government could consider seriously. Additionally, there were the voices of different interest groups asserting an array of prescriptions. Some of these included more school autonomy, more teacher power, more local community power, adequate facilities, more teachers, better teachers, a more appropriate curriculum tailored to Puerto Rico's needs, better support services. Responding to these public cries, the government under the PPD administration, Secretary of Public Instruction Awilda Aponte Roque, policy reseachers, and a group of students, teachers, and parents introduced an eight-point plan that formed the basis of the reform effort:

• Modification of the organizational and administrative structure of the school
• Actualization of teaching programs and cultural enrichment programs
• More efficient use of fiscal, physical, and human resources
• Parent and citizen participation
• Redefinition of the role of the student and a design for acquiring optimum development
• Redefinition of the role of supervisor
• Education and reeducation of adults and youngsters outside the school
• Revisions in recruitment practices, evaluation, participation, remuneration, and continued education of personnel.[8]

With these general points, the country struggled to get the reform off the ground. In January 1989 the Pre-Project was presented by the insular government. This section will address only those articles of the Pre-Project most clearly articulating the need for an expanded and tighter meritocratic system in the schools and the importance of high tech in the schools of the future. While not directly addressing the role that merit plays in the reform as it responds to a particular conception of development, the socio-economic relevance is implied. The following is a cursory presentation of what some of the articles proposed and some exploration of their meaning.

Article 4003 stated that learning shall focus on the goal of academic excellence of the student. Puerto Rico's Department of Public Instruction shall seek funds, donations, and economic aid from the insular government, the U.S. federal government, and private entities for the implementation, development, and monitoring of this project. The facilitator of any innovations under the newly created Institute for Educational Change and Innovation, provided for in the reform plan, will be the secretary of education of Puerto Rico[9]— a governor's appointee. In this article the meaning of excellence is not defined. Furthermore, the impact of the voice that different agencies will have on the development of excellence criteria will be significant in terms of how those criteria correspond to a host of socio economic needs. As an example of the difficulty with determining excellence, the Department of Public Instruction may try to emphasize the development of excellence criteria that respond to Puerto Rico's cultural and social values. Politically, the department may be compelled to respond to whatever ensures its position of power. The federal government may want to emphasize excellence consistent with the language in such reports as the U.S. Commission on Excellence in Education's report, *A Nation At Risk,* by reinforcing a highly meritocratic notion of excellence while responding to particular economic requirements. And the private sector may view excellence from the perspective of an essentially economic meritocratic system (consistent with *A Nation at Risk.*)

This is not to say that such views on excellence are as simple as they might seem to be. The intent of such simplification is to make the case that the use of terms like "excellence" in the reform language of the Pre-Project poses potential problems for a clear understanding of the reform aims and processes. Additionally, the issue of decentralization seems troubled when, in this instance and throughout the Pre-Project, the secretary of education becomes the facilitator for the development of an institute that is to address changes and innovations in the schools. Historically in Puerto Rico, the meaning and role of facilitator have conferred upon that person the power necessary to expedite or stall matters that call for facilitation. The two points separately and together suggest that much work to clarify the aims and processes of the reform in these two matters needs to be done.

Article 5001 stated:

The individual differences of the students who attend public schools require that alternative varieties of education be designed according to particular interests and necessities. Within the school population, for example, we have talented students, average, those economically disadvantaged, with learning disabilities, physical and emotional limitations, inclined toward vocational areas or the arts, sports, and other activities. In each of these groups, the field of experiences and necessities, like the familial or social conditions, varies significantly, for that we should provide different special services to attend to the differences between the students, enrich their experiences and provide them opportunities to accomplish maximum academic achievement, [and] by so doing, preparing themselves for incorporation into the work force and contributing to the development of the country.[10]

The article opens with the claim of individual differences predicated on choice and talent. It ends by making reference to the value that attention to these differences will have in the marketplace and Puerto Rican development. With the decline of enrollment in the public schools, at least among those sectors of the society economically able to enroll their children in private schools, public schooling is fast becoming a wasteland. The context in which Article 5001 was written appeals to a notion of equality of educational opportunity. Many understand this to be a pinnacle in the democratic character of a school system. Yet what does this article tells us beyond its assertion that a system of merit must be upgraded? Again, the meaning of such a statement is contingent upon numerous factors. One of these is an economic factor that may call for the need to develop excellence and talent that respond to the market. Another factor may be social. Here, students may be encouraged to accept their lot in life as a social necessity based upon the results of the "equal" opportunity afforded throughout their school experience. In any case, one of the problems with this article is its vagueness yet definiteness. On the one hand, the article takes for granted, and is vague about, what constitutes individual differences, talents, inclinations, and so forth. On the other hand, its conclusion makes it clear that the ultimate goal is incorporation into the labor force.

The preparation for incorporation into the labor force was reinforced by Article 5005 that lays out the process for student promotions from one grade to the next. This is an important component of a school system that relies heavily upon merit. The article states that testing for placement (read "tracking") will take place in grades one, two, four, and five in elementary schools, and grade eight in intermediate schools.[11] Upon completing the third and sixth grades, and also the ninth grade, all students will take a promotion exam. A pregraduation exam will be administered to all high school students in the tenth and eleventh grades, as a requisite for promotion. Finally, all students completing their high school requirements will take a graduation exam in order to obtain a diploma. If any of the above exams is failed, the student will have to attend summer school.[12] Such a barrage of exams throughout the child's school life has the potential for results that may benefit some sectors of Puerto Rican society and harm others, or may harm all of them.

First, in the elementary, intermediate, and high schools, according to this provision, tracking will occur. Those with the best results will receive preferential treatment. From a cost-benefit analysis, these students are the better investment opportunities— and in an underbudgeted and historically poorly managed school system, this could well mean that these students would have access to facilities that would make their transition into the labor force much easier, quite possibly providing them with a more comfortable outlook for the future. Second, there is the problem of teaching and learning for the tests. With so many tests, much of the students' attention may be drawn to them, which appear in many years of chidren's school life. Thus, chidren's intelligence and excellence will be defined by the test makers and the tests, and determined by the results of the tests. What is valuable in educational terms is reduced to how well students internalize the importance of testing as a measure of their intelligence. Article 5006 reinforced teaching and learning for the tests by proposing a series of honors and prizes for the "most talented student in the sixth, ninth, and twelfth grades."[13] The honors or prizes ranged from a plaque to vacations or trips— even cash.

In addition to the role that testing plays in the school life of the students, the teachers are subjected to a proficiency exam prior to certification.[14] Rewards for meritorious teaching will be conferred upon those recognized in the teaching field. The emphasis placed upon a meritocratic system became central to the language of the reform initiatives and the assertions by policymakers as they engaged in debates.

A year after the preproject was introduced, most of the fundamental points were still under debate. For example, the process for evaluating superintendents, principals, and supervisors, some believed, would leave them at the mercy of the governor. In all instances, the power for evaluating and appointment to those positions is in the hands of the secretary of education, a governor's appointee. In other words, those with tenure would be subject to a series of evaluations that if not satisfactory, could mean their appointment to lesser positions; and those without tenure would have to comply with the plans determined by the secretary of education and the governor.[15] The preproject document received much attention in the media and much response from educators throughout the country.

Educators Respond to the Reform

Early in 1990, a series of articles appeared in the daily *El Nuevo Día*. This paper, arguably the largest and most widely distributed in Puerto Rico, is owned and operated by the Ferré family, one of Puerto Rico's wealthiest families whose wealth is greatly attributed to their investements in cement and other industries during the early years of Operation Bootstrap. The patriarch of the family, Luis Ferré, was governor of Puerto Rico in the 1960s and a staunch promoter of statehood for Puerto Rico. The series of articles ran under the title, "The Goals of the '90s." The headlines stated that the Department of Public Instruction hoped to educate in a more scientific manner during the new decade.

Appointed by Governor Rafael Hernández Colón, the new secretary of public instruction, José Lema Moyá, asserted that children would need to learn computer skills early on. Furthermore, he stated:

This will be the generation of educational technology. Schools will have to compete with the means of communication. There will be fewer textbooks, and many more audiovisual, video, and computer diskettes. Before, the history teacher taught the number of battles during the Independence War in the U.S. This will be less important because the child will have such information readily available on video. Schools need to develop good communication skills in order for the child to make good use of the information at her/his disposal.[16]

Bearing in mind the thesis of this volume—that the language of school reform is locked into an orthodox conception of development that limits the possibilities of allowing for the legitimacy of alternative conceptions—variety of voices, some supportive and others challenging the secretary's assertion, came to the fore. Like many others, however, the position of the secretary reinforced an orthodox conception of development.

The director of the Center for Instruction and Modern Education, and former Secretary of Public Instruction (in 1977), Herman Sulsona, remarked, "Private schools have been more effective, in general terms, and it is unnecessary to reinvent the wheel, since the model of reform is already before us in the form of a revitalized private school sector."[17] Another former secretary, María Socorro Lacot, emphasized that schools no longer need to expand vocational education and technical programs because the textile and apparel industries, among others, have their own training programs. What is needed is basic skills applicable across a wide variety of fields; for example, much more attention needs to be dedicated to tourism. Given the proliferation of television and high tech in the schools, teachers would become observers and coordinators who examine students and promote them.[18]

Another former secretary posed a position that bordered on the margins of what might have been considered a real alternative. Angel Alfaro Quintana, suggested:

A true school reform has to be accompanied by profound changes in the social environment that diminish our great social differences and promote a solidarity position that would assist us in realizing the values subscribed to in the Constitution. . . . We must remember that our children are tied to the social system that educates them or corrupts them.[19]

Other voices focused on better teacher pay, longer school hours, more schools, more classrooms, better discipline, and a host of issues that might, but generally did not, challenge the present status of affairs governing the island's development.

At the university level, the presidents and other administrators held similar positions. José Alberto Morales, president of Sacred Heart University, affirmed that, "Quality will be emphasized and not quantity. Factors such as employability of graduates will carry much more weight in the design of the curriculum. The student will seek not a diploma, but preparation in order to compete in the employment market."[20] Agreeing with much of Morales' position, Pedro José Rivera, the former president of Interamerican University, noted that universities would have to seek other sources of income and not rely primarily upon tuition, as had generally been the case. He suggested that alternative forms of income be investigated such as the development of properties, businesses and appeals to philanthropy.[21] According to the president of the Ana G. Méndez Foundation, José A. Méndez:

It is necessary for the insular government to genuinely support those institutions of the private sector that have demonstrated evidence of progress and seriousness in their service to the community. Such support may come in the form of government donations to students in need in the private institutions; funds from a tax on private firms for long-term studies; some sort of tax-exempt savings account for studies, a kind of educational IRA; amend the tax laws so that private institutions receive a fair share of the tax revenue, since private universities and postsecondary schools service over 50 percent of those at this level of study.[22]

As for policy statements regarding the reform, there were many articles and references to the expansion of a system of meritocracy and the need to emphasize communications through, among other practices, use of and emphasis upon computers,[23] because this industry would become one of the major employers of the 1990s. The reform also would have a significant impact on the professional lives of the teachers. Both teachers and students would come under a system of careful scrutiny and evaluation not experienced in Puerto Rico since the early decades when English-language instruction policies were strictly enforced. Regardless of this, however, the reform plan has been unable to demonstrate that such changes constitute a progressive step in Puerto Rico's public school system. The outcome of the struggle of the public school system to strike a balance with the requirements of the private schools and private firms remains uncertain. In Puerto Rico, market demand, play a central role in the development of public school programs and reform initiatives. The pressures to expand the country's privatization campaign into many of the government firms places public schooling in a precarious situation. The language of the reform overwhelmingly reinforces such a campaign, and this has many Puerto Ricans worried.

Such changes may well mean that schooling will progressively become an opportunity for an exclusive few. Additionally, the focus of the universities and other postsecondary schools is on developing a curriculum that responds to the market; and though this is nothing new to Puerto Rico, this tendency— due, among other things, to the failing economy of the insular government and orthodox development in Puerto Rico—is becoming dominant at the country's public universities and colleges, consistent with U.S. plans for Puerto Rico under the CBI and 936 projections. This has important implications for college preparatory and secondary schools. These schools will tend to concentrate on responding to the requirements for college entrance as articulated by a postsecondary school system whose policies are informed by the changes in the employment market; and this market remains under the control of the United States and its private firms in Puerto Rico. With the growth of capital-intensive programs in Puerto Rico, and more recently with the intensification of the campaign toward privatization, the language of reform in the public school system, that relies upon the insular and federal governments for its existence, is fast becoming the same language as that of the private schools. We now turn to a look at some of the most recent initiatives which continue to represent administrative advocacy of privatization both in the economy and in education.

LAW NUM. 68: THE ORGANIC LAW OF THE DEPARTMENT OF EDUCATION OF THE FREE ASSOCIATED STATE OF PUERTO RICO

Despite the concerns and issues left unresolved by the Pre-Project, on August 28, 1990, Hernández Colón's adminstration approved the Organic Law of the Department of Education. Primary among many of the criticisms were the assertions that the project could not really be defined an educational reform project since it does not establish a reform initiative with the requisite processes. Instead, the project establishes the basis for a new structure for the public education system of Puerto Rico.[24] Because of this, instead of naming the initiatve a Reform Law, it was to be called the Organic Law of the Department of Education.

Generally, Law Num. 68 is grounded in the need to reaffirm a student-centered education system wherein the teacher is viewed as an agent for constructive change and the school is to be understood as the center of the learning process, and not the structures which support the system.[25] The law also asserts the need to defend school autonomy as the means through which schools can best respond to the development of efficiency and excellence.[26] Finally, the law articulates the need to develop a broader base of participation in the educational process.[27] These principles formed the basis of the law and the blueprint from which the concept of Autonomous Community Schools was developed. In order to effect the development of a reform in the school system, the law also provides for the establishment of the Institute for Educational Reform, which will assist in the design, implementation, evaluation, and modification of the new systems which will allow for the development of the autonomous schools. In sum, Law Num. 68 was passed in order to engender relationships between administrative personnel and the schools from those of supervision and control to those of support and facilitation. The definition of community school states that:

> The Community School is a community of studies made up of its students, its personnel, the parents of students, and the community it serves. . . . It is organized and administered in a democratic form. . . . The participation of the community in the school is intense and proactive in the detection and resolution of common problems. The community is that area within which the school and the neighborhood are located.[28]

The project establishing community schools lists a series of points outlining the powers of the schools. However, the appointment and administration of the school is ultimately under the power of the Secretary of the Department of Education (no longer referred to as the Secretary of Public Instruction), who is appointed by the governor, and who appoints the principals of these new autonomous community schools; and who is also in charge of the Institute for Educational Reform.

The Teachers Federation of Puerto Rico issued numerous critiques of the law including concerns that the law reinforced not decentralization, but a more centralized public school system—as the Secretary of the Department of Education exercises absolute powers and the exact definitions of participation and autonomy are obscured by such power. Furthermore, the accreditation of schools will depend upon a newly established Council of Education, a supervisory body. As García Blanco and Colón Morera note:

> The Secretary of Education remains in charge of establishing the basic curriculum and materials, defining the basic skills that students must have accomplished at each grade level, and controlliong the administration and upkeeping of buildings. . . . Although the law declares the need to restructure the system, it still maintains highly problematic hierarchical structures that depend on the Secretary of education and school superintendents.[29]

The Organic Law of the Department of Education (Num. 68) became the subject of intense debate and political rivalry. Its vagueness made it possible for proponents and adversaries to enter into relentless neverending debates over definitions and processes. Law Num. 68 never actually responded to the needs of Puerto Rico's population. Public Schooling in Puerto Rico needed to recreate an existence conducive and consonant with the changes in the political economic arena. The struggle became a desperate one. Puerto Ricans wanted and needed change. The disposition to seek change in the face of the ensuing crisis resulted, as often it does, in an administrative change in the country's ruling party. In 1992, Pedro Roselló of the PNP won the gubernatorial race. Soon after his inauguration, Roselló announced his project to reform public schooling in Puerto Rico.

The Privatization of Community and Education

On April 26, 1993, Governor Pedro Roselló presented his version of a school reform project aimed at reversing the failing public school system of Puerto Rico. The governor's proposal, Senate Project Num. 227 would personify him as a leader in the efforts to revitalize education by advancing privatization. Senate project Num. 227 included the following points:

1. Adopt Law Num. 18 creating the development for Community Schools
2. Create an Institute for Educational Reform.
3. Establish the composition and functions of the Institute for Educational Reform.
4. Establish an Advisory Council for the Institute of Educational Reform.
5. Arrange its composition and functions.
6. Amend articles 4.06 and 4.07 of Law Num. 68 (relative to School Councils).
7. Assignment of funds.[30]

Generally speaking, the proposal was no different than the already established Organic Law of the Department of Education (Law Num. 68). The two points most fervently advanced and likewise attacked by the projects opponents have been the meaning of Community Schools and an increased centralization of the Department of Education, now under the direction of José Arsenio Torres. Adding to the force of the issues have been the push to privatize schooling and the introduction of an educational voucher system.

The federation of teachers responded quickly as its President Renán Soto Soto affirmed that:

The project really represents the municipalization of education, with objectives including (1) ideological control of the educational system by the new political administration; (2) the preparation of the road to the privatization of education in Puerto Rico; (3) the restriction or elimination of rights acquired by teachers; (4) the destruction of teachers organizations in order to leave workers orphaned with no representation; (5) the elimination of public schools as an alternative.[31]

The new administration's educational reform proposal reinforces the centralization of the Secretary's power by placing in the Secretary's hands the final word on matters regarding the Institute for Educational Reform, which the Secretary will direct, control of all fiscal matters and appropriations of funds, the appointment of Community School principals, hiring and firing of faculty and other personnel, matters related to the design, development, and implementation of all procedures in all schools in the system, curriculum design and development matters, design of instruments for teacher evaluation, design and development of instruments for student evaluation and testing, salary scales and categories, advisor to the School Councils, establishment of school facilitators by schools, determination of services rendered to a Community School by the Department of Education, appoint the Executive Director of the Institute for Educational Reform, all curriculum matters related to systemwide standards for design and evaluation, among many other powers.[32] The primary concerns with the establishment and development of the Community Schools was community preparedness and commitment in the presence of a history of alienation and an ill-informed public.

Some two months after Roselló presented his plan to reform education, the daily, *El Nuevo Día*, ran a short but interesting article highlighting the World Bank's concerns that failing education systems in Latin America represent the "Achilles Heel" of this region's development.[33] Earlier in this volume some attention was given to how institutions like the World Bank's development projects, with their structural adjustment models often do more harm than good in advancing the cause of development for any nation's people.

Accompanied by fiscal crisis, like most other Latin American countries, Puerto Rico under Roselló, especially given its preferred status as a major player in the CBI project through its 936 corporations, is doing all it can to appease the colonizer, hoping to bring more investments to Puerto Rico and as such present Puerto Rico as the next best hope for a 51st state of the United States. For Governor Roselló, education's contribution, along with his proposed reform Senate Project Num. 227, will come in the form of an expanded privatized schooling system—one whose primary market is to be found in the failures of the public schools now to be transformed into sites ready and willing to respond to the future of U.S. finance capital in Puerto Rico.

The plan to advance the privatization of Puerto Rico's public school system is being executed by the governor's voucher plan. Roselló's plan is to issue vouchers of $1,500 to somewhere between 3,000 and 6,000 students among a student population of over 637,000 in Puerto Rico. These vouchers will be paid in the form of checks and credit vouchers. Those students transferring to the private school sector will receive a check. Those changing from one public school to another will receive a credit voucher. Among the many criticisms launched against this campaign has been the affirmation that such a voucher system takes local resources and locates them in particular schools. This obviously has serious implications for public schooling in Puerto Rico. The privatization of schools through a voucher system which actually contributes to a merit system by which schools will be evaluated and assigned funds does seem to reaffirm the municipalization of education noted by Renán Soto of the Teachers Federation. Not only this, such a move gives further credence to the notion of the maximization of rationalized behavior. That is to say, those schools and students that respond to the technological rationalistic demands under the proliferation of finance capital in Puerto Rico under U.S. colonialism, will be rewarded; while those that struggle to forge an understanding between development and the Puerto Rican national culture will suffer.

Two final notes on the Roselló administration's reform initiatives. First, the Secretary of the Department of Education, José Arsenio Torres, in an article in the daily, *El Nuevo Día* dated July 18, 1993, announced that his department would actively seek the development of agricultural vocational schools, called "special schools," in certain rural regions of the country. His rationale for such a project was grounded in the perception that the poor situation in which these schools found themselves and the fact that they fall outside the parameters of "ordinary district schools" has placed them in the "special" category. When requested by a farmer that this project include agroindustrial education, Secretary Torres staunchly refused the request.[34] Such a refusal reminds us of the history of attempts in Puerto Rico to initiate agricultural projects for national development, the response by farmers associations in the United States to Puerto Rican agricultural development, and some of James Dietz's assertions that agriculture and other industries could work together for Puerto Rico's development; that agriculture need not have been abandoned.

Lastly, Under the Secretary of the Department of Education, the new administration plans to embark upon a plan to establish separate schooling at fifteen public housing projects throughout the country. These schools will be, "less academic . . . we have to adapt the school to the situation," noted Secretary Torres. The costs for being poor will rise as Puerto Rico's pulic housing population will be categorically denied equality of opportunity and access— and their class standing will confine them to the ranks of secondary citizens. Like the Community Schools programs, privatization through vouchers, and the continued privatization of the public sector whether in education, health, utilities, transportaion, or whatever, the implications of this project might well serve the proliferation of the fractionalization of the Puerto Rican nation. The fabric of a culture is strengthened by the hands of educated and committed people in the service of the nation's development as a people. Those who resist Roselló's plans know this. But so too do those who support it. Puerto Ricans are much easier to control or manipulate politically when their interests are viewed, projected, and experienced individually, and not as part of the national or a collective character.

HIGH TECH IN THE SCHOOLS: A NEW PANACEA

Before examining the possibilities that an increased presence of high tech in the public school programs will provide Puerto Rico with some assistance in its development projects, let us look briefly at the environment in that such proposals are being fomented. The current unemployment and underemployment rate is dangerously high and growing. The percentages for the 1980s were articulated in Chapter 6. For example, unemployment in 1983 was at approximately 22 percent; this was primarily among those between the ages of eighteen and twenty four and, paradoxically, among those with the highest levels of schooling.

A study by Dr. Angel Ruíz, "The Demand for Human Resources by Occupation and by Industrial Sector for 1984, 1992, and 2,000," gave some interesting insights into the dynamics facing the "high tech in the schools" position as a contribution to Puerto Rican development and employment. For 1992, the study projects a need for an additional 47,295 positions requiring postsecondary schooling. It is estimated that the total graduating population of the University of Puerto Rico, the colleges, and other postsecondary institutions, both public and private, between 1985 and 1992 will exceed 154,680. In other words, during this period there will be an excess of 107,385 graduates in relation to the demand. This represents 10.5 percent of the labor force projections for 1992.[35] This high level of excess personnel indicates that the problem is more than just the reconciliation of the products of these institutions and the demand for them.

Much of the criticism being expressed by the private sector in regard to the public school system, including the University of Puerto Rico, is related to the perception that the liberal arts, humanities, and social sciences tend to produce personnel for unemployment. Yet the global indicators of supply and demand indicate that, independent of the distribution of the educational programs offered— academic, professional, or technical— postsecondary institutions have been producing a graduate total that is three times the demand.[36] Specific to the occupations most closely related to the school reform rationale for intensifying computer education in the schools, as an overall contributor to Puerto Rico's development needs, are the projections for employment in engineering and technical occupations. In 1985 there were 2,944 graduates specializing in technical areas such as medical technology, engineering technology, and computer operations and programming. For 1992 it is predicted that a total of 23,552 graduates will have the skills required for these positions. Thus, even in a field that alleges a great demand for the future in terms of employment, it is estimated that the supply will exceed the demand by ten times.[37] If the new high-status knowledge is not capable of responding to Puerto Rico's development needs, what is it capable of providing for the people of Puerto Rico? The language of the school reform, by appealing to high-status knowledge, becomes the driving force behind the legitimacy of a conception of development predicated upon the demands of certain market interests that nourish the relationship between language and development.

The importance of high-status knowledge as a component of the reproduction of an ideology informing a particular conception of economic development is significant inasmuch as such knowledge is challenged, generally speaking in the case of Puerto Rico, at its most superficial level. The call for computerized instruction as a response to the present and future industrial needs is generally challenged by those who take issue with such matters as the financing of certain projects, the scope and sequence of various curricular matters concerning the projects, or regarding matters of efficiency and the implementation of the projects in conjunction with supply and demand. Earlier in the chapter, former Secretary of Education Angel Quintero Alfaro was quoted as citing the need for "profound social change that would diminish our great social differences." This kind of language needs some clarification. Such a statement, as an example of a possible challenge to the proliferation of high tech as high-status knowledge in the schools, could also be viewed as consonant with such a proliferation. One need only argue that the high-status knowledge will contribute to the growth of participation in the work force and the development of high-tech industries in the country, thus having a positive effect on the society. The language of orthodox economic theory could easily be incorporated into Alfaro's statement.

Thus, like many of the attempts to challenge the colonial language of school reform in the past, today much of the challenge is constructed in such a way that its language lacks the clarity and precision that might protect it from being co-opted into the orthodox language of school reform that reinforces the colonial relationship and a conception of development that characterizes that relationship.

Michael Apple, paraphrasing Walter Feinberg's treatment of the notion of a high-status knowledge and rationality, reminds us that, "Production of a particular 'commodity' (here high-status knowledge) is of more concern than the distribution of that particular commodity. To the extent that it does not interfere with the production of technical knowledge, then concerns about distributing it more equitably can be tolerated as well."[38]

In Puerto Rico, though growth has been experienced at different points during its history, development remains poor. Likewise, though Puerto Ricans have had access to patterns of massive consumption, primarily as a result of federally subsidized transfers, Puerto Rico has been prevented or restrained from venturing beyond the production of a particular conception of development and the corresponding knowledge. Puerto Rico's profound economic problems are incorporated into the new high-status knowledge language and the school reform. First, the production of high tech as high-status knowledge is advanced by arguing that the most developed and richest countries in the world are also the leaders in communications and the computer industry, sometimes called the information industry. In order to take part and receive some of the benefits from such development, Puerto Rico's public schools must spend much time, effort, and money producing this high-status knowledge. Second, Puerto Ricans are led to believe that a school system that responds to such changes in high-status knowledge will necessarily mean an improved economic future for Puerto Rico. Lastly, once Puerto Ricans have produced this high-status knowledge, if it does not provide a brighter economic future, they will tend to view the problem as one reducible to a poor insular government, corruption, and a poor public school system.

However, though this is certainly part of the problem, the fact that issues of development continue to be separated from issues of status contributes to a disarticulated language of school reform. On the one hand, schools are asked to respond to the demands of the market. Historically, that is what schooling in the colony has done, and this has had poor results; most of the per capita growth, has been due to federal subsidies and not development in the public school system or its products in the market. On the other hand, the school system and the insular government are attacked for the failures in Puerto Rico's development. It would be safe to say that never has the language of school reform addressed the critical relationship that colonialism has to development. If it has, it has done so in a manner consistent with the colonial relationship and orthodox economic conceptions of development through some new political formula— whether in the form of a newly characterized colonialism, a state of the United States, or a neocolony called a republic of some sort.

The new high-status knowledge may in fact exacerbate the problem of colonialism, the reliance upon an orthodox conception of development, and the limitations that these present for the expansion of a language of school reform that allows for the legitimacy of alternative conceptions of development. Martin Carnoy offers an economist's view of some of the problems that education and the high-tech, high-status knowledge arguments might be forced to confront. In the following section I will examine his treatment of high technology and education as they relate to the economy. Through such an examination, the belief that the new high-status knowledge will necessarily yield benefits for Puerto Rico or Puerto Rico's public school system will be questioned.

High Technology and Schools: Martin Carnoy's Economic Argument

Referred to as the "information revolution," the new age of technology stands behind the argument that automation and robotization will "make it possible to increase high productivity, eliminate repetitive, low skill jobs, and virtually eliminate unemployment."[39] This will take place with the help of computer assisted instruction (CAI). The computers allow highly individualized learning at a pace suitable to the individual student. Yet, in the context of the language of school reform as it relates to the production of a particular high-status knowledge that reinforces a conception of development predicated upon a continued orthodox economic model of development, and that is now appealing to high technology as an important contributor to the alleviation of Puerto Rico's economic situation, the value of CAI for Puerto Rican development remains problematic.

Carnoy provides some interesting considerations relative to Puerto Rico's school reform initiatives and their call for high technology in the schools to respond to the market, and hence improve the economic situation. According to Carnoy's studies, high-technology industry has witnessed huge drops in the cost of the silicon transistor. Between 1964 and 1972 integrated circuit prices fell from between seventeen and thirty dollars to one dollar. Each of these units was able to carry out a larger number of tasks in 1972 than a decade earlier. Thus the price decline per unit underestimates the fall in cost per unit of quality.[40] Carnoy remarks:

The principal input in high technology products is highly educated, scientific/engineering human capital. It is this characteristic that distinguishes high technology industry from traditional manufacturing and services. . . . But most high technology products neither require inputs with high transportation costs, nor produce outputs that are expensive to ship. . . . The most important inputs are the skilled technicians who can develop new products, lower the production costs of a firm's output by developing new processes, or improve the reliability and quality control of existing products. . . . The new technology is "embodied" in engineers and technicians who move from universities, where government contracts subsidize state-of-the-art research, to industry, where the knowledge they have acquired is turned into profit making technology.[41]

In Puerto Rico, the school reform initiative, in its calls for the expansion and development of high technology in the schools, has run into, among other problems, the financing of such a project. While the private schools are demonstrating their success with the private sector of the economy, none of the private postsecondary schools is actually involved in the establishment of state-of-the-art research and development facilities that might contribute to local development. As noted earlier, the focus of most of these schools is on the expansion of those fields that respond to the management and clerical aspects of the high-technology industry. The ability to respond to economic development by establishing and encouraging research is mediated by problems of technological ownership and scant facilities. Furthermore, though private postsecondary vocational programs have increased enormously in number since 1975 (from 81 in 1975 to 479 in 1989),[42] these are low-level, semiskilled programs, not of the sort directly involved in the research and development of the new technologies or their profitable gains.

If the principal input is a highly educated scientific and engineering community, then the call for more high technology in the schools of Puerto Rico is legitimate. However, sustaining a high-technology school environment also requires, as Carnoy has pointed out, the presence of state-of-the-art research universities, laboratories, industries, and the capital necessary to finance such a venture. Without the technological research and development components, the presence of high-technology is likely to yield what the presence of other advanced technologies has offered Puerto Rico: some low-skilled jobs whose research and development sectors remain located in the United States or some other metropolis. Furthermore, even some facilities in Puerto Rico such as the pharmaceutical plants of Squibb, Johnson and Johnson, Eli Lilly, Searle, and others are primarily engineered from the United States; and beyond this, the focus of the high-technology plants in Puerto Rico is on profit making and not necessarily the technological needs of Puerto Rico's development.

The contemporary environment of the role of high technology in the so called Third World has not significantly changed the patterns of underdevelopment in the region in terms of high-skilled employment rates. Although those highly educated in technology are involved in research and development, marketing, and sales, the technology is largely characterized by subcontracting firms, many of them in low-paying Third World countries, that provide labor for the basic fabrication of parts that are later assembled and finished in the United States.[43] This production by cheap labor merely replaces one job with another while contributing little to the actual contribution that such a change makes to a country's development. Examples of this can be seen in Taiwan, Hewlett-Packard in Mexico, and Atari and RCA in Puerto Rico.

A second point should be raised regarding the relationship that foreign high technology has to Puerto Rico's development needs. This industry tends to be highly mobile. That is, the cost of transporting assembled inputs and finished products is relatively low making it easy to move if necessary; also, the research and development components remain in proximity to universities and other research institutions with advanced technological facilities that might attract highly educated labor.[44]

The mobility of the industry gives it a political strength not readily available to less mobile industries— it is easier a decide to remain in a country or to relocate. Foreign investment in underdeveloped countries often tempered by the political climate of the client country. The mobility of high technology makes it easier for firms in the industry to encourage countries to demonstrate how well behaved they can be, and thus deserving of the investments and economic benefits brought by new jobs, however temporary. This behavior covers anything from the client country's school system's emphasis upon high technology, to labor and tax incentives, to political stability and compliance with the firm's general ideology as exercised in its business. High technology as high-status knowledge plays an important political role inasmuch as it not only legitimizes the domain of high technology, but also reinforces a relationship based upon reliance on the foreign firms to control and decide, rather than upon mutual benefit, and rarely upon the development needs of the client country.

Yet while the role of the high technology industry in many Third World countries may be a replacement of one form of cheap labor with another, the drain of many engineers from this part of the world is significant. A study funded by the Mellon Foundation reported:

many graduate engineering programs, even at some of the most prestigious institutions, draw 70 percent or more of their students from abroad. Several engineering deans suggest that without foreign students they would have to close down their graduate programs in the short run and their whole operation ultimately. Since graduate students are essential labor in university laboratories, much research vital to the national interest would "grind to a halt" without foreign students.[45]

The availability of research facilities and lucrative positions has drained many countries of their best hopes for technological development. While some Puerto Rican engineers do find positions in the country, the facilities in Puerto Rico do not offer the research and development that attract many engineers; hence, Puerto Rico, too, is suffering from a massive brain drain. The United States absorption of Third World scientists and engineers is so significant that in 1988 the U.N. General Assembly passed a resolution urging a halt to "reverse transfer of technology" out of the Third World. The United States and other NATO powers voted against it.[46]

Exacerbating the brain drain experienced by many countries is the issue of increased employment at the lower levels promised by industry. Some of the more optimistic proponents argue that high technology will create many new jobs, raise productivity due to product adaptability in other industries, and lower costs, thus creating new jobs.[47] The pessimists argue that the new jobs will be few and that robotics and automation may eliminate jobs rather than create them. These arguments that a leveling off of employment will occur through automation and robotization do not reflect the recent history of labor projections. Yet arguments that jobs will be created through productivity increase in the high-tech industry lack any concrete evidence.[48]

Given the importance of the service economy in Puerto Rico, what do the optimists say about the kind of work and skills that high-technology industry will offer? Not only will many and new jobs be created, but the skills required will be increased. This reflects the position that the reform language in Puerto Rico is advancing. The optimists also assert that new opportunities will arise for developing countries by increasing job availability in industry and services supplying the rapidly growing industrial countries; and by increasing the efficiency of other domestic industries. Those arguing against this position note that the net growth of jobs will be slowed by the new technology; real wages will have to fall in industrial countries and in developing countries to combat substitution by falling costs of high-technology capital; industries will experience a general deskilling process even as a small percentage of highly educated and skilled jobs appears and these, combined, will exacerbate the polarization of workers in Puerto Rico and internationally. In Puerto Rico the dramatic increase in the number of technological schools and vocational programs has not resulted in the number of job opportunities asserted by the optimists. While the number of graduates from technological programs in postsecondary schools has increased dramatically, the economy has been unable to absorb them into the labor force. In other words, even though the new technology programs have grown in numbers of courses and graduates, unemployment in Puerto Rico remains dangerously high.

The optimists' promise of increased employment through high technology needs to be considered carefully. Carnoy offers three definitions of high-technology industry that can shed some light on the problem of claiming increased employment possibilities.

The broadest definition of high technology industries includes industries where the proportion of workers employed in high technology occupations (engineers, life and physical scientists, mathematical specialists, engineering and science technicians, and computer specialists) is at least 1.5 times the average for all industries. A narrower definition includes those manufacturing industries in that the proportion of workers employed in high technology occupations (those listed above) is equal or greater than the average for all manufacturing industries. An even narrower definition only includes industries with a ratio of R&D expenditures to net sales at least twice the average for all industries.[49]

Given the above definitions, new employment will depend upon how high technology is defined. While employment in all industries is expected to increase by 28 percent between 1982 and 1995, it is projected that even under the broadest definition of technology, one of six new jobs will be in high technology, whereas the nine-fastest growing jobs in absolute terms will all be service jobs, such as building custodian, office clerk, and secretary— requiring a high school diploma or less.[50] Considering the increasing problems of financing its public school system, the already high and rising dropout rate, and the brain drain of scientists and mathematicians, the arguments asserting Puerto Rico's possibilities for developing the technology and creating the jobs necessary for high technology development locally seem more like rallying calls than projections based upon careful and critical consideration of the country's development needs. Yet the production of the new high-status knowledge is important in other ways.

Chapter 2 introduced the importance that agreement upon a language of development has to a development program. In Puerto Rico such agreement could be found in the Americanization process through the schools and English as the language of instruction during the first forty years of U.S. occupation, along with a monocultural economy based upon the production of sugar. Between the 1940s and 1970s the industrialization of the country gave way to a new focus in the language of development. The new focus was on vocational schooling and this was accompanied by massive school expansion. The most recent face of high-status language now for incorporation and expansion of high-technology in the schools in order to meet the demands of a changing world. While the call for developing high technology is not in and of itself necessarily undesirable, its import on Puerto Rican development remains problematic.

First, Puerto Rico is not in a position to determine the goals and focus of high technology in Puerto Rico. Relying upon the firms, primarily from the United States, to determine the focus and goals of the industry places Puerto Rico at a disadvantage where decisions on the contribution that high technology can make to local development are concerned. By having to respond to the demands of the industry, which are capital-intensive, Puerto Rico is less likely to gain access to the power needed to implement development programs that focus on local needs. The character and dynamics of development remain in the hands of the colonizer. Second, the new high-status knowledge plays a significant ideological role. Without agreement, the above point would potentially run into considerable resistance. However, if the Puerto Rican people are convinced that the high-technology ushered in by the United States is legitimate, then, though some resistance will still remain, the language of development under the United States is sustained.

Furthermore, given Puerto Ricans' access to high levels of consumption of the products of high technology— television sets, computers, autos, kitchen appliances— agreement upon the new high-status knowledge was generally easy to come by. In an important sense, consumption or the availability of consumable goods is seen as an indication of development; and while according to the orthodox model this may be the case, much remains to be said about the impact that it has on a people's ability to distinguish between having something available, being able to acquire it, and creating or producing it. However, as expectations rise and responses to those expectations continue to diminish, Puerto Rico will more and more have to face its contradictions. Unable to provide Puerto Rico with the fringe benefits of an easily sustained language of agreement regarding development, the United States may have to seek new relations.

The disparities between the numbers of graduates and dropouts, the growing unemployment rate, the decline in the standard of living, and the expansion and apparent ability of private schools to respond to the new high-status knowledge have given many reformers the medium needed with that to call for school reform. Yet if in absolute terms, the supply of graduates remains high and the demand (absorption into the work force) remains low, how is a reform project going to receive approval and support? Most simply put, the new high-status knowledge need only incorporate a system in that the few in demand are viewed favorably, and rest are asked to respond to the remaining requirements in the development project. A system of meritocracy is thus expanded. The testing of students in virtually every grade of their school lives becomes the legitimizing instrument with that to argue that students receive what they merit. This, though, is more of a problem for a public school system, that is generally founded upon the premise that all will receive an education, than the criteria put forward by private industry, in which the notions of competition and merit play a more determinant role in the measure and appropriation of success and failure.

NOTES

1. Denis Goulet, "Development . . . or Liberation," In *The Political Economy of Development and Underdevelopment,* ed. Charles Wilber (New York: Random House, Business Division, 1988), 485.

2. Edwin Irizarry Mora in *Claridad* 31, no. 1921 (December 1-7, 1989)., vol. 4.

3. Miguel Hernández Agosto in *El Mundo*, Friday, March 6, 1987, 2.

4. Richard Carrión in *El Mundo,* Friday, March 6, 1987, 3.

5. Ibid.

6. Howard Simmons in *El Mundo*, Friday, March 6, 1987, 3.

7. For example,"*Al rescate de la escuela,* " sponsored by the Ana G. Méndez Foundation in May 1988. Central to this forum was the call for more government involvment in supporting private schools, more government assistance in seeking funds for private schools, the need for a merit system, and the need to respond to advances in the world of advanced technologies.

8. Awilda Aponte Roque in *El Nuevo Día,* June 28, 1987, p. 7.

9. Estado Libre de Puerto Rico, *Anteproyecto de Ley de enero de 1989,* 11th legislative Assembly, 1st sess., 31-34.

10. Ibid., 36.

11. Ibid., 38.

12. Ibid., 38.

13. Ibid., 39.

14. Ibid., 53.

15. Ibid., 27-30.

16. See José Moyá in *El Nuevo Día,* January 21, 1990, 3.

17. Ibid., 7.

18. Ibid.

19. Ibid.

20. Ibid., 8.

21. Ibid.

22. Ibid.

23. Ibid.

24. Federación de Maestros de Puerto Rico, "Ley 18: 16 de junio de 1993 escuelas de la comunidad, consejos escolares, facilitadores, instituto etc." June 23, 1993, Río Piedras, 1.

25. Ibid., 2.

26. Ibid.

27. Ibid., 6.

28. Ibid.

29. Ana María García Blanco and José Javier Colón Morera, "A Community-Based Approach to Educational Reform in Puerto Rico," in *Colonial Dilemma,* edited by Edwin Meléndez and Edgardo Meléndez (Boston: South End Press, 1993) p. 163.

30. Federación de Maestros de Puerto Rico. "Posición de la Federación de Maestros de Puerto Rico ante los Proyectos Num. 227 del Senado y Num. 548 de la Cámara." Río Piedras, Spring1993.

31. Ibid., 2.

32. Ibid.

33. La Agencia EFE. "Carencias en la educación," *El Nuevo Día*, June 9, 1993, 37.

34. Nestor Figueroa Lugo. "Revigorizan las aulas del agro," *El Nuevo Día*, July 18, 1993, 15.

35. Former Secretary of Education Awilda Aponte Roque, in an article in the newspaper, *El Nuevo Día,* Jan. 21, 1990, p. 5, remarked, "Computers are already being used as early as kindergarten in some Puerto Rican schools. Students learn to interact with the computer as it indicates to the student how to go about learning. According to former Secretary José Moyá, computers will be used in every classroom in every school by the year 2000."

36. Irizarry, 11.

37. Ibid., 15.

38. Michael Apple, *Ideology and Curriculum* (London: Routledge and Kegan Paul, 1990). See Walter Feinberg, *Understanding Education* (Cambridge: Cambridge University Press, 1983), for a detailed analysis of the notion of high-status knowledge.

39. Martin Carnoy "High Technology and Education: An Economist's View." In *Society as Educator in an Age of Transition,* ed. Kenneth Benne and Steve Tozer (Chicago: University of Chicago Press, 1987), 89.

40. Ibid., 90.

41. Ibid., 90.

42. *El Nuevo Día*, January 22, 1990, 8.

43. Carnoy, 1987, 93–97.

44. Ibid., 94.

45. Sekai, J. *Settlers: The Mythology of the White Proletariat* (Chicago: Morningstar Press, 1989), 141.

46. Ibid.

47. Carnoy, 1987, 94.

48. Ibid., 95.

49. Ibid., 97.

50. Ibid., 109.

One of the squatters in the community known as Villa Sin Miedo near Carolina (1982). From *Puerto Rico Mio*, photography by Jack Delano, published by the Smithsonian Institute. Washington, D.C., 1990.

CONCLUSION

*T*hroughout this volume we have examined some of the ramifications that development policies in Puerto Rico under the United States have had for school reform and the possibilities for changing the prevailing conceptions of Puerto Rican development. The chapters have advanced the contention that development is constituted by more than the criteria referred to by growth theory arguments. Even though schooling in Puerto Rico has expanded under colonialism, the contribution that such expansion has made to Puerto Rico's own development remains limited by this relationship. Part of the answer regarding development will require that Puerto Rico's colonial status be resolved.

Since 1898, the development of public schooling has been intimately joined to the economic programs articulated by Puerto Rico's relationship with the United States. If development is taken to mean "change in a particular direction," then at least two questions might be raised regarding that change. First, what direction will that change take? And second, Who determines the direction? This volume has asserted that the possibilities for Puerto Ricans to affect the direction of change is related to their ability to view themselves as capable of development beyond continued U.S. domination. This of course has different meanings depending upon the vision of Puerto Rico's political status. A change in the political status of Puerto Rico may well contribute to a redefinition of the direction in which change will occur. But one of the issues preceding the outcome of directional change, insofar as political status is concerned, is the decision-making process as it relates to an expression of development. This process has, throughout this volume, been referred to as self-determination. And development, throughout this volume has implied that a developmental process engenders and stimulates the creativity of a people as they struggle to grow and to survive as a culture—as they work to realize the ontological vocation Freire calls the effort to realize their subject being. Quite possibly, then, self-determination is the single most significant issue facing Puerto Rican development generally, and public schooling, in particular.

In Chapter 4, public schooling was examined as a socializing agency aimed at Americanizing Puerto Ricans and was, early on, a focal part of U.S. development plans for the island. The insistence upon English as a language of instruction, the implementation of U.S. policies that disallowed Puerto Ricans the celebration and commemoration of cultural events or national holidays, the many U.S. patriotic activities repeated daily in the classrooms, and the policies controlling school administration and curriculum development, among many other factors, were prominent in the attempts to divest Puerto Ricans of their cultural voice. In essence, everything Puerto Rican was to be subordinated. This is not the same as saying that Puerto Ricans should or can deliberate from the perspective of some cultural reality or construct divorced from U.S. influence. That influence has been pervasive and remains at the foundation of the decision-making process.

Puerto Rico has been greatly impacted by its colonial relationship with the United States. This impact, throughout Puerto Rico's history, has been characterized by various forms and degrees of agreement with and resistance to the United States. Agreement and resistance are usually, but certainly not limited to, political party affiliations and agendas. Generally, those favoring statehood, for example, argue that Puerto Rico's best prospects for development lie somewhere within a permanently integrated relationship with the United States as its fifty-first state. Yet even the staunchest proponent of statehood faces a dilemma when confronted by questions such as language and culture. For advocates of statehood, Puerto Rico has suffered from a colonial history. Colonialism in Puerto Rico, for statehooders, has deprived Puerto Ricans of their share of the wealth and opportunities available to Americans. Proponents of statehood have argued that only as a state can Puerto Rico realize its potential.

The pro-statehood party, the Partido Nuevo Progresista (PNP; New Progressive Party), has stood strong behind any initiatives that advance the English language while, for a time, affirming the development of a *jíbaro* state. That is, if Puerto Rico were to become a state of the United States, its cultural foundation as incarnated in the rural character would be preserved. The *jíbaro* in Puerto Rico is here defined as an identification with certain traditional cultural patterns embraced by Puerto Ricans. For the proponents of statehood, commonly called *estadoístas,* development and cultural preservation (here cultural preservation is synonymous with what the political economy paradigm considers as a need to incorporate a people's values in any development program) are compatible.

Statehooders do not view orthodox development as a threat to the overall principle of cultural preservation or cultural advancement. The notion of culture here is distinguished from development in that references to some tradition constitute the framework from which culture is defined. The impact that development or growth has on a people's values and cultural ways becomes divorced from the economic and social plan. In this case, culture might be viewed as that with which Puerto Ricans identify as a kind of objectified existence in the character of the *jíbaro*, a Puerto Rican tradition whose definition and form are fixed and stagnant, explainable independent of its material existence. Quite possibly such a reliance upon this definition of culture and its relationship to development would contribute to the continuation of a reified existence, as would the persistence of colonial culture, even as a state of the United States.

Those favoring the continuation of Puerto Rico's present status, the Estado Libre Asociado (Free Associated State) argue that some basic form of cultural autonomy needs to be preserved while development evolves under the aegis of the United States. The proponents of the commonwealth are a little more tenuous regarding the compromise between the Puerto Rican culture and strict growth needs. Generally members of the Partido Popular Democrático (PPD), ELA proponents assert a desire to increase Puerto Rico's autonomy while maintaining close economic and political association with the United States. Assertions favoring Spanish as the official language of the island, for example, provide evidence of a PPD initiative. To *populares* (the collective reference to those affiliating themselves with the PPD), maintaining different aspects of the cultural personality of Puerto Rico, while not threatening the economic fabric of U.S.-Puerto Rican relations, defines the parameters for the party's response to issues of development and cultural preservation. Economic growth under U.S. control is not necessarily viewed in opposition to overall development.

Like those favoring statehood, the *populares* distinguish culture from economic and social development. The dialectic of culture as a process and product of Puerto Rico developing with(in) the dynamics of external and its own influences is missing. The assumption is that as one culture enters, the other disappears. While this could happen, resistance to such a situation throughout Puerto Rico's colonial history has demonstrated that the uniqueness of the national identity, though surely influenced, maintains a strong sense of its national character. Thus, while one issue regards the question of U.S. domination and cultural imperialism, another, and quite possibly one of equal significance, is the ability and commitment of the people to preserve that identity in the midst of a colonial reality. If culture is also process, then that process must be engaging different factors and variables in the course of change.

However, if culture includes the development of a state of mind, of the process of this development, and of the means of the process, then clearly, whether Puerto Rico experiences the *jíbaro* state of the statehooders or the continuation of the colony, the direction and the development of economic and social change will be influenced by culture— and the Puerto Rican culture will be influenced by such change. Historically, in Puerto Rico this kind of simplified distinction between cultural development and economic growth has given birth to many contradictions and issues regarding such things as modernization and progress, as independence and dependence.

Independentists favor an independent Puerto Rico that might enter into economic relationships with the United States from a position of political sovereignty. The *independentistas* (here I am referring to those advancing that position most often representative of the Partido Independentista Puertorriqueño [PIP], the Puerto Rican

Independence Party) see development under colonialism and cultural preservation as a fundamental contradiction.

The history of Puerto Rican development has been characterized by the proliferation of economic policies aimed at attempting to strike a palatable balance between the presence of colonial exploitation and cultural preservation. Within the struggle to strike such a balance, strategies for the advancement of each political position are advanced, and each has significant meaning for public school policy. However, the development of new strategies for advancing statehood or a continued colonial status, called a commonwelath, or independence also gives rise to contradictions that contribute to the development and rise of other political organizations and strategies for addressing development and culture. In Puerto Rico, there are political and cultural organizations and movements that, while favoring independence, view participation in any electoral process as a legitimation of U.S. colonial presence. This has led to the development of grass-roots national liberation organizations in Puerto Rico and among Puerto Ricans in the United States. These movements, are creating and advancing economic, cultural and educational projects throughout Puerto Rico.

While Puerto Rico has been influenced by U.S. standards for economic development and cultural expression, the evolution of the Puerto Rican culture has grown out of resistance to that influence by the influence itself. Simply put, it may best be described in the saying, "The seeds of colonialism's destruction are built into the colonial structure itself"— and this is closely related to the question of self-determination and development. For example, the English language was imposed upon Puerto Ricans. The act of imposing one's will on another reduces the other to a subordinate role. The power of one to determine for another the latter's best interests disengages the other from participating in the development of both the determination of interests and the relationship that those interests have to development. Spanish, some may argue, was imposed on the indigenous peoples of Puerto Rico. Thus, an argument against English has to consider Spanish as another imposed language. The point here, however, is that Spanish constitutes an integral part of Puerto Rican language and culture. It, too, has developed in the context of struggle between various traits of the Puerto Rican identity (the forging of identity between the Spanish, the Taino, and the African). All three have contributed to the cultural and linguistic symbols and values known as Puerto Rican.

The assertion of the imposition of English as a colonial practice should not be analyzed independent of the role that language plays in the general context of culture. For some, English in and of itself is not a problem. And again, discursive activity is not experienced in a vacuum. The development of skills in different languages is beneficial for any people. However, when language is used to divest a people of their culture and to subordinate them to another, that is, according to international law, an act of genocide.[1] Today, the significance of English to Puerto Rican development is, according to international law, to be determined by Puerto Ricans. For the United States, Puerto Rico's situation is considered a domestic affair, not one falling under international jurisdiction. Resistance to the English language seems more representative of a resistance to cultural imperialism and colonialism than an attack on a language per se. That English is a central part of the ongoing debates regarding the decolonization of Puerto Rico, toward whatever form of political status, is evidence of the impact that Puerto Ricans feel English has had in determining the direction of change for Puerto Rico. Again, the language issue needs to be examined within the greater colonial context. To comment on language divorced from its material and concrete manifestations in the struggle for the development of the Puerto Rican nation is to reduce an examination of any language to mere verbalism.

The impact of language upon culture was central to the political philosophical work of Antonio Gramsci, who wrote that: "Every language contains the elements of a conception of the world."[2] Mental activity depends on the character of the available vocabulary; if abstractions like "democracy" and "liberty" are identified with existing institutions, this will present a barrier to the diffusion of alternative images of society. Thus, the influence of the English language in Puerto Rico has constituted a significant aspect of the issues surrounding development, education, and the nation generally.

However, language in and of itself is not the cornerstone upon which the definition of nation is based. Many nations speak different languages, and in some nation-states several languages are spoken officially. The development of a nation is defined over a long period of time in that values, customs, folkways, and mores evolve, giving a people a sense of uniqueness or culture. This uniqueness or culture is the product of these characteristics and others that evolve as a result of a dialectic between the people and their environment, between themselves and the material demands for their survival. Language then becomes a vehicle for the transmission of values and folkways. The determination of stateness is the right of every nation or people. In a colonial relationship such a right is violated by the colonizer. That such a violation is sustained is, in part, explainable through the history of the contribution that public schooling has made to that end.

Like language, one cannot have a good understanding of the public school's contribution to colonialism without examining the context and the dynamics within which public schooling was grounded and exists. The initial economic change in Puerto Rico, from coffee to sugar, and the maintenance of a monocultural economy under the first four decades of U.S. domination, had an enormous impact on the character of the nation of Puerto Rico. Sugar, controlled by the United States, became king, and the Puerto Rican workers its pawns. Thousands of people were displaced from their towns, forced to seek employment in the sugar regions and emigrate to the United States. Yet the majority of the people remained in poverty as Puerto Ricans became more dependent upon the movement of U.S. capital on the island for their livelihood. Concurrently, public schools, under U.S. control, launched a massive education campaign aimed at Americanizing Puerto Ricans. Here the notion of development as change in a particular direction was clearly understood by the United States. The need for a public school system that would engender the proper disposition toward the U.S. presence was central to the colonial project. The possibilities for Puerto Rican development were forced into a dependency upon the United States, and this alone truncated the human and material resources available to Puerto Ricans without U.S.

intervention. During the period of industrialization, the rationalization of production was intertwined with a logic sustaining the legitimacy of U.S. domination over Puerto Rico. The expansion of vocational education programs advanced the values and fixed the lenses with which Puerto Ricans were to make decisions regarding their vision of the future.

Again, we cannot evaluate the question of intervention without examining the history of Puerto Rico before the United States invaded, its development at the time of the invasion, and the impact that U.S. colonialism has had in determining the direction of change in the colony. In the words of Walter Rodney:

Dependent nations can never be considered developed. It is true that modern conditions force all countries to be mutually interdependent in order to satisfy the needs of their citizens; but that is not incompatible with economic independence because economic independence does not mean isolation. It does, however, require a capacity to exercise choice in external relations, and above all it requires that a nation's growth at some point must become self-reliant and self-sustaining. Such things are obviously in direct contradiction to the economic dependence of numerous countries on the metropoles of Western Europe, North America, and Japan.[3]

Furthermore, in order to understand Puerto Rican underdevelopment or development, we need to examine the impact that the exploitation of Puerto Rico had on the development of the United States. For this we need to understand the dynamics that propelled the United States into its age of imperialism.

The history of the United States in Puerto Rico and its influence in public schooling is fraught not only with exploitation but also with the resistance that such exploitation produces as a contradiction in the very character of capitalist colonial relations in Puerto Rico. Throughout the history of the United States in Puerto Rico, organizations, political parties, and individuals have resisted what they viewed as an imperialist presence. In the 1930s, the Nationalist Party spearheaded massive strikes against the exploitation of Puerto Rican workers by the United States. In the 1940s and 1950s, militant groups carried out attacks against the U.S. presence in Puerto Rico, including the attack on Blair House (the residence of President Harry Truman), the Grito de Jayuya of 1950 (a nationwide revolutionary insurrection), and an armed attack by nationalists on the floor of the House of Representatives in Washington in 1954. Throughout Puerto Rico's history, militant clandestine organizations aimed at advancing national liberation, have carried-out armed attacks on U.S. military and industrial sites. Such activities have occurred both in Puerto Rico and the United States and have been the work of numerous organizations who argue that their acts are justified under international law, including the U.N. Charter, the Protocols of the Geneva Convention, and various international legal documents which recognize the right to armed struggle in the case of anti-colonial movements. Some of the organizations engaged in such direct actions have included the Ejército Popular Boricua-Macheteros (the EPB; Popular Puerto Rican Army), the Fuerzas Armadas de Liberación Nacional (the FALN; Puerto Rican Armed Forces for National Liberation), the Organización de Voluntarios para la Revolución Puertorriqueña (the OVRP; Organization of Volunteers for the

Puerto Rican Revolution), the Fuerzas Armadas de Resistencia Popular (the FARP; Armed Forces of Popular Resistance), and the Comandos Revolucionarios del Pueblo (the CRP; Popular Revolutionary Commandos). These are only the more publicized acts in Puerto Rico's history of resistance to U.S. colonialism on the island. Other forms of resistance, like the development of educational, economic, and cultural projects continue to grow.

In Puerto Rico, and many other Third World countries, we need to juxtapose the metropoles' projects to divest the people of their culture and national identity alongside economic development projects initiated and controlled by foreign business. In Puerto Rico, for example, industries of different sorts are not encouraged to combine efforts for their mutual development and the development of local industry. The history of local industries in Puerto Rico under Operation Bootstrap, such as the Puerto Rico Paper and Pulp Company, the Puerto Rico Glass Corporation, and the Puerto Rico Clay Products Corporation, all brainchildren of Operation Bootstrap, were dependent at some point of production upon private U.S. capital, making it virtually impossible for them to contribute to local development. Their affiliation with the insular government made U.S. private capital nervous, which was a significant factor in their demise.

This volume has argued that development in Puerto Rico has been truncated by the controls promulgated in the colonial relationship with the United States, and that the history of public school reform policies and their language has been a major source of the contributions to a sustained colonial relationship. But this begs the question of underdevelopment. Yet "underdevelopment makes sense only as a means of comparing levels of development."[4] While we can examine Puerto Rico's development from the context of Puerto Rico alone, under a colonial system, or any other system characterized by a relationship to the presence of another country, such development needs to be examined comparatively. For example, all Third World countries today are exploited by other countries.

In a way, underdevelopment is a paradox. Many parts of the world that are naturally rich are actually poor and parts that are not so well off in wealth of soil and sub-soil are enjoying the highest standards of living. When the capitalists from the developed parts of the world try to explain this paradox, they often make it sound as though there is something "God-given" about the situation. One bourgeois economist ... accepted that the comparative statistics of the world today show a gap that is much larger than it was before, by at least 15 to 20 times over the past 150 years. However, the bourgeois economist in question does not give a historical explanation, nor does he consider that there is a relationship of exploitation that allowed capitalist parasites to grow fat and impoverished the dependencies.[5]

Public school reform initiatives, grounded in a language of sustained colonial rule, need to work toward the reconstruction of a language of development for Puerto Rico. The language of despair must reveal a language of possibilities, of self-determination and affirmation. Puerto Rico's public school system needs to address a host of issues relevant to Puerto Rico's future. These issues, however, need to be examined within the context of the colonial reality; to avoid this is to accept it. As a nation with a unique culture, and language, and definitive territorial space, some argue, only through independence can Puerto Rico experience its development. For others, U.S. statehood for Puerto Rico represents the culmination of the colonial experiment. For those favoring statehood, incorporation would mean that Puerto Rico would finally receive its long overdue share of the American dream.

Armed with the evidence of how successful private schooling has been, regardless of the insufficient publicity given to the analyses that might explain such success, private industry and private schooling have become a serious matter facing Puerto Rico's public school system. As the country's economy worsens, the budget for public schooling will remain a problem. Despite the assertions of policymakers and school reformers to the contrary, the battle and decisions to implement policies regarding schooling and general development in a particular direction constitute political acts; to avoid the political nature of any such issue is to commit the Puerto Rican people to a continuation of the historical problem facing many in the nation—that is, that decisions of development can be divorced from the question of status.

The thesis of this volume— that public school reform initiatives in Puerto Rico's history have generally contributed to a sustained colonial relationship with the United States— is grounded in an examination of the political-economic developments that have been fundamental to the context within which educational policy initiatives have appeared. In concluding this volume that raises issues of development, at least some mention of problems facing scholarship regarding decolonization and theoretical discourse on developing countries should be made.

Rarely is mention made of exploitation in understanding the development of the Third World, including the role of imperialism as a logical phase of capitalism. Most economic and political-economic paradigms generally define development within the context of factors of production: land, population, capital, technology, specialization, and so on. Historically, most paradigms, when not outwardly racist, tend to confuse the issues of development by giving as causes of underdevelopment the things that are really the consequences. While causes and effects come together to reinforce one another, Puerto Rico's brain drain, the exploitation of natural and human resources by the colonizer, and in general its colonial existence must be a focal point in any debate over development and education. Puerto Rico's contribution to its underdevelopment, examined in this comparative light, should help to reveal some of the contradictions in its history of momentary growth and underdevelopment.

The question of responsibility for underdevelopment lies, on the one hand, in the colonial efforts of the United States, which drains Puerto Rico of its wealth, both human and natural. On the other hand, responsibility rests in the hands of those in Puerto Rico who stand to gain through the continued exploitation of their own people. Puerto Ricans are ultimately responsible for breaking with any system that disallows the country's development; this precisely is what self-determination is. The development of the nation of Puerto Rico is dependent upon the development of, among other vital things, a public school system that prepares Puerto Ricans to critically encounter the contradictions that characterize its present reality, understand them, and act to transform them.

This constitutes a process of development, one in which the quantitative and qualitative factors of the Puerto Rican people enrich their contribution to human development.

NOTES

1. *United Nations International Convention on the Prevention and Punishment of the Crime of Genocide* (1948) art. 2. Of the five acts considered genocide, only one pertains to the killing we so often associate with genocide. The other four relate to state acts aimed at "destroying in whole or in part, a national, ethnic, racial, or religious group." Of these acts, the second point (causing serious mental harm) could here be argued. Other acts in the definition however, also are pertinent in the case of Puerto Rico.

2. Antonio Gramsci. Lettere dal carcere, vol. 6 (Turin: Einaudi, 1950). Quoted in Joseph Femia, *Gramsci's Political Thought* (Oxford: Clarendon Press, 1987), 44.

3. Walter Rodney, *How Europe Underdeveloped Africa* (Washington, D.C.: Howard University Press 1972), 25.

4. Ibid., 13.

5. Ibid., 21.

Class assembly at the Sábana Seca second unit school (1946). From *Puerto Rico Mío*, photography by Jack Delano, published by the Smithsonian Institute. Washington, D.C., 1990.

BIBLIOGRAPHY

Adamson, Walter L. 1980. *Hegemony and Revolution*. Berkeley: University of California Press.

Albizu Campos, Pedro. 1974. *La conciencia nacional puertorriqueña*. Edited by Manuel Maldonado-Denis. Mexico City: Siglo XXI.

Althusser, Louis, and C. Balibar. 1970. *Reading Capital*. London: Left Books.

Amin, Samir. 1976. *Unequal Development*. New York: Monthly Review Press.

_____. 1977. *Imperialism and Unequal Development*. New York: Monthly Review Press.

_____. 1980. *Class and Nation: Historically and in the Current Crisis*. New York: Monthly Review Press.

_____. 1985. "Modes of Production: History and Unequal Development." *Science and Society* 49, no.2 (Summer): 194–207.

Anderson, Paul. 1974. *Lineages of the Absolute State*. London: NLB.

Annual Report of the Commisioner of Education for Porto Rico 1916. 1917. Washington, D.C.: U.S. Government Printing Office.

Apple, Michael W. 1981. "Curricular Form and the Logic of Technical Control" *Economic and Industrial Democracy* 2, no. 3 (Aug.): 293–320.

_____. 1982. *Cultural and Economic Reproduction in Education*. London: Routledge and Kegan Paul.

_____. 1982. *Power and Ideology*. London: Routledge and Kegan Paul.

_____. 1990. *Ideology and Curriculum*. London: Routledge and Kegan Paul.

Arato, Andrew. 1982. "Esthetic Theory and Cultural Criticism" In *The Essential Frankfurt School Reader* edited by Andrew Arato and Eike Gebhardt. New York: Continuum.

Avineri, Shlomo. 1971. T*he Social and Political Thought of Karl Marx*. New York: Cambridge University Press.

Azize, Yamila. 1979. *Luchas de la mujer en Puerto Rico, 1878–1919.* San Juan: Litografía Metropolitana.

Baran, Paul. "Economic Progress and Economic Surplus." 1953. *Science and Society* 17, no. 4 (Fall): 289-317.

Baran, Paul, and Paul Sweezy. 1966. *Monopoly Capital.* New York: Monthly Review Press.

Beardsley, Clarence, 1987. "Se Implementarían cambios educativos en agosto." *El Mundo,* (Mar. 6): 2–3.

_____. 1987. "Menos dinero federal para la educación." *El Mundo,* (Mar. 6): 3.

Becker, Gary S. 1964. *Human Capital.* New York: Columbia University Press.

Berbusse, Edward J. 1969. *The United States in Puerto Rico, 1891–1900.* Chapel Hill: University of North Carolina Press.

Bernstein, Basil. 1975. *Class, Codes, and Control.* London: Routledge and Kegan Paul.

Bernstein, Richard. 1971. *Praxis and Action.* Philadelphia: University of Pennsylvania Press.

Berrios, Nelson Gabriel. 1990. "Cambios educativos de la 'A' a la 'Z'." *El Nuevo Día,* (Jan. 21): 4–5.

_____. 1990. "Incentivos a la excelencia pedagógica." *El Nuevo Día,* (Jan. 22): 7.

Bird, Esteban. 1941. *A Report on the Sugar Industry in Relation to the Social and Economic System of Puerto Rico.* Senate Document. no. 1. San Juan: Bureau of Supplies, Printing, and Transportation.

Blaut, James 1989. "Colonialism and the Rise of Capitalism." *Science and Society* 53 no. 3 (Fall): 260-296.

Blumberg, Paul. 1968. *Industrial Democracy: The Sociology of Participation.* New York: Schocken.

Bonilla, Frank and Ricardo Campos. 1981. "A Wealth of Poor: Puerto Ricans in the New International Order." *Daedalus* 110 (Spring): 133–176.

Bottomore, Tom. 1966. *Classes in Modern Society.* New York: Pantheon.

Bourdieu, Pierre. and John Passeron. 1977. *Reproduction.* Beverly Hills, Calif.: Sage.

Bowles, Samuel and Herbert Gintis. 1976. *Schooling in Capitalist America.* New York: Basic Books.

_____. 1982. "The Crisis of Liberal Democratic Capitalism: The Case of the United States" *Politics and Society 11, no. 1:* 51–93.

Brau, Salvador. 1966. *La colonización de Puerto Rico.* San Juan: Instituto de Cultura Puertorriqueña (Reprint).

Braverman, Harry. 1974. *Labor and Monopoly Capital.* New York: Monthly Review Press.

Brumbaugh, Martin. 1901. *Annual Report of the Commissioner of Education.* Washington, D.C.: U.S. Government Printing Office.

Brundenius, C., and M. Lundal. 1982. *Development Strategies and Basic Needs in Latin America: Challenges for the 1980's.* Boulder, Colo.: Westview Press.

Buchanan, Patrick J. 1991. "Don't make Puerto Rico 51st State." *Chicago Sun–Times,* (Mar. 16): 17.

Buitrago Ortíz, Carlos. 1976. *Los orígenes históricos de la sociedad precapitalista en Puerto Rico.* Río Piedras: Huracán.

Bureau of Insular Affairs. 1907. *Report of the Commissioner of Education for Porto Rico . . . , 1906.* Washington, D.C.: War Department.

_____. 1911. *Report of the Commissioner of Education of Porto Rico 1910.* Washington, D.C.: War Department.

_____. 1912. *Report of the Commissioner of Education of Porto Rico 1911* . Washington, D.C. : War Department.

_____. 1920. *Report of the Commissioner of Education of Porto Rico 1919.* Washington. D.C.: War Department.

Butts, Freeman R., and Lawrence A. Cremin. 1953. *A History of Education in American Culture.* New York: Henry Holt.

Cardoso, Fernando H. and Faletto, Enrique.1979. *Dependency and Development in Latin America,* Translated by Marjory Mattingly Urquidi. Berkeley: University of California Press.

Carnoy, Martin. 1974. Education and Cultural Imperialism. New York: McKay.

_____. 1987. "High Technology and Education: An Economist's View" In *Society as Educator in an Age of Transition.* Edited by Kenneth D. Benne and Steven Tozer. Chicago: University of Chicago Press.

Carnoy, Martin, and Henry M. Levin. 1975. "Evaluation of Educational Media: Some Issues," *Instructional Science* 4: 385–406.

_____.1976. The *Limits of Educational Reform.* New York: McKay.

Carr, Raymond. 1984. *Puerto Rico: A Colonial Experiment.* New York: New York University Press.

Carrasco, Olga. 1990. "Acortan la distancia para el sustento." *El Nuevo Día,* (Jan. 22): 8.

Carroll, Henry K. 1900. *Report on the Island of Porto Rico.* Washington, D.C.: Department of the Treasury, U.S. Goverment Printing Office.

Cartagena, Rafael. 1983. *Puerto Rico enfermo.* Río Piedras: El Roble, 51.

Centro de Estudios Puertorriqueños (CENEP). 1975. *Taller de migración.* New York: CENEP.

_____.*1977. Documentos de la migración puertorriqueña, 1879–1901.* No. 1. New York: CENEP.

_____. 1979. *Labor Migration Under Capitalism: The Puerto Rican Experience.* New York: Monthly Review Press.

Chomsky, Noam. 1987. *The Chomsky Reader.* Edited by James Peck, New York: Pantheon Books.

Claridad. 1989. 31, no. 1915 (June 24–30).

_____.1989. 31, no. 1917 (Nov. 3–9) 34.

_____. 1989. 31, no. 1921 (Dec. 1–7) 4.

Clark, Truman R. 1975. *Puerto Rico and the United States, 1917–1933.* Pittsburgh: University of Pittsburgh Press.

Clark, Victor S. et al. 1930. *Porto Rico and its Problems.* Washington, D.C.: Brookings Institution.

Coll y Cuchi, José. 1923. *El nacionalismo en Puerto Rico.* San Juan: Gil de Lamadrid Hermanos.

Colletti, Lucio. 1972. From Rou*sseau to Lenin: Studies in Ideology and Society.* New York: Monthly Review Press.

Colton, George. 1910. *Report to the Governor of Porto Rico.* 1910. Washington, D.C.: U.S. Government Printing Office.

Comité Interagencial de la Estrategia de Puerto Rico. 1976. *El desarrollo económico de Puerto Rico: Una estrategia para la próxima década.* Río Piedras: Editorial Universitaria.

Cordero Matos, R. 1901. *La instrucción pública en Puerto Rico.* Ponce: Imprenta de Manuel C. López.

Cordero, Rafael. 1952. *El progreso económico de Puerto Rico en los últimos 50 Años.* San Juan: Department of Public Instruction.

Cotto, Candida. 1989. "Aumenta la pobreza en Puerto Rico." *Claridad,* 31, no. 1921(Dec. 1–7): 4.

Curet Cueva, Agustín. 1977. *El desarrollo del capitalismo en América Latina.* Mexico City: Siglo XXI.

Dahl, Robert. 1956. *A Preface to Democratic Theory.* Chicago: University of Chicago Press.

Davis , George W. 1900. *Report of the Military Govenor of Porto Rico on Civil Affairs .* Washington D. C.: U.S. Government Printing Office.

Delgado, A. 1988, "Una economía improductiva y sin empleos." *Claridad,* 30, no. 1874, (June 24–30): 3.

Department of Education. 1941. *Tentative Syllabus in English for the First Three Years of the High School Course.* San Juan: Department of Education.

U.S. Department of War, 1899. *Report of the United States Insular Commision to the Secretary of War, Upon Investigations Made into the Civil affairs of the Island of Porto Rico with Recommendations.* Washington, D.C.: U.S. Government Printing Office.

Dewey, John. 1966. *Democracy and Education.* New York: Free Press.

Díaz Alcaide, Maritza. 1987. "Obsoleta la estructura de regiones educativas." *El Mundo,* (Mar. 6): 2.

Dietz, James. 1979."Imperialism and Underdevelopment: A Theoretical Perspective and a Case Study of Puerto Rico." *Review of Radical Political Economics* 11 (Winter): 16–32.

_____. 1984. "Puerto Rico's New History." *Latin American Research Review* 19 no. 1: 210-22.

_____.1986. *Economic History of Puerto Rico: Institutional Change and Capitalist Development .* Princeton: Princeton University Press.

Diffie, Bailey W., and Justine W. Diffie. 1931. *Porto Rico: A Broken Pledge.* New York: Vanguard Press.

Eaton, John. 1966. *Political Economy: A Marxist Tradition.* New York: International Publishers.

Edel, Mathew D. 1962. "Land Reform in Puerto Rico." *Caribbean Studies* (Oct.): 26–60.

Emerson, Rupert and D.K. Fieldhouse. 1968. "Colonialism." In the*International Encyclopedia of the Social Sciences.* Vol. C. (New York: Macmillan) 1–3.

Estrada Resto, Nilka. 1990. "Más educación que instrucción." *El Nuevo Día,* (Jan. 21): 6–7.

Estrada Resto, Nilka. 1990. "Los puestos transitorios politizarán al DIP." *El Mundo,* (May 24): 35.

Fanon, Frantz. 1963. *The Wretched of the Earth.* Translated by Constance Farrington) New York: Grove Press..

Faulkner, Roland P. 1909. *"Elimination of Pupils from Schools"* Psychological Clinic 2, no. 9.

Feinberg, Walter. 1983. *Understanding Education: Toward a Reconstruction of Educational Inquiry.* Cambridge: Cambridge University Press.

Feinberg, Walter, and Eric Bredo, eds. 1982. Knowledge *and Values in Social Science and Educational Research.* Philadelphia: Temple University Press.

Feinberg, Walter, and Jonas F. Soltis. 1985. *School and Society.* New York: Teachers College Press.

Femia, Joseph. 1982. *Gramsci's Political Thought*. Oxford: Clarendon Press.

Figueroa, Loida. 1977. *Breve historia de Puerto Rico*. 2 vols. Río Piedras: Edil.

Foner, Philip. 1972. *The Spanish-Cuban-American War and the Birth of American Imperialism*. New York: Monthly Review Press.

Foro Sobre la Reforma Educativa. 1988. *Al rescate de la escuela*. San Juan: Sistema Universitario Ana G. Méndez.

Frank, Andre Gunder. 1969. "Sociology of Development and Underdevelopment of Sociology." In *Latin America: Underdevelopment or Revolution?* New York: Monthly Review Press.

Freire, Paulo. 1985. *The Politics of Education*. Translated by Donald Macedo. Westport: Bergin and Garvey.

_____. 1990. *Pedagogy of the Oppressed*. New York: Continuum.

Freire, Paulo, and Donaldo Macedo. 1987. *Literacy: Reading the Word and the World*. Westport: Bergin and Garvey.

Freyre, Jorge. 1969. External and Domestic Financing in the Economic Development of Puerto Rico Río Piedras: University of Puerto Rico Press.

Furtado, Celso. 1970. *Economic Development of Latin America: A Survey from Colonial Times to the Cuban Revolution*. Cambridge: Cambridge University Press.

Fusfeld, Daniel R. 1982. *Principles of Political Economy*. Glenview, Ill.: Scott, Foresman.

Gallardo, José. 1946. *Annual Report of the Commissioner of Education, 1945-46*. San Juan: Department of Public Instruction, Bureau of Supplies, Printing, and Transportation.

Gayer, A. D., Paul T. Homan, and Earle K. Jones. 1938. *The Sugar Economy of Puerto Rico*. New York: Columbia University Press.

Gintis, Herbert. 1971. "Education, Technology, and the Characteristics of Worker Productivity," *American Economic Review* 61, no. 2 (May): 266–79.

Giroux, Henry A. 1981. *Ideology, Culture, and the Process of Schooling*. Philadelphia: Temple University Press.

_____. 1983. *Theory and Resistance in Education A Pedagogy for the Opposition*. Westport: Bergin and Garvey.

Gómez Tejera, Carmen and David Cruz López. 1970. *La escuela puertorriqueña*. New York: Troutman Press.

Gould, Carol. 1978. *Marx's Social Ontology*. Cambridge, Mass.: MIT Press.

Gould, Lyman J. 1969. *La ley Foraker: Raíces de la política colonial de los Estados Unidos*. Río Piedras: Universidad de Puerto Rico.

Goulet, Dennis. 1988. "Development . . . or Liberation." In *The Political Economy of Development and Underdevelopment*. Edited by Charles Wilber. New York: Random House, Business Division.

Gramsci, Antonio. 1971. *Selections from the Prison Notebooks*. Edited and translated by Quintin Hoare and Geoffrey Nowell Smith. New York: International Publishers.

Grundy, Shirley. 1987. *Curriculum: Product or Praxis?* New York: The Falmer Press.

Gutiérrez, Elías R. 1977. *Factor Proportions, Technology Transmission and Unemployment in Puerto Rico*. Río Piedras: Editorial Universitaria.

Habermas, Jürgen. 1981. *The Theory of Comunicative Action*, vol. 1. Translated by Thomas McCarthy. Boston: Beacon Press.

Headrick, Daniel R. 1988. *The Tentacles of Progress*. Oxford: Oxford University Press.

Held, David. 1980. *Introduction to Critical Theory*. Berkeley: University of California Press.

_____. 1989. *Political Theory and the Modern State*. Stanford: Stanford University Press.

Heller, Agnes. 1976. *The Theory of Need in Marx*. New York: St. Martin's Press.

Hofstader, Richard. 1965. *The Paranoid Style in American Politics and Other Essays*. New York: Monthly Review Press.

Huntington, Susan D. 1917. *Curso de estudio sen educación moral y cívica para las escuelas públicas de Puerto Rico*. 2 vols. San Juan: Bureau of Supplies, Printing, and Transportation.

Inkeles, Alex. 1966. "The Socialization of Competence"*Harvard Educational Review* 36, no. 3 (Summer): 265–83.

Inkeles, Alex, and David H. Smith. 1974. *Becoming Modern*. Cambridge, Mass.: Harvard University Press.

_____. eds. 1979. *Directions in Economic Development*. Notre Dame, Ind.: University of Notre Dame Press.

Institute of Field Studies, Teachers College, Columbia University.1950. *Public Education and the Future of Puerto Rico*. New York: Teachers College Press

Irizarry, Rafael L. Mayo 1987. "El desempleo de la población joven y la espiral inflacionaria de la educación en Puerto Rico." Unpublished paper. University of Puerto Rico, Graduate School for Planning.

_____.1987. "La población joven, el empleo y la educación: Perspectivas futuras." Unpublished paper.

Jaffe, A. J. 1959. *People, Jobs and Economic Development*. Glencoe, Ill.: Free Press.

Jameson, Kenneth and Charles K. Wilber. 1988. "Paradigms of Economic Development and Beyond." In*The Political Economy of Development and Underdevelopment*. Edited by Charles Wilber. New York: Random House, Business Division.

Junta de Planificación.1975. *Balanza de pagos*. San Juan: Junta de Planificación.

_____.1979. *Compendio de estadísticas sociales* San Juan: Junta de Planificación.

_____. 1984. *Informe económico al gobernador, 1982–83*. 2 vols. San Juan: Junta de Planificación.

Katz, Michael B. 1968. *The Irony of Early School Reform*. Boston: Beacon.

_____. 1971. *Class, Bureaucracy, and Schools: The Illusion of Educational Change in America*. New York: Praeger.

Kay, Cristóbal. 1989. *Latin American Theories of Development and Underdevelopment*. London: Routledge.

Kliebard, Herbert M. 1987. *The Struggle for the American Curriculum 1893–1950*. New York: Routledge and Kegan Paul.

Kolko, Gabriel. 1963. *The Triumph of Conservatism*. New York: Free Press.

Lal, Deepak. 1985.*The Poverty of "Development Economics"* Cambridge, Mass.: Harvard University Press.

Levin, Henry M. 1983. "Low Skill Future of High Tech" *Technology Review* 86, no. 6. (Aug./Sept.):18–21.

Lewis, Gordon K. 1963. *Puerto Rico*. New York: Monthly Review Press.

_____. 1974. *Notes on the Puerto Rican Revolution*. New York: Monthly Review Press.

Lidin, Harold J. 1981. *History of the Puerto Rican Independence Movement, 19th Century*. Vol. 1. Maplewood, N.J.: Waterfront.

Lipton, Michael. 1977. *Why Poor People Stay Poor: A Study of Urban Bias in World Development*. Cambridge, Mass.: Harvard University Press.

López, Adalberto, James Petras eds. 1974. *Puerto Rico and Puerto Ricans: Studies in History and Society*. New York: Halsted Press.

Luciano, María Judith. 1990. "Hueca la Reforma." *El Nuevo Día*, (Jan. 22): 7.

Lukács, Georg. 1971. *History and Class Consciousness.* Cambridge, Mass.: MIT Press

Luque de Sánchez, María Dolores. 1980. *La ocupación norteamericana y la ley Foraker: La opinión pública puertorriqueña, 1898–1904.* Río Piedras: Editorial Universitaria.

Madera, José R. 1982. "The Strategy of Development." *Industrial Newsletter.* (Puerto Rico Economic Development Administration). 22:1–2.

Maldonado Denis, Manuel. 1972. *Puerto Rico: A Socio-Historic Interpretation.* New York: Vintage Books.

_____. 1977. *Hacia una interpretación marxista de la historia de Puerto Rico y otros ensayos.* Río Piedras: Editorial Antillana.

_____. 1980. *The Emigration Dialectic: Puerto Rico and the U.S.A.* New York: International Publishers.

Marcuse, Herbert. 1961. "Language and Technological Society." *Dissent* Vol. 8, No. 1 (Winter): 66–74.

_____. 1968. *Negations: Essays in Critical Theory.* Boston: Beacon Press.

_____. 1969. *An Essay on Liberation.* Boston: Beacon Press.

_____. 1982. "Some Social Implications of Modern Technology." In *The Essential Frankfurt School Reader.* Edited by Andrew Arato and Eike Gebhardt. New York: Continuum.

Marx, Karl. 1963. *The Eighteenth Brumaire of Louis Bonaparte.* New York: International Publishers

_____. 1967. *Capital.* 3 vols. New York: International Publishers.

Massachusetts Institute of Technology. 1990. *Education That Works: An Action Plan for the Education of Minorities.* Cambridge, Mass: MIT Press.

Mathews, Thomas. 1960. *Puerto Rican Politics and the New Deal.* Gainesville: University of Florida Press.

McAfee, Kathy. 1990. "Hurricane: IMF, World Bank, U.S. AID in the Caribbean." *North American Congress on Latin America (NACLA)* (February) vol 23, no. 5: 13-26.

McCarthy, Thomas. 1978. *The Critical Theory of Jürgen Habermas.* Cambridge, Mass.: The MIT Press.

Mead, Margaret. 1935. *Report to the Committee of the Social Studies Commission on the Secondary School Curriculum.* Washington, D.C.

Memmi, Albert. 1984. *Dependence.* Boston: Beacon Press.

Méndez, José L. 1978. *La agresión cultural norteamericana en Puerto Rico.* Mexico City: Editorial Grijalbo.

Merrill-Ramírez, M. 1979. "Operation Bootstrap: A Critical Analysis of the Puerto Rican Development Program." Unpublished Master's thesis, University of Texas.

Miliband, Ralph. 1969. *The State in Capitalist Society.* London: Weindenfeld and Nicholson.

Miller, Paul. 1917. *Annual Report of the Commissioner of Education of Porto Rico.* Washington, D.C.: U.S. Government Printing Office.

Mintz, Sidney. K. 1974. *Caribbean Transformations.* Chicago: Aldine.

_____. 1977. "The So-Called World System: Local Initiative and Local Response." *Dialectical Anthropology* 2 (Nov.): 253–270.

Montilla de Negrón, Aida. 1977. *La americanización de Puerto Rico y el sistema de instrucción pública 1900–1930.* Río Piedras: Editorial Universitaria.

Mundie, John. 1960. "The Role of the Government Development Bank in Puerto Rico's Economic Program." Ph.D. diss., University of Texas.

Muñoz Meléndez, M. 1916. *Estado social del campesino puertorriqueño.* San Juan: Tipografía Cantero Fernandez.

Muñoz Rivera, Luis. 1898. *La Democracia.* Nov. 3.

Myrdal, Gunnar. 1971. *Economic Theory and Underdeveloped Regions.* New York: Harper & Row.

National Commission on Excellence in Education. 1983. *A Nation at Risk: The Imperative for Educational Reform.* Washington, D.C.: Department of Education.

New York Times Magazine. 1981 (staff) October 18.

Nyerere, Julius K. 1974. *Freedom and Development.* Oxford: Oxford University Press.

Osuna, Juan José. 1975. *A History of Education in Puerto Rico.* Río Piedras: University of Puerto Rico Press.

Outline for the Teaching of Social Sciences in the Eighth Grade. 1936. San Juan: Department of Education.

Pacheco, Osvaldo Rodríguez, Ed. 1976. *A Land of Hope in Schools: A Reader in the History of Public Education in Puerto Rico, 1940–1965.* San Juan: Editorial Edil.

Pateman, Carol. 1970. *Participation and Democratic Theory.* Cambridge: Cambridge University Press.

Peoples Press. 1979. *Puerto Rico: The Flame of Resistance.* San Francisco: Peoples Press.

Perloff, Harvey. 1950. *Puerto Rico's Economic Future.* Chicago: University of Chicago Press.

Permanent People's Tribunal. 1989. *Tribunal Proceedings and Findings.* Barcelona, Spain.

Petrovich, Janice. 1983. "Some Contradictions of School Expansion." *Homines,* Vol. 7 no. 1–2: 141–46.

Polanyi, Karl. 1957. *The Great Transformation: The Political and Economic Origins of Our Time.* Boston: Beacon Press.

Poulantzas, Nicos. 1978. *Political Power and Social Classes.* London: New Left.

Puerto Rican Policy Commission (PRPC). 1934. *Report of the Puerto Rican Policy Commission (Chardon Report)* San Juan: PRPC.

––––––. 1976. *Conflictos de clase y política en Puerto Rico.* Río Piedras: Huracán.

Puerto Rico Planning Board (PRPB). 1961. *Economic Development of Puerto Rico, 1940–1950, 1951–1960 .* San Juan: PRPB.

Quintero Rivera, Angel G. 1980. "La base social en la transformación ideológica del Partido Popular en la década del '40." In *Cambio y desarrollo,* edited by Navas Dávila. Río Piedras: Editorial Universitaria. 35-119.

Raffucci de García, Carmen I. 1981. *El gobierno civil y la ley Foraker.* Río Piedras: Editorial Universitaria.

Report of the Commisioner of Education in Porto Rico, 1901. 1902. Washington, D.C.: U.S. Government Printing Office.

Report of the Commissioner of Education for Porto Rico to the Secretary of the Interior . . . for the Fiscal Year Ended June 30, 1905 . 1906. Washington, D.C.: U.S. Government Printing Office.

Report of the Commissioner of Education to the Honorable Governor of Puerto Rico Year 1907-08. 1908. San Juan: U.S. Government Printing Office.

Ribes Tovar, Federico. 1973. *Historia cronológica de Puerto Rico.* New York: Plus Ultra.

Riche, Richard W., et al. 1983. "High Technology Today and Tomorrow: A Small Slice of the Employment Pie" *Monthly Labor Review* (Nov.): 50–58.

Rivera Quintero, Marcia. 1980. "Educational Policy and Female Labor, 1898-1930" In *Intellectual Roots of Independence: An Anthology of Puerto Rican Political Essays.* Edited By Iris M. Závala and Rafael Rodríguez. New York: Monthly Review Press.

Rodney, Walter. 1972. *How Europe Underdeveloped Africa.* Washington, D.C.: Howard University Press.

Rodríguez, Artemio P. 1934. *A Report on Wages and Working Hours in Various Industries and on the Cost of Living, in the Island of Puerto Rico, During the Year 1933.* San Juan: Bureau of Supplies, Printing, and Transportation.

Ross, David F. 1969. *The Long Uphill Path–A Historical Study of Puerto Rico's Program of Economic Development.* San Juan: Editorial Edil.

Ross, E. A. 1901. *Social Control: A Survey of the Foundations of Order.* New York: Macmillan.

Rowe, Leo S. 1975. *The United States and Porto Rico.* New York: Arno Press.

Ruccio, David. F.and Lawrence H. Simon. 1988. "Radical Theories of Development: Frank, the Modes of Production School, and Amin." In*The Political Economy of Development and Underdevelopment,* Edited by Charles Wilber. New York: Random House, Busines Division. 121–173.

Saldaña, Jorge. 1932. *El café en Puerto Rico.* Chicago: Aldine.

Sánchez Tarniella, Andrés. 1971. *La economía de Puerto Rico.* Madrid: Afrodisco. 5th ed., Río Piedras: Bayoán, 1973.

Santiago, K. Antonio. 1984. "La concentración y la centralización de las propiedades en Puerto Rico, 1898–1929. *Homines* 8 (Jan.): 129–56.

Sarason, Seymour B. 1971. *The Culture of the School and the Problem of Change.* Boston: Allyn and Bacon.

Sassoon, Anne S. 1987. *Gramsci's Politics.* Minneapolis: University of Minnesota Press.

Schultz, Theodore W. 1963. *The Economic Value of Education.* New York: Columbia University Press.

Schumpeter, Joseph. 1942. *Capitalism, Socialism, and Democracy.* New York: Harper & Row.

Seers, Dudley. 1969. "The Meaning of Development." *International Development Review* 11 (Dec.): 2-6.

Segarra, Pablo. 1989. "¿Le sale caro Puerto Rico a los Estados Unidos ?" *Claridad.* 31, no. 1917 (Nov. 3–9): 34.

Sekai, J. 1989. *Settlers: The Mythology of the White Proletariat.* Chicago, Morningstar Press.

Silén, Juan Angel. 1971. *We the Puerto Rican People.* New York: Monthly Review Press.

———. 1973. *Historia de la nación puertorriqueña.* Río Piedras: Edil.

———. 1978. *Apuntes para la historia del movimiento obrero puertorriqueño.* Río Piedras: Cultural.

Simon, Paul. 1991. "Commonwealth status for Puerto Rico is pre–packaged colonialism." *Extra,* (Mar.13) Chicago: 8.

Sivestrini, José Rivera. 1972. *Puerto Rico entre dos culturas: Desarrollo del capitalismo.* Río Piedras: Colección Mayoría Silenciosa.

Skelly, John T. 1990. "Bonanza para la educación superior." *El Nuevo Día,* (Jan. 22): 6.

Stead, William H. 1958. *Fomento: The Economic Development of Puerto Rico.* Washington, D.C.: National Planning Association.

Taller de Formación Política. 1982. *¡ Huelga en la caña !* Río Piedras: Huracán.

Tentative Outline for the Teaching of English in Grades One, Two, and Three. 1938–39. Department of Education, San Juan: Department of Education.

"The Towner-Sterling Bill." 1922. In the *Reference Shelf.* Compiled by Lamar T. Beman. New York: H. W. Wilson.

Thomas, C. 1976. *Dependence and Transformation.* New York: Monthly Review Press.

Todaro, Michael. 1969. "A Model of Labor MIgration and Urban Unemployment in Less Developed Countries." *American Economic Review* . (Mar.): 138–148 .

_____. 1981. *Economic Development in the Third World.* 2nd ed. New York: Longmans.

Tugwell, Rexford Guy. 1945. *The Puerto Rico Public Papers.* San Juan, Services Office, Government of Puerto Rico.

Ul Haq, Mahbub. 1976. *The Poverty Curtain: Choice for the Third World.* New York: Columbia University Press.

United Nations. 1948. International Convention on the Prevention and Punishment of the Crime of Genocide.

U. S. Department of Commerce. 1979. *Economic Study of Puerto Rico.* 2 vols.Washington, D.C.: U.S. Government Printing Office.

Wagenheim, Kal. 1958. *The Protestant Ethic and the Spirit of Capitalism.* New York: Scribner.

_____.1973. *The Puerto Ricans: A Documentary History.* Garden City, N.Y.: Anchor.

Weber, Max. 1946. "Bureaucracy," in *From Max Weber: Essays in Sociology* . Edited by H. H. Gerth and C. Wright Mills. Chapter 8. New York: Oxford University Press.

Weisskoff, Richard. 1985. *Factories and Food Stamps: The Puerto Rico Model of Development.* Baltimore: Johns Hopkins University Press .

Wells, Henry. 1969. *The Modernization of Puerto Rico.* Cambridge, Mass.: Harvard University Press.

Wessman, James W. 1977. "Towards a Marxist Demography: A Comparison of Puerto Rican Landowners, Peasants, and Rural Proletarians." in *Dialectical Anthropology 2* (Aug.): pp. 223–33.

_____. 1980."The Demographic Structure of Slavery in Puerto Rico: Some Aspects of Agrarian Capitalism in the Late Nineteenth Century." *Journal of Latin American Studies* 12 (Nov.): 271-89.

Wilber, Charles K., and Kenneth P. Jameson. 1988. "Paradigms of Economic Development and Beyond." In*The Political Economy of Development and Underdevelopment.* Efited By Charles Wilber. New York, Random House, Business Division.

Wilber, Charles K. ed. 1988. *The Political Economy of Development and Underdevelopment.* New York: Random House, Business Division.

Williams, Raymond. 1961. *The Long Revolution.* London: Chatto and Windus.

Wirth, Arthur G. 1972. *Education in the Technological Society: The Vocation-Liberal Studies Controversy in the Early Twentieth Century.* Scranton, Pa.: Intext Educational.

Index

About the Author

JOSÉ SOLÍS is Assistant Professor of Education at DePaul University in Chicago. He was born and raised in Puerto Rico and has taught in public and private schools as well as at the university level. He has written numerous articles and taught education in Puerto Rico.